THE GOLDEN HIND SERIES
Edited by Milton Waldman

DAMPIER

CAPTAIN WILLIAM DAMPIER
From the painting by Thomas Murray in the National Portrait Gallery.

Dampier

EXPLORER AND BUCCANEER

By

CLENNELL WILKINSON

NEW YORK
Harper & Brothers Publishers
MCMXXIX

PREFACE

O adequate life of Dampier exists. It is true that during the late eighteenth and early nineteenth centuries many biographical notices of him appeared, usually in those massive volumes of " collected voyages " so dear to our ancestors' hearts. But all of these that I have seen (and I cannot have missed many) consisted, as regards his private life, merely of those very few statements which he himself has vouchsafed to us ; and, as regards his adventures, of a summarized version of his own narrative and those of his fellow-voyagers.

The first with any claim to originality appeared in the *United Service Journal and Magazine* (Parts III and IV) in 1837, and has been generally attributed to Rear-Admiral Smyth, the distinguished writer on naval questions. Smyth had taken the trouble to look up some of Dampier's correspondence ; in dealing with his authorities he had compared the original manuscripts, many of which are in the Sloane Collection, with the published books ; and in this way had discovered the barefaced " doctoring " of Ringrose by Hacke, in the interests of Captain Sharp. Also he had found out when Dampier died, and had been through the files at Doctors' Commons and discovered his will. In addition to all this, his own comments and deductions are those of a shrewd and friendly critic. I am greatly in his debt. But he made one deplorable error, in denying indignantly that Dampier had ever been court-martialled. The only previous references to this unfortunate incident had been of a vague and general character, and Smyth does not seem to have taken them seriously enough to make any inquiry into the matter.

It was left to Professor Sir J. K. Laughton, in his otherwise rather slight and none too friendly account of Dampier in the *Dictionary of National Biography*, to supply this deficiency. Mr. Masefield, in his very valuable notes and appendixes to the new edition of Dampier's works, published by Messrs. Grant Richards in 1906, dots the i's and crosses the t's. He has, moreover, summarized Fisher's charges against Dampier, with Dampier's answers, and has also quoted at some length from the correspondence between Dampier and the Admiralty. But the whole business of the court-martial may be studied at leisure in the Public Record Office by anyone sufficiently interested. I have also found there the Master's Log of the " Roebuck," and much other interesting matter. No previous writer has made use of this log, which is often very valuable. It shows signs of having been in the water, and probably got a wetting when the " Roebuck " was lost off Ascension Island. The muster-book unfortunately went down with the ship. Such new information as I have obtained from the log will be found in the following pages.

The great value of Mr. Masefield's work lies in the

timely and well-informed editorial notes with which he has discreetly peppered Dampier's pages. After Smyth, my greatest debt is to him. I have also derived much pleasure and assistance from Sir Albert Gray's essay on Dampier in the Argonaut Press edition of the *New Voyage*, to which I shall refer again later. Mr. N. M. Penzer's bibliographical note in the same volume is of the highest value, and has, I believe, been adopted in the catalogues of the British Museum. Mr. G. E. Manwaring has gone out of his way to make many friendly and helpful suggestions. Finally, I cannot conclude without a word of thanks to the Rev. Maurice R. Bailey, vicar of East Coker, whose kind hospitality and keen interest in the subject gave me such a pleasant start upon my journey.

CLENNELL WILKINSON.

CONTENTS

ILLUSTRATIONS

NOTE.—The author and publishers are indebted to Messrs. Cassell
& Co. Ltd. for permission to reproduce Thomas Murray's portrait
of Dampier and Skelton's engraving of Captain Woodes Rogers
from Captain Rogers's *A Cruising Voyage Round the World* ; to
Lt.-Col. J. B. Batten, D.S.O., for permission to reproduce the

illustration of Hymerford House from his book *Historical and Topographical Collections relating to South Somerset* ; to Messrs. Martin Hopkinson Ltd. for permission to reproduce " The Island of Juan Fernandez " from their edition of *Anson's Voyage Round the World* ; and to Messrs. Halton and Truscott Smith and the Trustees of the Macpherson Collection for permission to reproduce " Panama about 1690 " and " The Battle of the Texel " from Frank C. Bowen's *The Sea : its History and Romance.*

WILLIAM DAMPIER

CHAPTER I

"PIRATE AND HYDROGRAPHER"

THE character to be presented in these pages is that of one of the great English explorers — one whose achievements surpassed those of any rival over a period of about a hundred years. From the accession of Charles I to the death of Queen Anne, it is hard to think of any English voyages of discovery at all comparable with Dampier's, or of any travel record half as valuable as his. Hakluyt died in 1616, and in the same year (it was also the year in which the Dutch rounded Cape Horn) the little barque " Discovery " left Gravesend on its famous voyage to Baffin's Bay. But between that date and Dampier's death in 1715— between the last of the Elizabethans and the great sailors of the mid-eighteenth century—this one figure stands out almost alone.

It is not that the English effort ceased entirely during this period ; except for the break caused by the Civil War, it was both continuous and successful. But it is as though the English explorers, moved by some common impulse, had given up sighing for new worlds to conquer, and agreed to concentrate upon exploiting and extending the discoveries already made. And that makes them rather shadowy figures from our point of view, limping far behind such gallant adventurers as the Dutchman, Tasman, or their own countryman, Dampier.

Again, it is not as though the scientific work of the

geographers and map-makers had been allowed to cease.
On the contrary, throughout the reign of Charles II,
we seem to have been actively preparing, whether con-
sciously or not, for the great effort that was to mark
the middle years of the succeeding century. Shipbuild-
ing design improved, being not a little encouraged by
the intelligent interest taken in the subject by the King.
Navigation was studied to some purpose. For the first
time it became possible to take accurate observations at
sea. And by 1713 that most efficient and industrious
of Royal Commissions, the Board of Longitude, had
begun its sittings in London, and was mightily smoothing
the way for Dampier's successors. In fact, the whole
atmosphere had changed. But Dampier himself bene-
fited little by all this. He was just too soon. He put
to sea in leaky ships and ill-equipped. He says himself
that the only maps which he possessed of the Pacific
were " all false." When he sailed the crazy " Roebuck "
to the unknown shores of Australia in 1699, and when
he piloted Woodes Rogers round the world, he did so
with surprisingly few technical advantages over his
Elizabethan predecessors. He had mutinous crews, and
an unfortunate " past " of his own, which probably
made it difficult for him to impose his authority on
subordinate officers. Only his natural genius and his
irrepressible spirit of adventure brought him through.

Yet in the face of this record it has been said of
Dampier—and it is implied in everything that is written
of him—that he was " not formed of the stuff of which
explorers are made." [1] There may be some truth in
that, and I do not know that I am much concerned to
deny it. After all, it only makes him more interesting.
Perhaps it is not really so easy to define precisely the
kind of material that goes to make explorers. Certainly
they have differed quite noticeably in the past. It

[1] W. Clark Russell in *English Men of Action*. Macmillan: 1925.

would be difficult, for instance, to imagine two characters more opposed than those of Drake and Raleigh—or Hawkins and Grenville. And, coming a little nearer to Dampier's own time, what greater contrast could there be than between that mad fellow Coryat, who preceded him, and the sagacious Captain Cook, who came after ? There are many different kinds of " stuff " here ; and it may very well be that you cannot say what constitutes a great explorer, any more than you can say what constitutes a great artist, except by looking at the results.

But Dampier was undoubtedly unusual. He has no counterpart in the whole history of English exploration. He lacked so conspicuously some of the most obvious characteristics which we expect to find in explorers, and without which it seems impossible that they should succeed. You have only to look at his portrait. It was painted by Thomas Murray, and has become increasingly popular in black and white reproductions during recent years. Some months ago, a very striking advertising poster [1] was displayed on the London hoardings, in which were grouped together figures representing most of the great English explorers from the Elizabethans to the present day. Dampier, of course, was among them ; and anyone who took the trouble to study that poster will surely agree that it was quite startling to come upon this dark, unhappy, brooding face amid the bluff, open, confident countenances of the other great discoverers of our Empire.

The original hangs in the National Portrait Gallery ; and, if it is not one of the most important works of art there, it is certainly one of the most interesting from the psychological point of view. It depicts a thin, slightly-built man in middle life, not so dark as the black and white prints would suggest—no swarthy gipsy—but a

[1] Published by the Empire Marketing Board.

man of ruddy complexion with brown (not black) hair and strangely dark blue eyes. There is a beak of a nose, a firm, round chin, and a jutting underlip, from which his critics no doubt deduced obstinacy and his friends strength. But the chief impression that one carries away is of a rather pathetic, battered look in his large eyes, as of one who had started out in life with high romantic ideals and got cruelly mauled by the world. It is a fascinating, appealing, baffling portrait. Plainly the artist, Murray, was keenly interested in his subject, for we do not find this quality in his other work. And underneath the portrait is the simple legend : " *Captain William Dampier : Pirate and Hydrographer.*" It is as though we were to describe a man as " John Smith, burglar and mathematician," or " Tom Jones, bushranger and astronomer." The description is not quite fair to Dampier, for, though he sailed with the buccaneers, that was a very different thing from turning pirate ; but the legend does at any rate give the measure of his astonishing versatility.

As for his faults, they are here written clearly in his face for all to see. We can perceive a sort of petulant discontent with life, and more than a hint of temper. On the other hand, the face is strong and purposeful, without being really commanding. There is not quite enough of the drill-sergeant here. It is plain from his record that Dampier did not understand how to manage men. He had not the habit of command. His only idea of keeping his crew in order was to swear at them. Nor can we forget that when he returned from Australia, a court-martial found him to be " not a fit person to be employed as commander of any of his Majesty's ships "— though it is, perhaps, equally important to remember that he was, as a matter of fact, given another command within the year ! Discipline in those days was not the simple matter that it is now. If punishments were severe, rules were less stereotyped : there was the recognized custom of consulting subordinates before taking big decisions ; and, on those long voyages, there was a readiness on the part of the ship's company to engage in intrigues against their superiors, which would bring swift retribution to-day. Drake had to hang a man for mutiny ; John Smith was nearly hanged for it himself ; Shelvocke, who was Dampier's contemporary (and also circumnavigated the globe) did not better but worse than he.

Yet I do not find it easy to explain this weakness in Dampier. It has been suggested already that his buccaneering past may have been against him, when in command of the King's ships. But to know that your captain was an old buccaneer, who had sailed with Sharp and Sawkins, seems no reason for defying him on his own quarter-deck. Rather the contrary ! It may possibly have led Dampier's people to underestimate his intelligence and distrust his intentions— no doubt a bad enough thing on a ship—but it is no adequate explanation of his failure as a disciplinarian.

Sir Albert Gray, in the masterly little essay on Dampier which he has contributed to a recent edition of *A New Voyage Round the World*,[1] suggests that though Dampier was with the buccaneers he was never of them ; that he neither sought nor desired high command in so disreputable a profession ; that this Somerset farmer's son, brought up as a shopkeeper, was, in fact, too much of a gentleman. It is a penetrating remark. Dampier never seems to have made any money out of these voyages ; nor out of any voyage except his last—which not he, but Woodes Rogers, commanded. He had other ideals. Alone among his associates, he was more

---

[1] *A New Voyage Round the World*. By William Dampier. With an Introduction by Sir Albert Gray, K.C.B., K.C., President of the Hakluyt Society. Argonaut Press. London : 1927.

interested in the countries they saw than in the amount of money they could make out of them.   The fact that his name is hardly mentioned by those of his early buccaneering companions who have left us accounts of their adventures, may not unreasonably be attributed to this detached attitude of his.

He had, moreover, a natural modesty, still more unusual in such company.   We see it everywhere in his writings.   And in his appearance, as we have just noted, there was little of the swashbuckler.   He was not, for instance, the kind of man to cut a figure in London society, and we shall gather nothing of his personality in private life from a study of contemporary memoirs.   But there is one invaluable reference by the diarist, John Evelyn, which cannot be omitted from any character sketch of Dampier.   Evelyn was evidently aware of the charges of violence and bad language brought against Dampier by his enemies.   Yet when he met him at dinner at the house of Samuel Pepys, the diarist, he found him " a more modest man than one would imagine by relation of the crew he had assorted with."   What interests us here is that the shrewd and discriminating Mr. Pepys should have thought well enough of him to invite him to dinner with his old friend, Evelyn ; and that a great gentleman like John Evelyn should have been so pleasantly surprised by his modest address.   If only Pepys's eyes had not failed him thirty years before, we might even have had one of his own characteristic comments upon this very exceptional buccaneer.

The truth is that it is just this weakness—-if we must call it a weakness—in Dampier's character that makes him so attractive.   It is more than a mere accident of a quiet, intellectual young fellow finding himself serving with the buccaneers. Indeed it was no accident. Dampier went to sea at an early age, against the wishes

of his father, because no other way of life would serve
him.   He has given us his own account of the matter,
and it requires no stretch of the imagination to picture
him struggling miserably with his Latin books in that
Somerset school, while all his heart was far away on the
Spanish Main.

What schoolboy would have felt otherwise in those
great days ?   The wonder is that they did not all run
away to sea !   Even to-day there is more of the world
undiscovered than most people are aware of ; but it is
a mere odd corner or two, compared with the wide
prospect which offered itself to adventurous youth in the
latter part of the seventeenth century.   Half the earth
and sea lay open to their endeavour.   Comparatively
few of the islands of the Pacific had been discovered ;
Africa had only been nibbled at ; great tracts of land
were imagined where in reality there was only sea ; it
was not even known that Australia was a continent.
Dampier, over his Latin books, may well have dreamed
of a time when his name would appear on every map—
as it does to-day.   That, I think, is the real clue to his
character.   He was not by nature a man of action, but
an artist and a dreamer.   He was a romantic schoolboy
whose dreams came true—came true because he *made*
them.   His great successor, James Cook, ran away to
sea in his early teens.   Cook, with his commanding
presence and tougher fibre, had every qualification for
the part.   Dampier had only his dreams.   Yet he got
to Australia just the same—we recall that jutting underlip !—and it was only by a chance that he missed being
acclaimed its true discoverer instead of Cook.

This is no fantastic theory of Dampier's character,
based upon the few words he has written about his early
life.   As we follow the story of his career, we shall find
evidence of it at every turn : of his restless longing for
adventure, his insatiable appetite for strange sights, of

the curiosity—that is the word—which has been the inspiration of all great travel since the world began. It is the one undisputed fact about him. He left Captain Edward Davis to go with Swan in 1685, " not from any dislike to my old captain, but to get some knowledge of the northern parts of this Continent of Mexico," and because Swan intended eventually to pass over for the East Indies, " which was always very agreeable to my inclinations." He left Swan for similar reasons in the following year, " knowing that the further we went, the more knowledge and experience I should get, which was the main thing I regarded." He only joined the buccaneers " more to indulge my curiosity·than to get wealth." Elsewhere there are contradictions. One hostile writer will assert that Dampier's crew were in the habit of calling him a coward to his face ; and a few pages later the same critic will complain that he was such a bully that he " would fly out in a passion " if anyone even ventured to differ from him. But in regard to his inspiration, there seems to be no doubt. He was no sooner back in England than he began thinking of his next voyage. That was the spirit that sustained him. The fact that his writings are so extraordinarily readable to-day is due, not only to his natural literary gift, of which he was quite unaware, but to this same passionate interest in the world and its inhabitants. The eager notes which he jotted down about everything he saw could have been written by no one else. Dampier may not have been a born leader of men ; but he was, at any rate, a born traveller, and a born travel-writer.

Such was the character of the man whose career we are about to study. The duty of his biographer is, as I understand it, simply to present him whole—to state the facts—without any attempt to judge him by twentieth-century standards, or to point the moral of his tale. Dampier is not up for judgment here. He is not before

" the bar of history." Indeed—it has been said before, but cannot be said too often—history is not a bar in the sense of being a police-court. It would be more reasonable to describe it as a bar in the sense of being a place where men assemble together to tell stories of those who have gone before, and drink their healths, perhaps ; but not to judge them. In such an atmosphere, Captain William Dampier, "pirate and hydrographer," would be at his ease. Yet because he was so human, we may find a special pleasure in his story. For with all his limitations, and in the absence (as it turned out) of any particular *flair* for the business of exploring, he did always keep his goal in front of him, and he did succeed in doing just those things which so many of us have longed to do and have not had the pluck even to attempt.

It is difficult to see how there can be a dull page in this book, even in the hands of the clumsiest editor. For, except in the first few chapters, where I have endeavoured to rewrite a part of Dampier's life which has never been fully dealt with before, editing is really all that has been required. Dampier always thought his story more important than himself—he says so, over and over again—and his present biographer very humbly agrees. I have therefore put the story first and left the man to take care of himself. It is the method he would have preferred. The bare facts of his amazing career make the best commentary on his character. And the story itself is such a good one, so prodigal of incident, so brightly coloured with effects of light and shade, seen in every part of the globe, that it is hard to believe it can have been made to appear uninteresting.

CHAPTER II

WILLIAM DAMPIER SERVES
THE KING

ILLIAM DAMPIER was born in the village of East Coker, near Yeovil, in Somersetshire, in the year 165–, but there, immediately, our troubles begin.

There is a certain prejudice nowadays against the discussion of such things as dates and birthdays. They are regarded as part of the dismal paraphernalia of Professor Dry-as-dust, as repulsive and inexplicable to the general public as footnotes, or even genealogical tables. Yet history is truly described in the dictionary as " a narration of facts," and we know very well in our hearts that all the fun and romance of it are gone unless we can be sure that it is accurate. Truth usually makes a better story than fiction. To tell any audience that the anecdote you are about to relate happens to be a true one is the surest way of gaining attention. But we shall not get that full flavour of the true story, which gives it its peculiar and delightful character, unless we are certain that it *is* true. In short, if we are going to mention the date of Dampier's birth at all, we might as well get it right.

Every authority that I have consulted gives 1652 as the year. There seems to be good reason to suppose that the correct date is 1651. If it may be said without offence, the biographers have apparently followed one another blindly in a sort of game of " Follow-my-leader," quoting a date which probably has its origin in one or other of the brief biographical sketches which appeared in the course of the eighteenth century. Our real authorities are but two—Dampier's own reference to the subject, in the second volume of his *Voyages* ; and the parish register of the village of East Coker. Dampier was one of the most modest explorers that ever sailed the seas, and his own description of his early days is characteristically brief. His statement of his age at the beginning of one of his early voyages is useful, but does not enable us to decide definitely as between 1652 and 1651, in fixing the year of his birth.

The parish register of East Coker, on the other hand, is as fascinating and eloquent a work as it has ever been my good fortune to read. And it has, of course, the virtue of precision. Our immediate concern is with the baptisms, and of these we have to decide between two entries : September 5th, 1651, William Dampier, son of George and Ann ; and June 8th, 1652, William Dampier, son of William and Joan. It has been assumed, on I know not what grounds, that the latter is our man. But Dampier, in his writings, makes allusion to his " brothers " at East Coker, and also to his " brother," and in later life he refers frequently to his " brother George." Now William, the son of William and Joan, had no brothers, according to the register ; whereas William, the son of George and Ann, had a brother (only one, it is true) born in 1648, whose name was George. Dampier mentions that when he was home from his earlier voyages he would stay with his family (once he says his " friends ") in East Coker, and it is reasonable to suppose that the family would be represented by this George, who, as the elder brother, would naturally have carried on the farm which the Dampiers held from the local squire, Colonel Helyar—of whom more hereafter. It is true that George is the only brother mentioned in the register. It is true, too, that we find no record of the death of George the elder, and that the death of Ann (his " widow ") took place in October, 1665, and not in 1668, the year mentioned by Sir J. K. Laughton (in the *Dictionary of National Biography*), Smyth and others as that in which Dampier's mother died. I suggest, however, that these authorities are wrong. As a matter of fact, there is no record at East Coker of the death of any Dampier, male or female, in 1668. William, the son of George and Ann, had at any rate one brother (which is more than we can say for the rival), and of the right name too ; and the fact that Ann, at her death, was referred to as a " widow " proves that the elder George was already dead, and fits in with Dampier's statement in his *Voyages* that his parents died in his youth. On the face of it, therefore, the evidence of the parish register favours the George-Ann parentage of 1651.

There is only one thing more to say about this parish register. The baptisms we are concerned with were not, of course, performed by the regular Church of England parson of the parish, but by some Puritan interloper of the Commonwealth period—in point of fact by one Henry Cackney, if I read his signature aright. Henry seems to have been a man of character, and it is amusing to note the dramatic effect of his entry upon the register. About a year after the execution of King Charles I, the small, neat, educated handwriting of the vicar, the Reverend Richard Gore, suddenly disappears, and we get in its place a bold scrawl, sprawling all over the pages. The entries become hurried, incomplete, not always even in chronological order. After October 20th, 1653, there occurs the following memorandum : " The Old Register Booke of East Coker was fild of names in the yeare of our Lord God 1654 and a nother made that same yeare by me Henry Cackney.   Anno Dom. 1654." By then, unfortunately, the damage had been done, so far as the Dampiers are concerned.   For it is precisely in 1652 (the commonly accepted year of our William's birth) that we find half a page that has apparently been trampled on, or rubbed over with a flat iron, and is almost illegible.   It would perhaps be unfair to blame the God-fearing Henry personally for this ; but, politics and religion apart, I could wish that another memorandum which follows closely after it had come only ten years sooner.   It reads : " Memorandum that Mr. Richard Gore Vicar of Coker did reade the Articles of the Church of England on the twentieth day of October Anno Domini 1661."   Thereafter we have only Mr. Gore's careful script.[1]   But in the meantime—and this is important for our purpose—it is to be noted that William Dampier, the son of George and Ann, who was born in 1651, might very well have had another brother born in the period covered by the illegible page of 1652 ; whereas this is impossible in the case of William, the son of William and Joan, since he himself was born in June of that same year.   I therefore conclude that William Dampier, the explorer, was baptized at East Coker on the 5th September 1651, being the son of George Dampier and Ann, his wife.[2]

[1] It is fair to add that a little later, between 1668 and 1678, there is a blank of ten years, the intervening space being occupied by a clumsy drawing of a man and some horses and cows, apparently executed by an irreverently-minded child.   But Mr. Richard Gore was dead by then. His dissenting rival, Cackney, had died as early as 1664 ; the triumph of the " malignants " at the Restoration was evidently too much for him.

[2] As to her being his wife there is, happily, no doubt.   " From his wife," says the register proudly.   Alas, that it should be thought a matter for boasting !—but the most casual glance at this village record shows the reason why.

East Coker is an altogether charming village, and Dampier must often have seen it (as I did) on a bright spring morning, with its lilac trees blossoming into every shade of mauve and violet round the old, grey, thatched cottages. Many, if not most, of the present houses must have been standing in Dampier's time. In the church a modern brass now commemorates his exploits ; but little else is altered, and over the old oak door there is still a hatchment with the Royal Arms, set up in 1660 to celebrate the Restoration, which must, when its colours were bright and new, have been an object of delight to his childish eyes. They have few traditions of him in the village : after all, he was there only for comparatively brief periods, and his family has long since disappeared. But they will show you the house where he is said to have been born—Hymerford House, a typical mediæval building of perhaps the fifteenth century, of which the great hall and the kitchens beyond the screen at one end have been interfered with scarcely at all. As usually happens, the hall has been divided inside into two stories, so that the tops of the old mullioned windows now give light to the passages on the floor above ; but the outside of the house is still so mellow and old and English that it is difficult to imagine even the wildest boy wanting to run away from it to sea. Hymerford House is a farm-house now (they called it Bridge Farm till a year or two ago, but the present occupant has reverted to the older name), and if Dampier was born there it must have served the same purpose in 1651, for his father was a tenant farmer—that we know. The Dampiers (or, as it was occasionally written, Dampeeries) seem to have been fairly substantial folk ; but what was the size and distribution of the family, and what became of them—whether, for instance, that Dr. Dampier who was promoted by George III to the Deanery of Rochester in 1782, and whose son was made

HYMERFORD HOUSE, EAST COKER, DAMPIER'S BIRTHPLACE

Bishop of Ely, came originally from East Coker, I am unable to say. Nor does it matter much.

When young William Dampier reached school age, he suffered the fate of most small boys. His biographers have assumed that he was put to school at Yeovil ; but there is a grammar school of an ancient foundation at the neighbouring Crewkerne, and it is at least equally likely that he was sent there. We do not know. All the evidence that we possess is contained in his own brief and almost apologetic reference to his schooldays referred to above. In it he says : " My friends did not originally design me for the sea, but bred me at school till I came to years fit for a trade. But upon the death of my father and mother, they who had the disposal of me took other measures ; and having remov'd me from the Latine School to learn Writing and Arithmetick, they soon after placed me with a Master of a Ship at Weymouth, complying with the inclinations I had very early of seeing the World."

It will be observed that his guardians, whoever they were, only took the rather strong step of sending him to sea, instead of to a trade, in compliance with his own wishes. It is a plain case of a schoolboy's dream of travel and adventure—not more romantic, nor less so, than a thousand others.

With this Weymouth skipper, young Dampier made a short voyage to France. He returned with his appetite for travel considerably stimulated, and almost immediately set out again upon his first long voyage—a trip to Newfoundland. He was now, as he tells us, " about eighteen years of age," his parents had been dead for years, and he was feeling well able to look after himself. Yet the voyage to Newfoundland was a failure. It occupied the whole of one summer. But Dampier was so horribly " pinched " by the rigour of that cold climate that he swore that he would never sail so far North again—and he kept his word. Indeed it came near to cooling his ardour for travel altogether. He returned to his friends at East Coker—no doubt to his brother George, who would now be a man of twenty-one or twenty-two—and he tells us of this with an air of finality which suggests that he fully intended to stay there.

But he could not sit quiet ; the thing was in his blood ; and presently he began to pay flitting visits to London. And there, of course—since the whole world is, happily, not so cold as Newfoundland—he presently got an offer of what he calls a " warm voyage " (and a long one too) " both which I always desired," and was off to sea again.

This time he entered himself aboard an outward-bound East Indiaman, the " John and Martha " of London (Captain Earning), and was employed before the mast—for his apprenticeship days were over, and he was now an able seaman. Of this third voyage, like the first and second, we know very little. Dampier's East Indiaman would be a vessel of perhaps six hundred tons burthen.[1] She would carry a crew of about two hundred men and would be heavily armed. It is true that merchantmen of this period enjoyed a security at sea such as the Elizabethans had never known. Cromwell had suppressed the Algerian pirates (after cutting off the King's head for trying to raise " ship money " for the same purpose !), and had made the Mediterranean safe for our shipping. The capture of Jamaica had given our trade a fillip in the West. Spain had her tail down ; the Portuguese were no longer dangerous in India and the East. But, alas, we live in an envious

[1] Fifty years before this date, the East India merchants had supplied themselves with a new fleet of four ships of 650, 500, 300 and 200 tons respectively. Some of these may still have been afloat when Dampier went to sea ; in any case, they give a rough clue to the probable tonnage of the " John and Martha."

world ! No sooner had our ancestors got rid of the rivalry of the " cruel Spaniard " and the " treacherous Portingall " than another trade competitor arrived upon the scene—the equally cruel (and, if we may believe the English chroniclers, equally treacherous) " Hollander." The first Dutch war broke out in the year after Dampier's birth. Before he died he was to see the Dutch, in their turn, fall behind in the race, and become our allies against our next hated rival, France.

In the meantime, however, he was brought up in an anti-Dutch atmosphere. When he sailed on the " John and Martha " for the Dutch Spice Islands, there were old sailormen in the inns of Weymouth and London who could remember the so-called " Massacre " of Amboina in 1623, when the Dutch arrested all the Englishmen at one of the East India Company's factories, tortured them cruelly, and upon the unwilling evidence thus obtained publicly executed ten of them for conspiracy, with an indecent haste and a disregard of justice which English seamen would not easily forget. Bickerings had continued ever since, whether the two nations happened to be officially at war or at peace. Hence the guns on board the " John and Martha."

Captain Earning, on his owners' instructions, sailed direct for the port of Bantam, in the Dutch island of Java. He made a good passage, and stayed at Bantam for about two months, during which time he and his crew managed to keep out of trouble with the local authorities. He returned to England in little over a year, having called at only two intermediate ports—St. Iago in the Cape Verde Islands on the way out, and Ascension Island on the return journey. Dampier confesses regretfully that he kept no journal of this voyage, and there will be few of his readers to-day who do not share that regret. On the other hand, he learnt a great deal about practical navigation, a subject in which he

B

was eventually to excel all his contemporaries. How a seaman serving before the mast found time and opportunity for such studies is not easy to see ; but it is one of the most striking features of Dampier's career that he never ceased to " improve himself " in this way—not even when serving among the buccaneers.

Dampier returned to England at a somewhat critical moment in his country's history. He says : " We arrived at Plymouth about two months before Sir Robert Holmes went out to fall upon the Dutch Smyrna fleet." This dates his arrival ; because Holmes set sail on that indefensible [1] and, as it turned out, unsuccessful raid on the 23rd March 1672. The " John and Martha " must therefore have arrived about February. Dampier went home to East Coker, and stayed with his brother George, who was probably still at Hymerford House. He remained there taking his ease, watching the lilac trees bloom and fade, till spring turned to summer, and autumn to winter, by which time, as he tells us, he was once more " weary of staying a-shore." But, when he began looking out for another ship, he found the situation altogether altered. The Second Dutch War had broken out—not upon the declaration of the Dutch, as one might have expected after Holmes's exploit, but upon that of the King of England—and the rival fleets were preparing to put to sea. For a young man of twenty-one in search of adventure there seemed only one course to pursue, and Dampier took it. He " listed," as he calls it, on one of the King's ships, the " Royal Prince," commanded by Sir Edward Spragge.

It is necessary here to say a word about the naval situation. The great battle of Sole Bay (or Southwold) between the English and French on the one side and the Dutch on the other, had been fought in the previous summer while Dampier was still resting on his brother's

---

[1] The two countries were still officially at peace.

farm. The Duke of York (afterwards James II), who commanded the allied fleet, had shown creditable seamanship, and was not responsible for the indecisive result. For that the blame must rest chiefly upon the French, whose Admiral, D'Estrées, went off on a different tack at the critical moment, thus separating the allies' fleet, and then allowed himself to be " held " by a small Dutch detachment while the main battle was being fought between the British and Dutch. His conduct in the affair gave rise to the strong suspicion that he was under orders from Paris not to do more than he could help to assist a nominal ally in whom the French Government already began to perceive a future enemy. But between Sole Bay and the renewal of fighting in the following year, the Test Act had been passed, and the Duke of York had been obliged to give up his command—not because he was incompetent, but simply because he was a Roman Catholic. Rupert had taken his place, amid loud popular cheers for " the Protestant Prince." Rupert was the more experienced naval commander of the two, but in the forthcoming operations he certainly did no better than the Duke, and in particular showed little of that dash which characterized his cavalry tactics on land.

The French fleet, which was preparing to join ours, was still commanded by D'Estrées, in spite of (or as a reward for) his conduct at Sole Bay. The great De Ruyter again commanded the Dutch. On shore in Holland there had been changes. The two De Witts, the Republican leaders, had been murdered, and the Prince of Orange (afterwards William III of England) was now Captain-General and Admiral of the United Provinces, which gave him the supreme direction of the war. Happily for Holland, however, he did not take from De Ruyter the command of the fleet. Finally, there was a force of 6000 English troops at Yarmouth, waiting to be embarked for Holland, if we should succeed in eliminating De Ruyter's ships.

De Ruyter had about fifty-five ships of the line, as against fifty-four English and twenty-seven French. In these circumstances, he adopted a policy which may be described as one of active defence. It was decided that the Dutch fleet " should be posted in the passage of Schooneveldt, or a little farther south towards Ostend, to observe the enemy, and if attacked, or seeing the enemy's fleet disposed to make a descent upon the shores of the United Provinces, should resist vigorously by opposing his designs and destroying his ships." [1] This was the Dutch strategy. The English policy, on the other hand, may be described, in the words of a modern statesman, as that of " digging them out like rats."

But first, at the end of April, before he finally settled down to the defensive, De Ruyter made a spirited sally, with the object of blocking the mouth of the Thames by sinking ships in the fairway. On May 2nd, 1673, he was off the Thames, with his " sinkers " (as the English called them) ready to put his plan into operation. But a thick fog kept him inactive, and when it suddenly lifted on May 4th, he saw Rupert's fleet waiting for him, lying off the Middle Ground. De Ruyter at once refused action, and sailed back to Holland with his " sinkers." On the 20th May, Rupert followed him.

Dampier, as we have seen, was serving on board the " Royal Prince." We are not to visualize one of those clumsy " overbuilt " Elizabethan warships. Naval architecture had greatly improved since Charles I's " Royal Sovereign " (built for him in 1637 by Phineas Pett) had inaugurated a new and better school of ship construction. The Dutch, and afterwards the French, were, generally speaking, our equals in design ; but the

---

[1] Brandt : *Life of De Ruyter*, quoted by Mahan.

superiority of English oak over other European timbers, and the still more marked superiority of English seamen, gave us two enormous advantages.   Phineas Pett, when he built the old " Prince Royal " in 1610, had been the first to abandon the high beak, or prow, and the square buttock, or tuck.   At the end of the seventeenth century, the Dutch and French still had square tucks, but in English ships they were rounded.   The raised stern, which gave to Elizabethan warships an appearance of toppling forward on their noses, was reduced in height by English, Dutch and French designers alike, and was built in such a way as to conform with the general sweep of the ship's lines.   It was no longer (nor was the forecastle) an irrelevant excrescence upon the deck of the ship.   Indeed, the general appearance of a warship of 1673 was surprisingly like that of one of Nelson's vessels, and surprisingly different from Drake's.

The men, happily, were the same.   Admiral Mahan quotes the remark of a French critic, Chabaud-Arnault, who writes that " the undeniable superiority of Ruyter in experience and genius could not compensate for the weakness or incapacity of part of the Dutch officers and the manifest inferiority of the men under their orders." Yet the amazing fact is that a large proportion—probably most—of the English crews were composed of pressed men.   The captain of the " Royal Prince " found it as difficult to collect his crew as Nelson did on the " Victory " !   Volunteers like Dampier were probably in a minority.   Pepys tells us that in 1665, when the Fleet was in harbour, the Duke of York had to send for soldiers " to go keep pressmen on board our ships." He twice mentions the " mutinous " spirit of the men, which is not surprising when we consider how often the pay of these poor conscripts was in arrears.   Pepys, as an Admiralty official, sometimes found it impossible to

work at his office, " because of the horrible crowd and
lamentable moan of the poor seamen, that lie starving
on the streets for lack of money, which do trouble and
perplex me to the heart ; and more at noon, when we
were to go through them, for then above a whole hundred
of them followed us, some cursing, some swearing, some
praying to us." Dampier, however, had made his bed,
and there is nothing in his writings to show that he did
not willingly lie upon it.

His immediate commander, Sir Edward Spragge, of
the " Royal Prince," was quite a character in his way.
A turbulent, intriguing, hard-living, recklessly courage-
ous leader of the Cavalier type, his personality seems to
have made a considerable impression upon all who came
into contact with him. Pepys met him at dinner at Sir
William Penn's, and found him " a merry man that sang
a pleasant song pleasantly." Pepys would forgive much
to a boon companion who could also sing ; but unfortunately Spragge was Prince Rupert's favourite, and
used his influence there with characteristic indiscretion ;
whereas Pepys was always a Duke's man. In the end,
the diarist came to distrust Spragge's judgment, and
even his honesty. It is clear, however, that he was a
very popular commander on board the " Royal Prince." [1]

Rupert, then, followed De Ruyter, to the Dutch coast,
where he was sheltering in the Schooneveldt. The idea
was to send forward a detached squadron, with fire ships,
to attempt to draw him out. It was a dangerous game
to play with De Ruyter. Choosing his moment, he
sallied out vigorously, and Rupert's leading squadron
was rather badly mauled. De Ruyter withdrew before
the main body could come up. It is amusing to note
that on this occasion the French, under D'Estrées, were

[1] It is a coincidence, perhaps worth noting, that the previous commander of the " Royal Prince " was Pepys's friend, Lord Sandwich,
who was killed on board of her at Sole Bay.

placed in the centre so that they could not sheer off, and that, finding themselves in this position, they stoutly resisted the Dutch attack.   After De Ruyter's retirement, Rupert held his ground and maintained a blockade of the Dutch coast.   It appears that Spragge disapproved of the position of the allied fleet, and wanted the Prince to alter it, but Rupert refused.   On June 4th De Ruyter made another sally.   Again he was too weak to press home his attack ; but this time he did enough damage to cause Rupert to return to England to refit.   Another reason for the return may have been that the transports were not yet ready for the troops on shore.

At any rate, the Fleet did not put to sea again till July 22nd.   Once more they made for the coast of Holland, and about August 9th Dampier was taken ill, and was " put on board a hospital ship."   The very fact that there were hospital ships in attendance on the Fleet seems to show that Pepys's well-known reference to " this confounded business " of what to do with the wounded did not indicate quite such a state of unpreparedness as might be supposed.   Dampier was well out of the ensuing engagement, commonly known as the Battle of the Texel.   He tells us, however, that he watched it from the deck of the hospital ship.

Seen thus, at a safe distance, it must have been a fine and inspiring sight.   The whole panorama of the battle, just as Dampier saw it, may be studied in the large coloured maps—or rather pictures—done by contemporary artists, and now in the possession of the Earl of Dartmouth.   Reproductions of these spirited works of art, with Sir Julian Corbett's editorial notes, are to be found in the British Museum.[1]   The battle began about

[1] Sir Julian Corbett thinks that these drawings are " designs prepared by a tapestry draughtsman from bird's-eye views specially drawn by William Van der Velde from his original sketches, after they had been corrected by officers who were present at the engagement."   Some of

seven or eight in the morning of August 11th. As the hostile fleets approached each other, it was seen that Tromp, who commanded the Dutch right, was making a dead set at Spragge, who, as Admiral of the Blue, was in command of the English left, or rear. They were old enemies, having been " opposite numbers " before now. Accordingly when Spragge saw Tromp heading for him, he promptly hove to. He has been severely criticized for this action, the effect of which, of course, was to hold back the Blue Squadron and thus divide the English Fleet in two (D'Estrées, it should be added, was far on ahead with the extreme right and managed once more to keep out of the fighting altogether !) Spragge's officers in their report of the battle after his death, offered a number of technical (and not very convincing) reasons for his action ; but there seems to be no doubt that he waited for Tromp in a purely sporting spirit. Among the last words that he wrote in his journal on the night before the battle were : " Tromp is now in the rear (or right) . . . he will, I hope, fall to my share in the Blue Squadron to-morrow." He always referred to Tromp as his " consort." Anyhow, the result of his action was that a long and stationary duel took place between the " Royal Prince " and Tromp, with the other vessels of their respective squadrons joining in ; while the vans, under Rupert and De Ruyter, gradually drew farther and farther away. And it was probably this separation of the battle into two parts, even more than the defection of the French, which deprived Rupert of victory.

Dampier must have watched the duel with considerable excitement from the decks of his hospital ship. It was an Homeric contest (indeed it would technically, perhaps, have been better placed in the Iliad than in a

them also depict the two earlier sea-fights (referred to above) at which Dampier was present.

From a colour print lent by Messrs. T. H. Parker

THE BATTLE OF THE TEXEL, AUGUST 11TH, 1673

scientific modern sea-fight) and Dampier's shipmates seem to have done well. " For three hours (says an eye-witness) they lay braving one another with their topsails to the mast : Tromp was well seconded by several stout ships, from whence a gun was not fired at anybody but Sir Edward (*i.e.* his ship) as long as they could bring any to bear." In the end, the " Royal Prince " was completely disabled, and Tromp's " Golden Lion " was in little better case. In the Dartmouth pictures, we see them both drifting out of the fighting line, like birds with broken wings. Spragge made a desperate attempt to get back at Tromp about 10 a.m., but just then both his main mast and mizzen went by the board ; and, seeing that nothing could be done with the shattered " Royal Prince," he shifted his flag to the " St. George " and afterwards to the " Michael." Tromp and several other Dutchmen then surrounded the " Royal Prince," like vultures round a corpse ; but Dampier's shipmates again put up a great fight (" few finer defences of a disabled ship are on record," says Sir Julian Corbett) ; and presently Vice-Admiral Kempthorn, and after him Lord Ossory, intervened with their divisions to save the " Royal Prince " from capture. Eventually, in the evening, she was safely towed out of the battle.

Spragge was killed about 7 p.m., while shifting his flag yet again—this time to the " Royal Charles." He had the flag with him in a small boat, and when they pointed out to him that the Dutch would probably see it, and that it would be safer to go on board a frigate, he " scorned to be governed by arguments of fear." The Dutch did see it. They opened fire on the boat, and sank it ; and when the gallant Spragge was picked up out of the water he was found to be dead. We are told that he could not swim ; but his lieutenant and coxswain had held him up by the arms, and it is not clear whether his death was due to drowning or the enemy's fire.

So ended this confused and unsatisfactory Battle of the Texel, in which neither side lost a single ship and both claimed the victory. Dampier was put ashore at Harwich, with the rest of the sick and wounded, and " having languished a great while " in hospital, he went home once again to his brother to recover his health.

CHAPTER III

HE GOES TO THE WEST INDIES

BOUT this time—either just before or just after William Dampier's return from the Dutch War—his elder brother George moved from East Coker to a neighbouring estate, presumably that "Porton, near Breadport, Dorset" which is mentioned as George's place of residence in William's will. It was at Porton, I think, not at East Coker, that Dampier spent most, if not all, of his sick leave. He now decided not to return to the Navy. A treaty of peace, in which the Dutch conceded most of the English demands, was signed in 1674 ; but months before that it became apparent that all was over except the shouting, both nations being heartily sick of the war. Moreover Dampier had never quite " got the hang " of naval ways and naval discipline, as he himself admitted in after years, when he came to command a king's ship. He was not an easy man to place, as we shall presently discover ; for the fact is that he was equally out of his element in a king's ship and in the noisy fo'c'sle of a buccaneer.

Dampier, however, was rapidly recovering his health ; and " with my health I recovered my old inclination for the Sea." In fact, the South was calling, and he began to look round for another " warm voyage." On this occasion there was no need to visit London. He got in touch with a " neighbouring gentleman," Colonel

Helyar, of East Coker, his father's old landlord.[1] Colonel
Helyar happened to be interested in the West Indies.
He owned property there, and he seems to have imported
negro servants into East Coker, for a " black-a-moor "
of his is recorded as having been baptized in the parish
church in the year of Dampier's birth. He had taken a
fancy to young William, and now came forward with
what the latter calls " a reasonable offer " to go and
manage a plantation of his in Jamaica, under one Mr.
Whalley. Dampier was now twenty-two years of age ;
he had never been in the West Indies ; and he needed
no persuasion. He immediately booked his passage with
Captain Kent, in the " Content " of London, and sailed
from the River Thames " in the beginning of the year
1674 "—by which he means March or April [2]—thus
embarking with a good heart upon his fifth voyage. One
clause in his agreement with Captain Kent throws an
interesting light upon the evils of the system of deporting
criminals to Jamaica for forced labour. To avoid the
danger of being " trepaned," as he calls it, and sold as a
slave, Dampier agreed with Captain Kent to work his
passage out as a seaman, though, in view of the employment he was going to, he could doubtless have paid his
fare. At the same time, he was careful to get the
captain's written agreement to discharge him formally
after he had landed.

The " Content " met with favourable winds from the
start, and " went merrily along " until they had put the
Atlantic behind them, and came in sight of Barbadoes.
It would appear, however, that the passengers on board
were but a mean-spirited crowd. When they came in
sight of the first island, the Captain made them a sporting

[1] The Helyars continued as Lords of the Manor at East Coker down
to our own time.   The last male heir, Captain Helyar, was killed in the
Great War of 1914-18.
[2] " 1674 " is O.S.

offer.   The place was not included in his itinerary, he
said, but it was a long time since they had seen land ;
and if they would club together and pay the port charges,
he would anchor in the roads, and remain there " whilst
they got refreshment " ashore.   But he found them—
wealthy merchants for the most part—" not caring to
part with their money " ; and so bore away for Jamaica.

It is about now that we realize that Dampier has
begun to keep that famous " journal " of his, upon which
all his subsequent writings were based.   He delights in
describing every detail of the voyage, and delights us
no less by his descriptions.   Sailing from Barbadoes, the
" Content " passed between the islands of St. Lucia and
St. Vincent, so that they came near enough to observe
smoke rising from among the trees, and sent a boat
ashore to investigate.   Presently the boat returned,
loaded with plantains, bananas, pineapples and sugar-
cane which the sailors had purchased from the natives.
They were accompanied, too, by a canoe containing three
or four Indians ; and thus Dampier, leaning eagerly
over the bulwarks, made his first acquaintance with these
harmless folk, whom he was to know so well in later
years.   Characteristically he launches out into a lively
description of the Carib Indians, who love " to rove on
the sea in Periagoes or large Canoes, moving from one
island to another according to the season of the year."
He explains that the British occupation had driven them
out of Barbadoes into the lesser islands not yet settled
by Europeans.   But even St. Lucia was in 1674 " often
visited by the English " for the sake of its valuable
timber.

These particular natives had very little to say.   Apparently they spoke no English.   But they frequently
repeated the name " Captain Warner " and " seemed to
be in some disquiet about him."   Dampier did not
understand their meaning at the time ; but later he

heard a remarkable and tragic little story of life in those far-off seas, which he has happily preserved for us in his journal. I give it in his own words :

" This Captain Warner whom they mentioned, was born at Antego [Antigua], one of our English islands, and the son of Governor Warner, by an Indian woman, and bred up by his father in the English manner ; he learned the English language [? Indian] also of his Mother ; but being grown up and finding himself despised by his English kindred, he forsook his Father's House, got away to St. Lucia, and there liv'd among the Caribbe Indians, his Relations by the Mother's side ; Where conforming himself to their customs he became one of their Captains, and roved from one Island to another, as they did. About this time the Caribbes had done some spoil on our English Plantations at Antego : and therefore Governor Warner's Son by his Wife took a Party of Men and went to suppress those Indians ; and came to the place where his Brother, the Indian Warrior, lived. Great seeming joy was there at their meeting ; but how far it was real the Event shewed ; for the English Warner providing plenty of liquor, and inviting his half-brother to be merry with him, in the midst of his Entertainment ordered his Men upon a signal given to Murder him and all his Indians ; which was accordingly performed. The reason of this inhuman Action is diversely reported ; some say that this Indian Warner committed all the spoil that was done to the English ; and therefore for that reason his Brother killed him and his men. Others that he was a great Friend to the English, and would not suffer his men to hurt them, but did all that lay in his power to draw them to an amicable commerce ; and that his Brother killed him for that he was ashamed to be related to an Indian. But be it how it will, he was called in question for the

Murder, and forced to come home to take his Tryal in
England.   Such perfidious doings as these, beside the
Baseness of them, are great hindrances of our gaining an
interest among the Indians."

It is both unpleasant and unexpected to find colour
prejudice, which in general may be termed a modern
growth, so strong among our seventeenth-century
countrymen in the West Indies.   But it is fair to add
that such crimes as Warner's were rare.   Most Englishmen, whether honest traders or buccaneers, would have
agreed with Dampier's shrewd comment upon the inconvenience of such incidents from the business point of
view.   And we shall see, in following his adventures,
that even the most reckless followers of Sharp and
Sawkins fully appreciated the importance of keeping on
good terms with the Indians, if only as the readiest means
of obtaining guides, when they set out to attack some
unsuspecting Spanish town.

Leaving St. Lucia and St. Vincent behind him,
Captain Kent set his course across the Caribbean Sea,
until he fell in with the south coast of Hispaniola, or
Haiti, along which he coasted until he reached Cape
Tiburon, the westernmost point of the island.   Here
he sent men ashore to look for the orange groves reputed
to be there ; but they returned without having found
any.   Dampier remarks, however, that at a later date
he was able to satisfy himself of the existence of these
orange groves.   From Tiburon the " Content " made a
quick passage to Jamaica, where their arrival at Port
Royal must have been very welcome, since " we brought
the first news they had of peace with the Dutch."

Captain Kent kept his promise to Dampier, who was
duly discharged, and went ashore with his papers all in
order to meet his new employer, Mr. Whalley.   They
met in Spanish Town, probably at some picturesque old

inn—alas, that so little of all this remains to-day !—and later proceeded to Colonel Helyar's estate which was situated near the south coast at a place called Sixteen-Mile-Walk. The journey had formerly been considerably longer, the road winding round the foot of " a large mountain." But one day that " very ingenious gentleman," Mr. Cary Helyar, the Colonel's brother, had happened to take a walk that way with his dog, and perceiving the animal nosing about and apparently " finding a hole to creep through the rock," it occurred to him that perhaps there was " a hollow passage " through. Sure enough, there was ; and by blasting with gunpowder they made a passage large enough for a man on horseback to pass.

Our wandering William boasts that he lived with Mr. Whalley at Sixteen-Mile-Walk for " almost six months "—a long time for him. He then entered the service of a certain Captain Heming, who owned a plantation at St. Ann's on the opposite, or north, side of the island. It was a three-days' journey from south to north, and at nights, especially when crossing the Blue Mountains, a ridge which divides the island from east to west, Dampier was very cold " for lack of cloathes to cover me," and must have reflected bitterly upon this unexpected result of his latest " warm voyage." Arriving at the new plantation, he found himself " clearly out of my element there," and as soon as he was able to see Captain Heming he obtained his discharge, and took passage on a coasting vessel back to Port Royal.

Once more he was out of a job. But there was no unemployment problem in Jamaica in those days, and Dampier soon entered himself on board another coaster, commanded by a man who rejoiced in the name of Fishook, and with him went trading round the islands. We must remember that he still occupied quite a subordinate position ; he was apparently no more than an ordinary foremast hand ; but he remarks that " by those coasting voyages I came acquainted with all the ports and bays about Jamaica . . . with the benefit of the land and sea-winds." In fact, he has now definitely turned his attention to the study of pilotage and hydrography. From now on we find his journal full of notes of a highly technical character, which could only have been recorded by a young sailor who had developed a genuine scientific interest in his profession.

The English planters treated the crews of these coasters very " civilly." They allowed them to wander about their estates and help themselves to " plantains, yams, potatoes, etc.," upon which they seem to have subsisted almost entirely when on board their ships. But, at the end of " six or seven months," Dampier had again had enough of it. Perhaps the vegetarian diet began to pall. At any rate he now took a step which, as things turned out, had a decisive effect upon his career. He shipped with one Captain Hudsel (or Hudswell), who was bound from Port Royal to the Bay of Campeachy, to load logwood there.

Now the logwood-cutters of Campeachy Bay had long been a thorn in the side of Spain. Most of them, in their spare time, were buccaneers, preying upon Spanish trade ; and Spain was annoyed to find that under the treaty of 1670 with England (which contained a *ubi posseditis*, or " remain-in-the-place-you-already-possess " clause) she had apparently legalized the position of these ex-buccaneers in Campeachy Bay. She therefore proceeded to make things as unpleasant as she could for them, and the logwood-cutter's life was by no means a bed of roses. He slept with his hanger and his pistol by his side, and he lost no opportunity of " getting one back " on the Spaniards. To join the logwood-cutters at this date was to enter a profession of doubtful legality, and one in which hard knocks might be expected on a

c

generous scale. It was, in fact, "no profession for a gentleman"; but our young adventurer was not to be deterred by that. He may have been one of Nature's gentlemen; so far as there is any meaning in the term, I think he was; but he never in his life chose any course of action because he thought it was gentlemanlike.

Dampier's new vessel, a small ketch, carrying a crew of "only six men and a boy," sailed from Port Royal in August, 1675, in company with two even smaller ships. After coasting the southern shores of the island of Cuba, they entered the Gulf of Mexico, and approached the mainland of Yucatan (Dampier taking his usual careful notes all the way of everything he saw and heard), until they crossed the Bay of Campeachy, and cast anchor off the island of Triste (now known as Carmen Island), in the lagoon of Terminos, after a voyage of only fourteen days. Here were the headquarters of the logwood-cutters, and Dampier describes the country in some detail. He explains the methods by which the native fishermen caught tarpon—evidently as exciting a sport then as it is now—and he interrupts his narrative to tell us another amazing anecdote of life in those latitudes. It appears that the country in the neighbourhood of Seisal on the Yucatan coast was particularly rich in game; and, as it had very few human inhabitants, the English "privateers" (the tactful local name for buccaneers) from Jamaica were in the habit of landing there and roaming about hunting at their will. But one day a small party of six or seven men, who had come ashore in a canoe and got so far along the coast that their vessel was out of sight, were suddenly surprised by a detachment of Spanish soldiers from the neighbouring fort—a sleepy-looking, white building, drowsing among the palm-trees, which the English had been accustomed to ignore.

These poor sailormen were dragged before the

governor of the fort, who began his examination by demanding to know which of them was the captain. At this " they all stood mute," for the captain was not among them, and they were afraid to tell the Spaniards so, for fear of being hanged as " straglers "—which I take to mean masterless men, and therefore presumably pirates. On the other hand, none of them cared to assume the title of captain, since they had no papers with them, and it is characteristic of those times that no English captain ever dared to go ashore without carrying his commission in his pocket, for the protection both of himself and of his men. So there was an awkward pause. " At last," says Dampier, " one John Hubock cocked up his little cropt hat, and told him that he was the Captain," adding that he had inadvertently left his commission on board. The Spaniards accepted this explanation—apparently their intentions were not so hostile as the English had supposed—and the joke was that from now on Hubock was treated with special honour, given handsome lodgings and captain's food ; and when the whole party were marched overland to Campeachy town, a distance of about a hundred English miles, he was provided with a horse, while his indignant companions had to walk. At Campeachy he was " frequently regaled with chocolate, etc." and was then taken alone to interview the governor, upon whom the fellow's native wit seems to have had some effect, for the whole party was presently able to return to Jamaica. Hubock was " ever after called Captain Jack."

From Triste, Captain Hudsel sailed across the lagoon to One-Bush-Key, a landing-place on the mainland, which had acquired its name from the fact that there was only one " little crooked tree " growing on it. Dampier describes the landing as all covered with oyster shells, and adds that he never tasted better oysters any-

where.   He affirms that " the mangrove-roots that grow
by the sides of the creeks are loaden with them (*i.e.* with
oysters) ; and so are all the branches which hang in
the water." [1]

At One-Bush-Key Captain Hudsel got in touch with
the logwood-cutters, and hired from them a periago to
bring the logwood on board.   This was Dampier's first
acquaintance with that jovial confraternity, with whom
he was afterwards to live for a period of nearly three
years.   Characteristically he at once made it his business
to find out as much about them as he could.   He
frequently visited them in the " huts " or shelters in
which they lived, when " I and those with me were
always very kindly entertained by them with pork and
pease, or beef and dough-boys."   There were about two
hundred and fifty of these logwood-cutters, mostly
Englishmen, who had settled themselves in the neighbourhood of One-Bush-Key.   A large proportion of
them were undoubtedly old buccaneers : former associates of Morgan's, perhaps, who, now that that redoubtable leader had settled down and turned respectable as
Lieutenant-Governor of Jamaica,[2] had taken to logwood-
cutting, as being a dangerous, lawless and lucrative trade,
and in that respect not entirely unlike their former
profession.   Others would be escaped " servants," or
slaves, from the plantations, with a few independent
adventurers of the Dampier type.   They were a hard-
living, hard-swearing crowd—in fact about as " tough "
as their own logwood.

The great value of this commodity had been discovered some years before by an Englishman, Captain
James, who had taken a cargo of it back to England
and sold it at a high figure.   Since then the price had

[1] Here is a reasonable explanation of the Elizabethan legend, in which
Raleigh, among others, was a firm believer, of oysters that " grew " on
trees.   [2] See below, page 61.

risen to about £100 a ton, with the result that a successful logwood-cutter might now expect to make his fortune in a few years—if he survived. There was, however, always that unhappy doubt. The wood, which was very hard and burned with a clear and lasting fire, only grew at its best in pestiferous and swampy places. As illustrating the appalling hardships of the logwood-cutter's life, Dampier remarks that when they tumbled out of their miserable beds of a morning (beds which were hermetically sealed within a close-fitting " pavilion," probably of sail-cloth, to keep out the mosquitoes), they would often step straight into two feet or more of water, and would remain in it all day, under the tropic sun, working at their heavy task of cutting and hauling wood. (For the season of the floods was the best time of year for their purpose.) They are described as vigorous, powerfully built men, and one can understand that they needed to be. When they required food, they hunted the wild cattle, which abounded on the mainland (as on many of the islands thereabouts), sometimes stalking the animals on the open savannahs, sometimes catching them at their drinking-places by the rivers and pursuing them across the water in canoes—a hazardous business, comments Dampier, if a bull chanced to turn at bay ! It was the usual plan to go hunting every Saturday, in order to provide themselves with beef for the following week.

Amid such alternations of dangerous excitement and unremitting toil, and living in this perpetually humid atmosphere, it is not altogether surprising to hear that the logwood-cutters raised a thirst which the surrounding waters were far from satisfying. Indeed the reception accorded to visiting ships, and the terms upon which the valuable logwood was sold to them, were largely conditioned by the quantity of rum the skipper had brought with him and the generosity with which he dispensed it. A small local trader, such as Dampier had arrived in, would bring no money at all, but the captain, after standing drinks all round to establish a friendly atmosphere, would proceed to barter his rum in return for the logwood. When a full cargo of the latter had been obtained, the remainder of the rum [1] would be sold for money to the thirsty woodsmen—in this case, in the form of punch, " wherewith," says Dampier, " they grew frolicksome."

They must have been rather trying visitors on board ship, for it was apparently their practice to insist upon the firing of the ship's guns every time they drank a health.   Unfortunately (or perhaps fortunately), Captain Hudsel's little vessel had no guns on board.   " We had none but small arms to fire," confesses Dampier, " and therefore the noise was not very great at a distance ; but on board the vessel we were loud enough till all our liquor was spent."   After that, of course, there was no more to be said ; and towards the end of September Captain Hudsel decided that it was time to make a move.

So with one last parting cheer, and perhaps a last toast or two, and with much waving of hands and shouting of farewells, he up-anchored and put out into the lagoon, leaving Dampier's new friends ashore, still carrying on their wild carouse which would probably last for days.   Which practice, as Dampier's Victorian biographer[2] very properly remarks, "in that ungenial climate was carrying imprudence and folly to the last pitch."

But Dampier, meantime, was thinking hard. He was, in fact, making up his mind to return to this wild place. It was not simply that the life attracted him. Love of adventure was indeed his ruling passion and was to take him into many even stranger places than this ;

[1] There were also some other despised and unspecified " commodoties " on board, but they were evidently of no account.
[2] Smyth.

but, except for that, he had little enough in common with the ex-buccaneers and other riff-raff who made up this strange community. He has told us himself that he "did ever abhor drunkenness," and though his detractors have tried to cast doubt on this pious profession, it is clear that he was, on the whole, a "steady," temperate sort of man. But what he had plainly perceived at One-Bush-Key was, in the first place, a new opportunity of acquiring fresh "experience," and, in the second, to quote his own words, "a great prospect of getting money here, if men would be but diligent and frugal."

In the meantime, however, he had to get back to Jamaica, and that was not to prove so easy as it seemed. Captain Hudsel was a singularly feckless commander. First he sighted two sail in the Bay of Campeachy, and, mistaking them for Englishmen from Jamaica, wanted to heave-to and try to get some liquor from them, his own having all been left behind at One-Bush-Key, and his crew again athirst. Just in time they discovered these ships to be Spaniards, and escaped with difficulty after a long chase. A fortnight later they were still in the Bay, struggling against adverse winds, for the ketch was a "heavy sailer."

One night Dampier was on deck, it being his turn at the helm from 6 to 8 p.m. The night had that velvety warmth of the southern latitudes, the sky was purple overhead, and the stars were shining with the brightness of jewels, such as East Coker never saw. "All our men were layn down on the deck and fallen asleep"; "my Captain was just behind me on the quarter deck, fast asleep too." Young Dampier, characteristically, was occupying his time in speculating upon the reason why the sea had suddenly become so smooth, and why the ship, which had been steering very badly, was now steering well. Indeed he had just been looking over the side, trying unsuccessfully to discover the cause. Suddenly, without the slightest warning, the ship struck, throwing our young adventurer flat upon his back. They were ashore on the Alacranes Islands ! It was, indeed, a liberal education for a budding navigator to go to sea with poor Captain Hudsel.

Next morning they managed to get the ship off, and anchored among the islands, which Dampier visited, and describes with his usual care. There were opportunities of hunting here, and Dampier tried to persuade his companions to salt down some of the flesh of birds and seals, which abounded ; but they were lazy, and refused. Sailing on again, they sighted the coast of Cuba (being then no less than two months out from Triste !) and shaped a course for Jamaica, but were driven back to Cuba again, and decided to land on the Island of Pines in order to obtain meat. This was always dangerous work ; for just over the way at Cape Corientes there was a Spanish garrison, the soldiers of which, being mostly "mulatoes or some other sort of copper colour Indians," possessed a large canoe, in which they were in the habit of sallying out and robbing harmless merchant ships, sometimes murdering the crews "for fear of telling tales." [1]

The shore party from the ketch met no Spaniards, but neither did they meet with any game. Their whole bag consisted of a young swordfish, which was captured by the man whom they had left on the beach to look after their boat. Hungrier than ever, they departed from the Island of Pines, and immediately ran into a fierce gale, which continued for two days and left them— it is true—in the latitude of Jamaica, but without a mouthful of food on board. It was now a question of

---

[1] Dampier adds, with his usual fairness, that, of course, the Spanish "merchants and gentry" knew nothing of this—only the "soldiers and rascality of the people."

whether to beat for Jamaica (in this terribly " dull
sailer ") or to bear away before the wind for the South
Keys.   Dampier was for the former course, but he was
out-voted, and thereupon " turned into my cabin " in a
huff, declaring that they would all be starved.   The
incident is not without interest, as introducing us for
the first time to the celebrated Dampier temper, which,
in after years, was to form the subject of inquiry before
an Admiralty court-martial.

But all things come to an end, and this unlucky
voyage was no exception to the rule.   They reached
Jamaica at last, and made harbour, literally with their
tongues hanging out.   The captain, who with all his
faults seems to have been a man of generous instincts,
immediately sent ashore for suitable refreshments, and
invited them all to the cabin to drink a bowl of punch.
Alas, there was yet one more stroke of ill fortune in
store !   Two other skippers from neighbouring ships
had been asked to join the festive gathering ; and one
of these, lifting the bowl of punch in his hands, observed
that he was under an oath to take only three draughts
of liquor each day, and therefore liked them long ; and
so quaffed the whole bowlful before anyone could stop
him.   Whereat, says Dampier, with admirable restraint,
" we were disappointed."

We perceive that he is a man who enjoys telling a
funny story.   Of the voyage in general he observes that
probably no ship ever had so many misfortunes in
coming out of the Bay, " having first blundered over the
Alcany (Alacranes) Riff, and then visited those islands ;
from thence fell in among the Colorado shoals, after-
ward making a trip to Grand Caymanes," and so on.
But " in all these matters we got as much experience as
if we had been sent on a design."   That is the secret—
experience, experience !   As yet he has asked no more
of life.

CHAPTER IV

JOINS THE BUCCANEERS

OW this second, or return, visit of Dampier's to the logwood-cutting community in Campeachy Bay, which I am about to relate, marks a turning-point in his career. It definitely classes him among the adventurers of that period—men who did not care much where they sought excitement and riches, so long as it was at the expense of the King of Spain ; nor how many laws they broke, if they were only Spanish laws.

No doubt the Spanish claim to a monopoly in a trade which they themselves had done little to exploit was absurd, and would have been untenable in any age. The legal position was, in fact, rather complicated. Spain, as we have seen, since her treaty of peace with England, no longer claimed that the whole of the West Indies trade belonged to her alone. But in practice she stopped foreign trade whenever she could, and it was notorious that the local Spanish authorities were particularly down on the logwood-cutters. These latter had moved away from the inhabited parts of the coast to the lonely creeks round Terminos Lagoon precisely because it was unsafe to carry on their business anywhere within reach of a Spanish fort. And I am afraid that our William, when he deliberately returned to Campeachy, with visions of quickly acquired wealth before his eyes, had set his foot upon a slippery slope which, in the end, must land him inevitably upon the lawless deck of a buccaneer.

Anyhow, one Captain Johnson, of New England, being bound from Jamaica to Campeachy, agreed to take Dampier with him as a passenger (rather a step-up in the world) ; and on this ship our hero embarked, with an elaborate outfit of hatchets and saws and machetes, his " pavilion " to sleep in, his gun, powder and shot, and all the other impedimenta of the logwood-cutter. Sailing from Jamaica about the middle of February, 1676, they made a quick passage to the Terminos Lagoon, and Dampier " settled himself " in the west creek, on the west side of the lagoon, at a point about four leagues distant from One-Bush-Key. He did not at first set up on his own, but hired himself out under some of the old hands, to learn the trade from them.

Among his very first notes on the surrounding country are references to the strained relations between the log-wood-cutters and the Spanish authorities. He observes that there was, near Campeachy Town, a large and valuable salt pond. The Spaniards used to make the local Indians rake this salt ashore during the " kerning " season, and pile it up in heaps. Then the Indians would go off home, leaving the Spaniards to collect the salt at their leisure. Which was " jam " for the Spaniards, of course, since, as Dampier says, " I know of no other salt ponds on all the coast." But the English logwood-cutters, on their voyages between Jamaica and Terminos, would not infrequently pay casual visits to this salt pond, when they would " make bold to take and sell both the ships (which they found in harbour there) and the Indian sailors that belonged to them." This, they explained, was " by way of reprisal," for alleged injuries received from the Spaniards. The Governors of Jamaica (including the virtuous Sir Henry Morgan !) of course " knew nothing " of it. But, says

Dampier—and it is a point worth noting : " . . . neither durst the Spaniards complain ; for at that time they used to take all the English ships they met with in these parts, not sparing even such as came laden with sugar from Jamaica and were bound for England ; especially if they had logwood aboard. This was done openly, for the ships were carried into the Havanna, there sold, and the men imprisoned without any redress." In this connection I may quote the case of the unfortunate Captain Buckenham, related by Wafer,[1] who had formerly sailed with him. About five years after the date we are now dealing with, Buckenham was captured by the Spaniards while on a voyage from Jamaica to Campeachy, for logwood, and was carried prisoner to Mexico City. There he was seen by one, Russell,[2] another English prisoner, who afterwards escaped, and told Wafer the story : " He told me (Wafer) he saw Capt. Buckenham, with a log chained to his leg and a basket at his back, crying bread about the streets for a baker his master. The Spaniards would never consent to the ransoming him, though he was a Gentleman who had friends of a considerable fortune, and would have given them a very large sum of money." As a matter of fact, the Spanish were almost literally cutting their own throats by this dog-in-the-manger policy. Dampier's comment is a shrewd one : " It is not my business (he says) to determine how far we might have a right of cutting wood there, but this I can say, that the Spaniards never received less damage from the persons who

[1] *A New Voyage and Description*, etc. By Lionel Wafer. London : Knapton, 1699.

[2] There is a later allusion to Russell in Dampier's writings. He was an old logwood-cutter who was captured by the Spaniards and sent to Mexico City ; and after his escape he proceeded to " get his own back " in the usual way, by turning buccaneer. In fact, he drew interest as well, for Dampier tells us that " about the year '85 he captured the town of Vera Cruz."

generally follow that trade than when they are employed upon that work." Which is very true, for nearly every man at Terminos was an ex-buccaneer. The whole trade, as Dampier says, " had its rise from the decay of privateering," which the British authorities were just as anxious to stop as the Spaniards were. No doubt the logwood-cutters were a nuisance. At first they merely stole the logwood which the Spaniards had already cut. But when soldiers were sent against them to prevent that, they moved down the coast to places like Triste and One-Bush-Key, where, one would think, they might have been allowed to stew in their own juice. It is true that they frequently got drunk, and that they often sallied out against neighbouring Indian villagers, and " brought away the Indian women to serve them at their huts "—but what was that to the Spaniards ?

The Spaniards, however, would never leave the log-wood-cutters alone. They were always looking out for a chance to suppress them. Occasionally, " encouraged by their careless rioting," they would pluck up enough spirit to make a sudden descent and capture a few of these intoxicated Englishmen, and sell them as slaves in Mexico. Dampier tells us that, after he left the Bay, the logwood-cutters that remained there were all " routed or taken " in a big Spanish raid. He adds that his continual dread of a similar fate was one of the reasons which eventually led him also to abandon logwood-cutting—and take to buccaneering instead !

Well, Dampier lived with the logwood-cutters, and cut and hauled all the week, and went out hunting of a Saturday night like the rest of them. One of these week-end jaunts nearly proved fatal to him, for he got separated from his companions (he says he " gave them the slip," being perhaps bored by their profane conversation), and was unable to find his way back. He passed an unpleasant night with the mosquitoes, but no larger enemy appeared, and next morning he got safely home.

About this time, the " nature notes " in his journal are profuse and lively. " The monkeys that are in these parts are the ugliest I ever saw." " The fowls of this country are humming-birds "—which is to say " a pretty little feathered creature no bigger than a wasp." In fact there are enough ornithological observations to make a whole chapter. The tailor-birds, with their hanging nests, which so vex and tantalize marauding snakes, are said to be called in English " subtle-jacks." There is a kind of shellfish, too, " called by the English Horse-hoofs," and said to be " very good meat " ; but Dampier never tasted it, and its name is certainly against it. Other local fish are the " garr-fish," who " skip along a foot or two above the water for the length of twenty or thirty yards," and will " dart themselves with such force that they strike their snout through the sides of a cotton tree canoe " ; and the " sea-devils " who " make an odd figure when they leap out of the water."

As for the " tiger cats," " they prey on young calves and other game, whereof here is plenty ; and because they do not want food they are the less to be feared, but I have wished them farther off when I have met them in the woods." He also discusses the difference between crocodiles and alligators at considerable length. I am afraid he was not desperately interested in food ; but he does remark that he had the curiosity to try the snake flesh, which the Indians enjoyed so much, but " cannot commend it "—a point on which modern gastronomic opinion is entirely with him.

At the end of his first month Dampier received his wages, in the form of a consignment of the logwood which he had helped to cut and bring down to the beach. With the proceeds of this, and some more money that he had borrowed, he proceeded to set up on his own account, going into partnership " with some of my former masters." His immediate associates were three men named Price Morrice, Duncan Campbell and " George," whose surname we never learn. Campbell presently took passage on a visiting ship and went to New England to sell their existing stock. In his absence Dampier was worried to find Price Morrice " not very intent at work." It is always the same, he complains. " Those who have been well-bred are generally most careful to improve their time when there is any proba-bility of considerable gain," but " those who have been inured to hard labour and got their living by the sweat of their brows " no sooner acquire a little money than they begin to waste their time " in drinking and making a bluster." In addition to these troubles, Dampier now made his first acquaintance with the " jigger " worm— that familiar enemy of the modern traveller. He describes, with a wealth of distressing detail, how it " bred " in his leg, and made him feel very ill indeed, until a negro servant evicted it by means of some simple local remedies.

And then—" to complete my misfortune "—came the worst storm that any Englishman had ever known in those parts. Dampier gives a dramatic account of this storm in his *Discourse on Winds*.[1] It happened " some time in June, 1676." Two days previously, the wind had " whiffled about to the South, and back again to the East," blowing very faintly, and the weather fair and clear. Then came multitudes of men-of-war birds, flying over the land, whereat Dampier's companions were vastly pleased, for did not the appearance of these birds always portend the arrival of ships ? Some of the men said they had lived at Barbadoes, where it was a well-accepted fact that as many of these birds as passed over the town " so many ships there were coming

[1] Part III of volume ii of his *Voyages*.

thither." But on this occasion, as Dampier sarcastically observes, it seemed "impossible that they could
imagine there could be the hundredth part of the ships
arrive that they saw birds fly over their heads."

The next unusual phenomenon was that the water
ebbed for two days without a flood, till the creek where
they lived was almost dry. Then, about four o'clock
one afternoon, the sky rapidly blackened, and without
further warning the great storm burst. In less than
two hours all their huts but one were blown away. By
ten o'clock next morning the creek was over its banks.
The forest, says Dampier, presented an astonishing sight,
with the trees torn up and thrown across one another in
every direction, so that there was no passing through.
Multitudes of fish were cast up on shore, or floated
dead on the surface of the lagoon. At noon on the
second day, our party of logwood-cutters managed to
get their canoe to the side of the one remaining hut,
where they tied it to a stout tree. That night the storm
at last abated, and by two o'clock in the morning there
was a calm.

Dampier and his companions now found themselves
in a condition of the greatest misery. All their food
was spoilt, except the beef and pork, and as the highest
ground anywhere near them was two or three feet under
water, it was impossible to do any cooking, "unless we
had done it in the canoe." At last, in despair, they all
embarked, and sailed away in their canoe to One-Bush-
Key, where they found only a single vessel remaining
of the four which had been at anchor there before the
storm. And this was unfortunately a "dry" ship, for
other refugees had been there before them and had
drunk up all the rum ! The unhappy, wet quartette
therefore launched out upon the lagoon, in search of
the other ships and more heartening fare.

Approaching Beef Island, they were surprised to see

" a Flag in the Woods, made fast to a pole and placed on the Top of a High Tree " ; and coming near to land, there was an even more astonishing sight—the topmasts of a ship standing up among the trees, at least two hundred yards from the shore ! It was one of the missing ships from One-Bush-Key, which, flying in with the gale behind it, had dashed ashore and ploughed a " pretty clear passage through the woods " until it reached its present unnatural resting-place. There, all amidst the humming-birds and the monkeys and the mangroves, it was held bolt upright by the broken stumps of trees which were sticking through its sides !

There was no salvage to be done here, but Dampier and his friends went on board, and found there most of the crew who hospitably entertained them. Apparently none of these hardy adventurers felt any the worse for their startling experience. Then, hearing the sound of guns, and supposing it to be another of the British vessels in distress, Dampier's party put to sea again, and found a ketch, commanded by one, Captain Chandler, run ashore " on a point of sand " in the lagoon, where they had stuck immovably and were feeling very lonesome. These people welcomed the logwood-cutters with open arms, and persuaded them to stay for two days and help them get the cargo off.

Before leaving the subject of this mighty storm (this very notable " South," as Dampier calls it), it is of interest to collect together some of the further references to the subject which are to be found scattered about in his writings. Most of them are of a highly technical character, suitable only to a work on hydrography ; but he does mention that, in addition to the four English ships at One-Bush-Key, of whose fate we have heard, there were four more anchored off the island of Triste. Three of these were driven from their anchorage out into the Bay, and one of them was never heard of again.

D

This, we may infer, was the only English loss ; for it was an extraordinary feature of this storm that it " did not reach 30 leagues to windward of Triste," and an English ship which had sailed for Jamaica three days before felt nothing of it, though the captain saw black clouds behind him in the west.

The Spaniards were not so fortunate. Dampier mentions two Spanish " King's ships " as being driven ashore in the Bay. One of them, the " Piscadore," which had run on a sandy beach, near the River Tobasco, was there captured by Hewet, the English privateer captain. The Spanish loss in merchant ships must have been considerable. Dampier says that they always lost more heavily than the English, and he goes on to explain that this was due to their habit of " bringing their ships to under a foresail and mizzen " (instead of a mainsail and mizzen, or mizzen only, as the English did), which " must be an extraordinary strain to a ship, especially if she be long." What is more, " when the wind comes up fierce," the Spaniards " put right afore it " (for in their case " 'tis but halling up the mizzen and the foresail veers the ship ") trusting to luck and the goodwill of the saints, " and so continue till the storm ceaseth or the land takes them up "—which evidently happened not infrequently.

After helping Captain Chandler off with his cargo, Dampier and his friends returned to Beef Island, which now became their headquarters. Beef Island was, at this time, full of friendly Indians, who were very pro-British (and correspondingly anti-Spanish) in their sympathies. I fear it can hardly be maintained that the logwood-cutters, in removing large numbers of the neighbouring Indian women (as noted above) from the care of their natural guardians, were inspired by motives which would have commended themselves to the Aborigines Protection Society ; or were even scheming to get the Indians on their side. But the fact remains, as Dampier remarks with his usual air of detachment, that it was these women who " after their return made known the kind Entertainment that they met with from the English and persuaded their friends to leave their dwellings near the Spaniards, and settle on this island."

So that it was in a thoroughly friendly and cordial atmosphere that Dampier once more found leisure to open his journal and record a few notes. Beef Island seems to have had an unusual history—and Dampier always had an eye for the unusual. It originally belonged to a Spaniard called " John d'Acosta " of Campeachy Town, who seems to have had more resilience than most of his countrymen ; for, perceiving the impossibility of keeping the English out altogether, he made a compact with them, whereby he supplied them with as many head of cattle as they cared to ask for, on condition that they never came farther inland than the beach, and never did any hunting themselves. This was a wise provision, for, as Dampier observes, the Spaniards would " pick and choose only the bulls and old cows, and leave the young cattle to breed," whereas the English and French (especially the French) destroyed recklessly.[1] But the pig-headed governor of Campeachy, getting to hear of this arrangement, threw poor John d'Acosta into prison, where he remained many years. That was in '71 or '72. Thereafter, of course, the English shot cattle at their will and treated the island as their own property. Moreover, as we have seen, it had become an asylum for anti-Spanish Indians.

[1] So much so that very shortly after our capture of Jamaica there were no cattle left on that island, and the soldiers of the garrison, who had slaughtered them all, were like to die of hunger. As a matter of fact, adds Dampier, " had it not been for the great care of the Spaniards in stocking the West Indies with hogs and bullocks, the privateers must have starved "—a curious reflection !

Dampier did a good deal of shooting on Beef Island, and found the cattle grown wilder and fiercer. When attacked, they would run together as buffaloes do to-day, with the cows in the middle and the bulls showing a fence of lowered heads to the enemy. It was about this time, too, that, in crossing a stream, he stepped on an alligator, and in trying to scramble ashore (his companions all having run away at the first alarm), he twice stumbled over the same (or another) reptile, which so terrified him that he took an oath never to ford a river on foot again. He has several notes on the habits of the Indians—on their dress, for instance, in which " with their hair tied up in a knot behind, they think themselves extream fine." They also overrated their local drink, a beverage made from tartilloes. " If they treat a friend with this drink," remarks Dampier disparagingly, " they mix a little honey with it ; for their ability reaches no higher." Yet " this is as acceptable to them as a glass of wine to us." Their sleeping " hammocks," however, were very comfortable—as British sailors were already beginning to find out. Dampier expresses a strong view that the converted Indians, living near the Spanish towns, were very sincere Christians ; and, summing the Indian question up, he expresses this evidently typical opinion of an Englishman of his time : " They are a harmless sort of people, kind to any stranger ; and even to the Spaniards, by whom they are so much kept under, that they are worse than slaves : nay, the very Negroes will domineer over them ; and are countenanced to do so by the Spaniards."

I do not know how long Dampier remained on Beef Island. But we notice about this time that his journal begins to take on a more travelled air. His notes range far afield. He discovers, for instance, that there is a good opening for the hatters' and haberdashers' trades in the Spanish settlements along the coast. Why, " an old English beaver " hat, if it be " new-dressed " would fetch twenty dollars ! He exclaims at the stupidity of the English " privateers " in always trying to get across Mexico to the Pacific side—for instance to Tehuan-tepec—" supposing, as many do still, that the South Sea shore is nothing but Gold and Silver." He describes the failure of Hewet and Rives in their expedition from Triste to the River Goazacoalcos, designing to attack a town near there, but they had to give it up because of floods. Also the repulse of Hewet from before Estapo.[1] In fact the doings of the privateers begin to occupy an inexplicable amount of space. Then suddenly comes the frank confession. He himself is a privateer—has been one for months. The die is cast !

But Dampier, though he offers few excuses for his conduct, is not sufficiently proud of his new profession to give us the description of how he actually crossed the Rubicon. There are several such deliberate omissions in his books ; but this is the one that I regret most of all. What is certain is that he could hardly help himself. The storm had destroyed everything he possessed ; logwood-cutting was at a standstill for at least a year ; and there was no reason why ships should continue to visit the lagoon in the interval. With the aid of his gun a man might possibly have succeeded in keeping himself alive among the Indians on Beef Island ; but it was too much to expect that any sane person should choose this alternative while any other offered. In fact, as the excellent Smyth puts it, Dampier, who

---

[1] I borrow the following extract as it stands from Mr. Philip Gosse's *Pirates' Who's Who*: " Hewett, William, or Hewet, or Hewit, of Jamaica. One of Major Stede Bonnet's crew. Tried for piracy at Charleston in 1718, and hanged at White Point on November 18th, and buried in the marsh before low-water mark." Was Dampier by any chance with Hewet in the Bay ? He never mentions the name of his commander.

after nearly three years among " such dissolute associates as the logwood-cutters " had yet " escaped the moral contamination of their vices and excesses," was now driven into even worse company " by imperious necessity." Or, in Dampier's simpler language, " I with many more in my circumstances was forced to range about to seek a subsistence in company with some privateers then in the Bay."

The story of Dampier's first voyage with the buccaneers is quickly told. " In these rambles," he says (" rambles " is a good word, by the way), " we visited all the rivers from Triste to Alvarado ; and made many descents into the country among the villages there." But he gives us very few details, except in regard to their one serious encounter with the Spaniards. This took place at Alvarado, a town near Vera Cruz, across the Bay to the west. Here there was a real battle. In two boats, holding thirty men each, the buccaneers attacked the Spanish fort, and captured it after fierce fighting, in which ten or eleven Englishmen were killed—only to find that in the meantime the inhabitants of the town had escaped in boats with all their money and movable property. This was a nasty blow. The English, however, took away with them some salt beef and numbers of yellow and red parrots, which pleased Dampier particularly " because they would prate very prettily."

Now, what with beef, " chests, hencoops and parrot-cages," the English ships were " full of lumber," when, having rested themselves, and licked their wounds, the buccaneers at last set sail again. As they left the river, they encountered seven Spanish " armadilloes," which had been sent from Vera Cruz to intercept them. But, " heaving all the lumber overboard "—a sad end to the parrots' prating—" we drove out over the bar " ; and after a confused fight with this vastly superior enemy, who, however, showed no great stomach for it, both privateers got clear away. According to Dampier, the two English ships had only eight guns between them, and not above fifty men left after the fight on shore, while the seven Spaniards had some ten and some four guns, and crews of sixty to eighty men apiece. So that there was nothing disgraceful about the buccaneers' retreat.

Dampier had now been cruising and fighting for a period of about twelve months. A new logwood-cutting season had begun, and the effects of the late storm were " almost forgot." He, and most of his immediate associates, accordingly bade farewell to the privateers, and returned with well-lined pockets to Terminos. Dampier resumed operations on the eastern side of the lagoon, as far removed as possible from One-Bush-Key.

He was as much attracted as ever to this " most profitable " trade ; but he had made up his mind to pay a visit to England at the first opportunity, " with a design to return hither." At the beginning of April, 1678, he therefore sailed from Triste, and landed in Jamaica, where he took passage for England with a Captain Loder, and arrived there, after an uneventful voyage, at the beginning of August of the same year. He had been away four and a half years.

CHAPTER V

AND SINGES THE KING OF
SPAIN'S BEARD

N anonymous author of the late seventeenth century who, for reasons connected with the sale of his book, apparently desires to be mistaken for that rather backboneless buccaneer, Captain Bartholomew Sharp,[1] makes the following interesting reflection in his book called *Voyages and Adventures* : "That which often spurs men on to the undertaking of the most difficult adventures is the sacred hunger of Gold ; and 'twas Gold was the bait that tempted a Pack of merry Boys of us, near three hundred in number, being all Souldiers of Fortune, under command (by our own election) of Captain John Cox, to . . ." in short, to become buccaneers.

Regarded as a general proposition, there is much truth in that. Gold has been the stuff of romance in a sense never dreamt of by misers. Dangled before the Spanish *conquistadores* and the Elizabethan adventurers, it recast the map of the world, and made such a change in human mentality as has never taken place, before or since, in so brief a period of time. But what " Captain Sharp " appears to mean is simply that gold was the

---

[1] *The Voyages and Adventures of Captain Bartholomew Sharp in the South Sea* : Being a Journal of the Same. London : 1684. Sharp's own manuscript journal is in the Sloane Collection. See page 66.

lure that attracted the buccaneers.   This is not strictly
fair.   The early buccaneers were, in the words of Andrew
Lang, " the most hideously ruthless miscreants that ever
disgraced the earth and the sea."   But to describe them
as mere " go-getters " after wealth in the approved
modern manner, is to inflict an injustice on their
memories.   As with the logwood-cutters, they could
hardly help themselves.   Indeed, the cases of the buccaneers and the logwood-cutters were very similar, as I
shall presently show.

But the first thing we have to do is to get out of our
heads the idea that " buccaneer " was only another and
politer word for " pirate."   Many of the pirates were
no doubt ex-buccaneers.   But there would certainly have
been piracy in the West Indies, in the circumstances of
those days, if the buccaneers had never existed.   The
rise of the buccaneers was a considerable movement,
almost a rebellion, of men of all nations—former slaves,
criminals, adventurers and what not—against the Spanish
authority.   To class them with the pirates is like comparing the Spartacists of Ancient Rome with the foot-
pads of the eighteenth century.   The pirates were
ordinary sea-robbers—small gangs of men, usually
mutinous seamen, who went about thieving and murdering in a hole-and-corner way, and were shot at sight by
every honest man who happened to have a gun.   But
the rise of the buccaneers was an insurrection of all the
discontented elements in the West Indies, directed
primarily against the Spanish rule.   They fought both
by land and sea.   They were formidable foes.   The
pirates were their unworthy offspring.

We find the buccaneers first on the island of Hispaniola, or Haiti, engaged, like the logwood-cutters in
Campeachy Bay, in a highly lucrative, if dangerous,
trade, which the Spanish authorities were determined to
put a stop to if they could.   Hispaniola was full of wild

cattle, not only " beeves " (as the wild bulls and cows were called) but horses and wild boars, and the buccaneers were simply hunters. They are believed to have got their name from the *boucans,* or places where they salted their meat. Their leading historian is the Dutchman, Esquemeling, who does not pretend to have been happy in their company. He landed in Hispaniola in about 1669, and describes the buccaneers as a savage and dirty people, fearing neither God nor man, wearing coarse linen garments which they steeped in the blood of·the animals they slaughtered, armed to the teeth, and ready to murder any stranger who came among them. Like the logwood-cutters, they spent all their money in lewd and riotous living whenever they could get near a town. Like them, too, they had a wonderful thirst. They drank brandy " as liberally as the Spaniards do clear fountain water." Sometimes two of them—for they commonly hunted in couples, sharing everything they possessed—would combine to buy a pipe of wine, and this, says Esquemeling, " they stave at the one end, and never cease drinking till they have made an end of it." Nor, unfortunately, were the " beastly delights " of the " goddess Venus " forgotten. The chronicler spares us nothing.

Esquemeling's narrative undoubtedly has the ring of truth, and his story of the subsequent exploits of the buccaneers when they left the island is among the classics of seventeenth-century travel literature.[1] But though I do not believe that he lied intentionally, it is difficult to resist the impression that he did " pile on the agony," when it came to describing the cruelties practised upon the inhabitants of captured Spanish towns. He was a most unwilling recruit among the buccaneers, and probably repeats a good deal of camp-fire gossip.

[1] *The Buccaneers of America.* By John Esquemeling. English translation, 1684-85. New edition : Routledge, London, 1926.

At any rate, there was war to the knife between the Spaniards and these islanders. The latter, most of whom at this time were Frenchmen, would retire to the neighbouring island of Tortuga, when they found things getting too hot for them on Hispaniola, and from thence make sudden descents to collect more cattle. The Spaniards, with their usual shortsighted obstinacy, were prepared to go to the length of slaughtering all the cattle on the island rather than that the French should make any profit out of them. At last, the inevitable happened. The buccaneers, despairing of earning their living by any peaceful means, took finally to the sword, and were engaged for the rest of their history in an irregular and predatory warfare both by land and sea— yet something quite distinct from common piracy— against the Spanish authority throughout the West Indies.

And with the occasion, there arose the men. At Esquemeling's landing, there were not more than three hundred buccaneers in Tortuga ; but, scattered about the different islands, their numbers were rapidly increasing, and leaders of first-rate ability had already appeared who were well able to make a deadly use of this tremendous fighting instrument.

These leaders, in the beginning, were not necessarily seamen, nor were their principal exploits performed at sea. Lewis Scott, who appears to have been the first to operate on the grand scale, captured and sacked Campeachy Town—with what kind of following, French, English, or mixed, we are not told. Mansvelt, and John Davis of Jamaica, also deserve mention. Davis coolly walked into the town of Nicaragua with a mere handful of followers, and began to pillage the principal houses, and rob the churches of their sacred vessels, "without any respect or veneration." When he had collected as much as he could carry away, he made his escape before the town guard could rally against him. But L'Olonois, the Frenchman, who had been sold as a slave in the Caribbee Islands, and escaped to lead the buccaneers, was an abominable villain, whose cruelty overshadows even his courage and skill. He had a fleet of eight vessels, and captured many towns and villages, torturing and murdering the inhabitants without compunction. On one occasion he is said to have cut open the breast of a captured Spaniard, and " pulling out his heart with his sacrilegious hands, began to bite and gnaw it with his teeth, like a ravenous wolf." [1] This " infernal wretch," as Esquemeling calls him, met a suitably horrible death at the hands of hostile Indians. Others of standing among these early buccaneers were the Dutchman, Roche Brasiliano, who had been ill-treated by the Spaniards, and cherished an inveterate hatred against them ; and Bartholomew Portugues, who deserves to be remembered for his escape from imprisonment at Campeachy Town, and his long journey overland to the Terminos Lagoon, covering a distance of forty leagues in a fortnight, and having nothing to eat on the way but a few shellfish.

But the greatest of all the buccaneers was undoubtedly Henry Morgan—" our English-Jamaican hero," as he is magnificently styled on the title-page of the English translation of Esquemeling. And it is when we come to consider Morgan's career that we begin to doubt Esquemeling's simple view of the wicked buccaneers— or, at any rate, to realize that there are two sides to the case. Morgan was a big man, in every sense of the word. He commanded fleets of fifty sail, or more, and guns enough to oppose any armament that could be brought against him. In fact, he frequently held undisputed command of the seas in those parts. He led land armies. as in his famous expedition across the Isthmus

[1] Esquemeling.

of Panama, which no local authority could hope to with-
stand. Apart from the magnificent fighting quality of
his men, collected from every country in Europe except
Spain, they were numerous enough to enable him to
conquer whole islands, hoist the English flag over them,
and occupy them for as long as he found convenient.

It is significant, by the way, that the buccaneers seem
invariably to have fought under the national flag of their
leader, whoever he might be, whereas their piratical
descendants flew the Jolly Roger, or (more commonly,
I think) a disreputable blood-red flag. Relations were
nearly always perfectly friendly between each leader of
the early buccaneers and his own particular national
authorities. De Busco was made Governor of Tortuga,
and the French authorities, on at least one occasion,
employed a buccaneer fleet against the Dutch. Morgan
had the support of the Jamaican authorities, and he ended
up with a knighthood and a comfortable billet as Lieutenant-Governor of the island.

Yet Esquemeling accuses him of every imaginable
atrocity, of burning and slaying without distinction of
sex or age, of hanging up his prisoners over " slow fires "
in order to make them tell him where treasure lay hid,
of having Spanish ladies carried off to his tent, and, in
general, of running a good second to L'Olonois in
villainy. Morgan, however, has not been without his
defenders. In Sharp's *Voyages and Adventures*, for
instance, it is pointed out, with some plausibility, that
Morgan's forces were always well disciplined ; that
mere idle destruction and cruelty were not in his own
interests ; that he was not an escaped slave with a
passion for revenge (as Esquemeling alleges), but a man
of good family from Monmouthshire, who had gone out
to the West Indies as a soldier ; and finally that there
was, in practice, a state of war between ourselves and
Spain in the West Indies (though no formal declaration

had been made) right up to the settlement in 1670 ; and
that anyhow Morgan held a commission from Sir Thomas
Muddiford,[1] the Governor, and was therefore to be
regarded as doing what he did in the service of King
Charles.

To sum up, I do not think that we can believe Esquemeling in regard to details. There is no evidence but
his for the allegation that Morgan enjoyed torturing
prisoners. What may have happened in the heat of
battle is quite another story. The men of the seventeenth century were not naturally and coldly cruel like
those of the sixteenth ; but we have only to remember
Tilly in Germany and Cromwell in Ireland to realize
that they were capable of almost anything when their
blood was up. Morgan was a brutal soldier, but he
was not a pirate. Pirates would as soon have robbed
and murdered an English crew as any other ; they were
enemies of society, common felons, their hand against
every man, and every man's hand against them.[2] To
describe such a man as Morgan as a pirate is as foolish
as it would be to call Long John Silver a pickpocket.[3]

One word as to the state of the buccaneering profession at the moment when Dampier decided temporarily
to join its ranks. " Privateering," as it was now called,
had lost its character of an armed rebellion, and was
rapidly settling down as a regular line of business in
the West. On the other hand, it had not yet become
too disreputable for a man like Dampier to touch. The
wholesale crimes of L'Olonois had not yet given place

[1] His Jamaica estate, the Angels, happened to be next to that of
Colonel Helyar, where Dampier had worked.

[2] Yet we learn that, as late as 1718, the Governor of North Carolina
had the bad taste to be present in person at the wedding of that worst of
pirates, " Blackbeard " Teach.

[3] As Coleridge remarks, à propos of the Elizabethan adventurers,
" No man is a pirate unless his contemporaries agree to call him so."
Table-Talk, Mar. 17th, 1832.

to the paltry rascalities of a Captain Kidd.   In fact, the business was for the moment almost respectable.   We shall find these later buccaneers piously observing Sundays and Christmas Day, and hear from an eye-witness how one of their commanders indignantly threw overboard the dice with which he found some members of his crew profaning the Sabbath.   Dampier, as we have seen, professedly joined them for no other purpose than to see the world : and everything that we know of his character seems to support that profession.   Andrew Lang, in his famous denunciation of the buccaneers, was careful to make an exception of Dampier, singling him out by name ; but the truth is that there must have been scores of others in Sharp's company who were no more to be classed as criminals than Dampier was. Basil Ringrose, who has written the best description of the voyage, was a gentleman, and even something of a scholar.   And others who have left records behind, like Wafer the surgeon, were obviously decent men, who never dreamt that they were doing anything morally wrong.   They were not proud of being buccaneers, and their governments were not proud of them ; but they certainly never expected to be punished for it by any-one, except possibly the Spanish monopolists whose trade regulations they defied.   It was, perhaps, rather like being a rum-runner on the American coast to-day.

We left Dampier enjoying a brief holiday in England. But brief as it was, he found time to get married—a sort of " war-marriage," though more successful than most of them.   The lady was from the household of the Duke of Grafton, and her Christian name was Judith, but that is literally all we know of her.   Apparently she never bore him any children.   In the following spring (1679) he was off again on his wanderings, booking as a passenger on board the " Loyal Merchant," of London, bound for Jamaica. His intention was to revisit the Bay of Campeachy, and trade with the logwood-cutters, for which purpose he brought with him a consignment of such goods as he knew would have a ready sale in those quarters—hats, for instance, sugar, saws, axes, stockings, shoes and, of course, rum. But after landing at Port Royal, he changed his plans, "upon some maturer considerations," the nature of which he does not confide to us. He sold his goods at Jamaica, and remained there for the rest of the year, looking about for suitable employment.

In the end, he very nearly returned to England. He happened to hear of " a small estate in Dorsetshire, near my native county of Somerset," and promptly bought it from the title-holder, intending to sail for England about Christmas time, in order to see his new property. In fact, he was just about to embark, when a certain Mr. Hobby proposed to him a short trading voyage to the country of the Mosquito Indians, and Dampier, thinking it advisable to raise a little more money before returning to England, consented to go with him. Though he did not know it at the time, this was one of the most important decisions of his career. For Captain Hobby, after leaving Port Royal, happened to put in at Negril Bay, at the western end of the island of Jamaica. To his surprise he found the harbour full of ships. Closer investigation revealed a whole fleet of the " privateers," who had recently made a rendezvous there. There were nearly a dozen ships in all, mounting about fifty guns, and the crews numbering 477 men. The commanders were Sawkins, Coxon, Harris, Sharp, Cook and others, assisted by two French privateers.

It was a lively scene ; for the little fleet was in high fettle. This new concentration of forces was reminiscent of the great days of Sir Henry Morgan ; and the leaders were, as a fact, at that moment planning a descent upon the unfortunate town of Porto Bello, which Morgan himself had sacked only a few years before. Provisions were abundant, rum flowed freely, and we can believe that a hearty welcome was accorded to Hobby's ship, the latest arrival, when it appeared in their midst. Boats plied to and fro. Hobby's men mingled with the buccaneers, and, learning that a long expedition was being " contrived," they at once deserted in a body, " leaving," says Dampier, " not one with him beside myself." Dampier stuck by the unfortunate Hobby for three or four days, and then he too was " persuaded to go with them." Whereupon Mr. Hobby disappears from our history. A few days later, the buccaneer fleet set sail for Porto Bello.

Before entering upon this new episode in Dampier's career, let us glance at our " authorities," who happen to be numerous, varied and entertaining. The first is Dampier himself—clear, concise, disinterested, so aloof from his companions that he might almost be describing a voyage he never saw ; and alas ! so brief. The second and best—because by far the fullest and as honest as Dampier himself—is Basil Ringrose, gentleman and scholar, whose knowledge of Latin once enabled him to save the lives of a whole boat-load of British buccaneers, by acting as interpreter between them and the Spaniards. " He had no mind to this voyage," says his friend, Dampier, " but was necessitated to engage in it, or starve." His artless narrative is as good a thing of its kind as can be found anywhere in our travel literature. Unfortunately, Ringrose was killed in action at the taking of Santiago in Mexico, in 1686, and never got back to England to see his book through the press. In the meantime, a friend of Captain Sharp's (probably William Hacke) [1] got at the manuscript, and, in addition to a lot of quite unnecessary editing, inserted here and

[1] See Smyth.

E

there passages in praise of Sharp, whom Ringrose had very seldom mentioned, and probably despised. I shall note some of the more humorous of these interpolations as we go along. Ringrose's book, as it first appeared [1] (as a second volume of Esquemeling) and as it has recently been reprinted in a very handy form for modern readers,[2] is therefore, unfortunately, not his own ; but his original manuscript happily exists and may be seen in the British Museum.[3]

Captain Sharp has given his own account of the affair—brief but lively.[4] Then there is the excellent Cox,[5] a simple sailorman of New England, who dedicates his journal—it is, for the most part, only his day-to-day log—to the Duke of Albemarle, explaining that " a formall epistle " would be " a task beyond the capacity of a sayler " ; and, therefore, begs his lordship " to accepte this journal in the Plaine Tarpaulin Habbitt in which you will find it." Sharp hates Cox, describing him as a man whom he (Sharp) had helped to advancement " from old acquaintance " and not " from any valour or knowledge he was possessed of." Cox, on the other hand, is notably fair to Sharp. Sharp, in fact, is a typical smooth-tongued " climber," a man who could always talk his shipmates round, but could never lead them in a fight. Cox is an ordinary, thick-headed sailorman.

Lionel Wafer, whose journal has already been quoted,[6] was a young chemist's assistant, who went to sea as a surgeon's mate. There are some curious similarities

[1] *The Buccaneers of America*, vol. ii., containing the dangerous voyage and bold attempts of Captain Bartholomew Sharp. From the original journal of the said voyage, written by Mr. Basil Ringrose, gent. London : 1684.

[2] *The Buccaneers of America*. New Edition. Routledge : 1926.

[3] Sloane Collection, No. 3820.

[4] Sloane Collection, No. 46 a and b.

[5] Sloane Collection, No. 49.   [6] Page 44.

between his career and Dampier's.   His first long voyage
was to Bantam, and his second to Jamaica, where he
had a brother employed by Sir Thomas Muddiford, at
the Angels plantation, next door to that of the Helyars
at Sixteen-Mile-Walk.   He was in practice as a surgeon
at Port Royal when he fell into the society of the
privateers.   He was about ten years younger than
Dampier and evidently made a hero of him ; for his
rather rambling account of this voyage—obviously
written some time afterwards—makes frequent and
admiring references to " Mr. Dampier," whereas in the
other journals we are dealing with Dampier is hardly
mentioned at all.   We must remember, however, that
Dampier's book, which had a great success, was being
widely talked about at the time when Wafer wrote.   It
would, therefore, be unsafe to assume that Dampier
played quite the prominent part in these adventures
which Wafer assigns to him.

Finally, there are two less reliable authorities.   In an
additional chapter, appended to the second edition of
the *History of the Buccaneers*, there is an account of the
voyage said to have been written by one of those present,
and wearing, in places, the appearance of having been
compiled by Sharp himself ; but this can hardly be, for
the story ends with a description of Sharp's discreditable
disappearance from England, after committing an act of
piracy in the Channel and stealing some cattle from
Romney Marsh.   And lastly, there is the unknown quill-
driver whom I quoted at the opening of this chapter,
and who seems to have " cribbed " nearly all his facts
from Cox.   So much for our authorities.

The Porto Bello affair was soon over.   The buccaneers landed two hundred men, who crept through the
surrounding forests, and by a sudden dash succeeded in
surprising the place.   The town surrendered promptly—
it was becoming a habit with it—and the conquerors

divided among themselves booty to the value of £40 a head, not counting the extra shares awarded according to custom to the various commanders. They were now free to attempt some more arduous adventure elsewhere. After many conferences, in which Dampier certainly took no part, a really sporting decision was arrived at. It was resolved to march by land across the Isthmus of Darien, and try their luck " upon some new adventures in the South Seas." They were sure in advance of the support of the Darien Indians, who hated the Spaniards as much as they had loved the English ever since a certain Captain Wright, fifteen years before, had be-friended an Indian lad, clothed him, and fed him, christened him with the curious name of John Gret, and sent him back to his kindred.

But they were sure of nothing else. Of the country they had to traverse, its jungles and rivers and fever-laden swamps, of how long the march would take them, what provisions they might require, and what resistance they must expect from the Spaniards of the coast towns, when they reached the other side, they knew nothing whatever—except from the vague descriptions of their Indian friends. Nothing deterred by this, the fleet assembled at an island called the Golden Island, in the Gulf of Darien, which had been appointed as their rendezvous ; and here the English prepared to make their landing on the mainland, leaving a strong party behind to protect their ships in their absence. The two French privateers, however, parted company, misliking the idea of this inland voyage.

The English rowed ashore, and proceeded to draw up by companies upon the beach. They made a brave show, as their captains marshalled them in their ranks under the blazing sun. The dress of the men would conform to no fixed rule ; but then, as now, a sailor was easily distinguishable by his clothes, and of these we

may obtain some rough idea from the list of " slops "
provided for the Royal Navy at that time. For the
Navy had no uniform yet ; it wore, like the buccaneers,
the ordinary seaman's garments of the period. These
would consist of jackets of grey kersey, a kind of coarse
woollen cloth ; blue waistcoats ; wide petticoat breeches,
striped " crosswise " in crimson, and reaching to the knee ;
under them linen drawers ; black stockings and shoes ;
and red caps, with loosely tied white neckcloths.[1] Not
a bad dress for this particular occasion, provided that
the stockings were thick enough to keep out mosquitoes.

Captain Sharp had been ill (I suspect him of sea-
sickness), but as commander-in-chief, he was given the
van. His company marched first. They had a red
flag with a bunch of white and green ribbons. Next
came Sawkins's men, with a red flag striped with yellow.
Then two companies under Captain Peter Harris, having
two green flags ; then John Coxon, with two companies,
flying red flags ; and finally Captain Edmund Cook,
whose colours were " red, striped with yellow, with a
hand and sword for his device." The men were armed
with fusee, pistol and hanger, and carried three or four
" doughboys," or hard dumplings, boiled in sea-water.
" For drink," says Ringrose, " the rivers afforded
enough." There were 327 [2] men in all, with six Indians
to guide them. Dampier was with Sharp's company.

And so, turning their backs upon the white beach,
they marched into the dark shadow of the tropical
forests. Their ships moved away, and for all that any

[1] See *Mariner's Mirror*, January, 1924, " Dress of British Seamen,"
by G. E. Manwaring. There is no idea yet of " Navy-blue." Indeed
officers were often dressed in scarlet, and there seems to have been some
danger that red would come to be regarded as the characteristic seaman's
colour. The familiar blue and white uniform was not adopted until 1748.

[2] Cox says 330 English and 7 French.

Spanish cruiser could have seen a few minutes later, there might never have been an Englishman on that deserted shore.

This famous march began on the 5th of April, 1680 ; and that very first night some showers of rain fell. But it cleared up later, and the little army slept comfortably enough, " having," as Cox says in an unusual burst of eloquence, " the cold ground for our bedding and the spangled firmament for our covering." The temperature would be about 90° in the shade. On the 6th they continued their march, climbing a steep mountain, where the paths were so narrow that only one man at a time could pass, and descending towards evening into a valley on the other side. About noon on April 7th they reached a native town and were handsomely entertained by the chief, whom they called " King Golden Cap." His garments appear to have consisted almost entirely of beaten gold—which made John Cox's mouth water ! After a short rest, they continued their march along the banks of a river, and on April 9th, Sharp, Coxon, Cook and sixty others embarked in canoes which the Indians provided, but found this even more fatiguing than travelling by land, because of the fallen trees and other obstructions in the water. However, they got well ahead of their companions, and on the 12th were close to Santa Maria, a town on the river of that name, which runs into the Bay of Panama, by the Gulf of San Miguel. They saw many wild beasts, but were afraid to fire at them, lest the sound of the shots should give warning to the Spaniards. Bartholomew Sharp was particularly interested in the wild hogs, and no wonder, for he " observed that the navels of these kinds of animals grew upon their backs." [1] Next day the main

---

[1] Shelvocke, the privateer commander, claims to have noted the same phenomenon thirty years later. See his *Voyage Round the World*, London, 1726.

body joined them, and after a night's rest, the advance upon the town of Santa Maria was begun.

The entire force, with the addition of fifty more Indians, was carried down the river in a fleet of sixty-eight canoes, and landed at midnight at a point about half a mile from the town. The banks were so thick in mud that it was only by clinging to the branches of the trees that the men could drag themselves ashore, after which they had to hew their way through the tropical undergrowth in the dark till they reached a spot where they might rest unperceived by their enemies until dawn. But very early in the morning, almost before it was light, they were startled to hear a discharge of fire-arms in the town, followed by the beating of a drum, which showed pretty plainly that the Spaniards had been warned. The English, therefore, armed themselves in haste, and emerging from the wood, with a loud cheer advanced rapidly across the open.

The Spanish garrison retired before them into " a large palisaded fort, having each pale or post twelve foot high," and from thence " began to fire very briskly at us as we came." The buccaneers' advance guard, or " forlorn," under that particularly gallant fellow, Sawkins (Sharp claims to have been with them, too, though it is not clear why, and, in view of his subsequent record, not very likely), went ahead at the double, and, coming up to the palisades, forced their way in, and in a few minutes were masters of the fort. According to Ringrose, there were 260 Spaniards inside, and not above fifty assailants. The Spaniards lost over forty killed and wounded, the buccaneers only two. There was no further resistance, and our adventurers rushed eagerly into the town, in search of loot.

Alas ! it turned out to be but " a little pitiful place," very different from the wealthy metropolis which the imagination of their Indian allies had conjured up.

Worse still, the Governor and all the chief men had made a timely "get-away," taking with them most of the gold and valuables. The only people who got any satisfaction out of the capture were the Indians, who amused themselves by taking the Spanish prisoners out into the adjoining woods and murdering them there, until their European allies put a stop to it. Moreover, King Golden Cap's daughter, who had been held captive here by the Spaniards, was released and restored to her fond parent's bejewelled breast—a romantic little incident certainly, but of secondary interest to a party of hard-headed Englishmen whose minds were running on pieces of eight.

With their appetites no more than whetted, the buccaneers left Santa Maria, and pressed on eagerly towards the coast. The end of their long march was now approaching. On the second day out from Santa Maria, a faint blue ribbon was seen upon the far horizon. "About eleven of the clock," says Sharp, "we had a sight of the fair South Sea"; and, like Xenophon's Greeks two thousand years before, they must have hailed it with cries of joy. Apparently they had hardly any sick on this long march, though the climate of the peninsula is notoriously dangerous for Europeans.

It should be explained that they had come down the river in their canoes, and their first vague intention was to proceed in them against the important town of Panama, the scene of Morgan's most resounding exploit.[1] Near the mouth of the river they captured a small ship, and there was, not unnaturally, something of a rush to get on board of her, especially among those who were in the less seaworthy canoes. Ringrose in his MS. says simply that "there got in 137 men with Captain Sharp and Captain Cook." The published (and doctored)

[1] He captured and sacked the town in 1670, and then slipped away with nearly all the booty, leaving his followers in the lurch.

PANAMA ABOUT 1690

From the Macpherson Collection

(Showing vessels of the type in which Dampier served with the buccaneers)

edition of his work says : " There embarked thereon
to the number of 137 of our company, together with
that sea-artist and valiant commander, Captain Bartholomew Sharp "—and adds slightingly that " with him went
also on board Captain Cook." As a matter of fact,
Cook was by far the more " valiant commander " of
the two.

But it soon became apparent that the Spaniards had
again received warning of their enemies' approach.
When the canoes came in sight of Panama on the morning
of April 25th, they found the garrison standing to arms,
and a fleet, consisting of five " great ships " and three
" pretty big barks " of the armadillo type, drawn up
outside to receive them. There followed a brisk sea-
fight, which Ringrose vividly describes. The English
were not in full strength, Sharp with some of the canoes
having been detached on a minor expedition, and failing
to return in time. Ringrose indeed asserts that not
68 Englishmen were engaged against a Spanish fleet
which must have carried at least 200 men on the
armadilloes alone. In fact, the Spanish ships were
unwisely overcrowded.

As the canoes approached in line, the three armadilloes advanced boldly to meet them, and the first,
commanded by Don Diego de Carabanal, broke through
the English line, firing destructive broadsides to right
and left as she passed. But as the Admiral, Don
Jacinto de Barahona, attempted to follow, a shot from
one of the canoes killed his helmsman, so that his ship
ran into the wind and lay for a moment helpless, just
between the canoe commanded by Sawkins and that in
which Ringrose was. Instantly the canoes clustered
round the Spaniard like angry wasps. The buccaneers
discharged volley after volley from their small arms into
the Admiral's crowded decks. The third armadillo
approaching in its turn was met by Sawkins's canoe,

which closed with it, and a desperate struggle ensued. A powder barrel exploded in the Spanish ship, throwing several men overboard, whereupon the gallant captain, Don Peralta, though himself badly burned about the hands, sprang into the water and rescued them. Immediately afterwards, however, there was another explosion, and Sawkins, a dashing leader, taking instant advantage of the confusion, succeeded in boarding the ship and forcing the survivors to surrender. In the meantime, the Admiral had been killed and his ship boarded by Coxon and Harris, the latter of whom was shot through both legs and mortally wounded. Here, too, the Spaniards surrendered. The slaughter had been terrible. On Captain Peralta's ship only twenty-five Spaniards were left alive out of eighty-six.

The buccaneers had lost eighteen killed and twenty-two wounded. But apart from this loss in man power, which they could ill afford, they had every reason to be satisfied with their performance. They now possessed two roomy and convenient vessels in which to go a-cruising in the South Seas ; and they had evidently produced a considerable moral effect, for it is to be noticed that the first armadillo, after breaking through their line, was careful not to return to help its consort ; while the three " great ships," one of which had a crew of 300 men, sat tight in the harbour, and never even came out. The captured Spaniard, Captain Peralta, " would often break out in admiration of our valour," declaring that Englishmen were " the valiantest men in the whole world, who designed always to fight open, whilst all other nations invented all the ways imaginable to barricade themselves and fight as close as they could."

After this engagement, the buccaneers landed on the island of Perico, partly to bury Captain Harris and other dead, and partly to rest themselves, and wait for the

arrival of Sharp, with whom, I think, was Dampier.   It
should be mentioned that, after the affair at Santa Maria,
the smooth-tongued Sharp had been deposed from the
chief command,[1] which was given to Coxon.   Sharp
says that this was done as a bribe to induce Coxon to
continue with the expedition, he being a discontented,
quarrelsome fellow, who was always threatening to turn
back.   That description of Coxon is true enough.   On
one occasion, he had attempted to murder Harris by
shooting at him in consequence of some altercation.   He
now became more troublesome than ever, and, finally,
left the expedition with his company, announcing his
intention of returning overland by the way they had
come.   His departure was particularly discreditable, for
he left many of his wounded on their hands, and he took
away with him the best surgeon and nearly all the
medicines they had.   Sawkins, the popular hero of the
sea-fight, was appointed in his stead.   The buccaneers
were a discontented, mutinous, muddle-headed crowd,
who changed their commanders every few months just
for the sake of change ; but they knew a brave man
when they saw one.   They seem also to have been
genuinely fond of Sawkins.   He never had to face the
familiar charge of trying to cheat his men.

The buccaneers remained near Panama for ten days,
during which time they captured several Spanish merchant ships, and sent away " all the meanest of the
prisoners " on one of them.   Then they moved on to
some of the other islands, making further captures as
they went.   In the interval, Sawkins exchanged messages
with the Governor of Panama, from whom he demanded
a heavy tribute and a promise " not any further to annoy
the Indians."   The Governor, in reply, demanded to

[1] Ringrose says for his " backwardness in the fight," but these words are
deliberately suppressed by Hacke in the published version of Ringrose's
narrative !

see his commission ; whereupon Sawkins answered, with a fine Elizabethan flourish, " That as yet all his company were not come together ; but that when they were come up we would come and visit him at Panama, and bring our Commissions on the muzzles of our guns, at which time he should read them as plain as the flame of gunpowder could make them."

But no such triumph was in store for poor Sawkins. Shortly after this, growing tired of wandering among the islands, the buccaneers determined to make an attack in force upon the town of Puebla Nueva, near the mouth of the river on the mainland. They found the Spaniards well prepared. For a mile below the town, they had blocked the river with fallen trees, and they had raised three strong breastworks before the town itself.[1] Attacking with their usual impetuosity, the buccaneers met with a severe repulse. They could not reach the breastworks, and Sawkins, their leader, and many others were shot dead (May 25th, 1680).

Dampier, who briefly describes the engagement, came off as usual without a scratch. But the death of Sawkins was a terrible blow : "a man," says Ringrose, "as valiant as any could be." [2] He was not only a first-class buccaneer, but a person of high principles, and a strict Sabbatarian. Sundays were always observed on his ships. It is of him that Ringrose tells the curious story that, as he walked the decks one Sunday morning, he observed to his horror certain members of his crew engaged in play, and of how he immediately seized the dice and threw them overboard, declaring that " he would have no gambling aboard his ship." As to his

[1] Sharp says that a " renegade Frenchman " showed the inhabitants how to build these defences. The use of the word " renegade " is interesting as showing the attitude of other nationalities towards the Spanish in the West.

[2] And Hacke adds : " next to Captain Sharp " !

courage, even Sharp, the deposed commander, usually a most ungenerous critic, refers regretfully to the death of " the brave Captain Sawkins." Evidently a great " character," who might have become one of the most famous of all the buccaneers, had he lived.

It was not easy to replace him, and fresh dissensions immediately broke out. Sharp went aboard " La Trinidad," the biggest of the captured armadilloes, and there with his usual eloquence addressed the assembled buccaneers, setting forth the facts of the situation. Would they stay with him or attempt the overland march again back to their ships ? At the conclusion of his speech, those who from motives of loyalty or greed, or merely because (like Ringrose) they were afraid to trust themselves among the Indians ashore, had resolved to remain under his command, were distributed among the various ships ; while the malcontents, to the number of sixty-three, returned homewards in Coxon's footsteps, taking with them the remainder of the Indians. Dampier, as always, chose the adventurous course, not because he had any respect for Sharp, but in the hope of new experiences. It is possible that he may have had some influence on the next important decision, which was to leave the neighbourhood of Panama, and sail southward for the coast of Peru.

The principal commanders were now Sharp, Cook and John Cox, one of the chroniclers of the voyage, who had been given the command of a prize. Ringrose describes him as " a kinsman of Captain Sharp." [1] The captured Spaniard, Captain Peralta, was still with them, and seems to have acted very willingly as their pilot.

The southward voyage began on June 6th, and on

---

[1] But Hacke alters Ringrose's text to read : " John Cox, an inhabitant of New England, who forced kindred, as was thought, upon Captain Sharp, out of old acquaintance, in this conjuncture of time, only to advance himself."

the 17th they came in sight of the island of Gorgona,[1] where they went ashore, and regaled themselves on a varied menu of " Indian conies, monkeys, snakes, oysters, conches, periwinkles and a few small turtle, with some other sorts of good fish." Here too they cut away the roundhouse and upper works of the poop on the " Trinidad," which were built very high in the Spanish manner, also " all the high carved work belonging to the stern of the ship, for when we took her from the Spaniards before Panama she was high as any third-rate ship in England "—*i.e.* much too high for her size, according to English ideas of seamanship. Sailing on southward, with the intention of attacking the town of Arica on the mainland near Tacna, they had the mis-fortune to part company with Cox's ship, which was not seen again for a month, when they found him at anchor off the Isle of Plate. Here they killed a number of tortoises [2] and goats for salting.

Leaving this island, they sighted a Spanish merchant ship, gave chase and captured her after a stiff fight. They found 3276 pieces-of-eight on board ; but for some reason this does not seem to have improved their tempers, for two days later they disgraced themselves by murdering an unfortunate priest who had been chap-lain of the prize, shooting him and " casting him over-board before he was dead." Ringrose (and we can believe him) " abhorred such cruelties," but dared not interfere. Dampier, who must have shared his senti-ments, never mentions the incident, nor does he even allude to any of the captures made at sea. It has been assumed by his biographers that this was because he

---

[1] According to one of Hacke's interpolations in Ringrose, Sharp had the cool cheek to change the name Gorgona into " Sharp Island." Sharp himself says nothing of it.

[2] The inevitable Hacke rushes in with the assertion that Captain Sharp showed himself especially " ingenious in striking them."

was ashamed of them ; but in regard to the mere capture of Spanish ships, I think it more reasonable to accept his own explanation, which is that he had not space for details, having deliberately decided to compress this part of his voyage " in this short compass," and hurry on to later events of more importance from the point of view of geographical exploration. That he saw nothing wrong in taking Spanish ships in peace time is shown by his frank allusions to such captures in other parts of his writings. He was much too honest a chronicler to " doctor " his records.

Unfortunately, pieces-of-eight are of little use upon the high seas, and a week later the buccaneers found themselves so short of provisions that they were reduced to an allowance of " only two draughts of water " each day. They captured a small Spanish ship, but as it was necessary to cut away all her masts except one, lest she should reach the coast ahead of them and give warning of their coming, they had not the heart to deprive her crew of their water supply, and so sailed on towards Arica thirstier than ever.[1] On September 29th their rations were still further reduced to three and a half pints of water and one cake of boiled bread.

On October 26th they at last arrived off Arica, and sent in their canoes in the hope of surprising the place. But they found " a general alarm through the whole country," six ships riding at anchor with their guns ready, and a large force drawn up to oppose their landing. So they landed at another point, farther up the coast, and sacked the small town of Hilo, carrying off quantities of provisions in full view of a force of mounted Spaniards who looked feebly on.[2] Unfortunately these provisions

[1] Ordinary pirates would have felt no such compunction.
[2] It turned out afterwards, however, that they were mere boys, half of them unarmed, and commanded, surprisingly, by a local English resident.

included very little fresh meat, and when the southward
voyage was resumed, it was found that the crews were
suffering from scurvy. But they had luckily seized a
small quantity of chocolate, " whereof the Spaniards
make infinite use," and it was presently discovered that
" a dish of this pleasant liquor "—yet so strange to the
buccaneering palate—was an efficacious remedy, if taken
first thing every morning.[1]

They now fetched a compass, and, giving Arica a
wide berth, steered S.S.E. for the town of La Serena on
the mainland, some six hundred miles farther south.
Arriving there on December 2nd, they landed in their
canoes, and advanced against the town, which turned
out to be a considerable place, containing seven churches.
But once again the Spaniards (who must have out-
numbered the buccaneers by at least five to one) had
been warned of their approach, and had fled, taking
with them " the most precious of their goods and jewels "
and everything else they could carry. They had also
killed most of their Chilean slaves, in order to save them
from the temptation to help the invaders ! In these
circumstances, the disappointed buccaneers must have
found the empty town of La Serena serene to the point
of boredom ; and they would probably have destroyed
it out of hand if the Spaniards had not sent in a flag of
truce on the following morning, offering to ransom the
place rather than see it burnt. But it was only a ruse ;
and after two days of profitless haggling the English
marched back to their ships, contemptuously brushing
aside a Spanish ambuscade which they encountered on
the way. They found that in their absence an ingenious
attempt had been made to burn their principal ship.
Ringrose gives the following account of this stratagem :

" They (the Spaniards) blew up a horse's hide like a

[1] Some thirty years later we find Shelvocke's men drinking it regularly.

bladder, and upon this float a man ventured to swim from shore and come under the stern of our ship. Being arrived there, he crammed oakum and brimstone and other combustible matter between the rudder and the stern-post. Having done this, he fired it with a match, so that in a small time our rudder was on fire, and all the ship in a smoke. Our men, both alarmed and amazed with this smoke, ran up and down the ship, suspecting the prisoners to have fired the vessel, thereby to get their liberty and seek our destruction. At last they found out where the fire was, and had the good fortune to quench it, before its going too far. As soon as they had put it out, they sent the boat ashore, and found both the hide aforementioned, and the match burning at both ends, whereby they became acquainted with the whole matter."

Having concluded this gallant but profitless affair, the buccaneers drew off surlily from the coast, and sailed for the island of Juan Fernandez to refit. This, as it turned out, was their " farthest south." The inevitable quarrels broke out afresh. Sharp attributes the whole trouble to " that dissembling New Englander," John Cox. Cox, on the other hand, says that the men having now plenty to eat and drink, " nothing will serve their turn but a new commander " ; so " a party of refractory fellows " went ashore and signed a paper to put in Watling instead of Sharp. This Watling was an old buccaneer, a rough, blustering bully, with little else to recommend him. The first thing he did was to put his colleague, Capt. Cook, in irons, on a disgraceful charge. Another of his gestures was to insist upon the strict observance of Sundays, which had been allowed to lapse since Sawkins's death. Then he sailed north, direct for Arica, their original objective, determined to crack that hard nut or die in the attempt. His departure

F

was hastened by a rumour that Spanish warships were approaching to intercept him.

The more educated members of the party, such as Dampier and Ringrose, seem to have doubted this new leadership from the start. At Iquique they took some prisoners, and Watling, doubting the information given by one of them, had him summarily shot.[1] Three days' sail brought them to Arica, and Watling at once made preparations to attack. The date was January 30th, the anniversary of the martyrdom of King Charles I, and Cox attributed the ensuing failure to this unfortunate choice of date. Dampier points out that Arica was " a strong town advantageously situated," and hardly to be taken by so small a body of men, except on a surprise. Watling, however, as ignorant of sentimental as of military considerations, advanced boldly to the attack. Forty men were detailed to attack the fort. The main body stormed the principal breastwork, but immediately came under a heavy fire from three other breastworks which commanded it. " We faced about," says Cox, " and with a small party of men took them (the breastworks) also." He adds significantly that they " left the party that guarded them all fast asleep that they might do no further mischief, for they were of a copper complexion which never give quarter themselves."

Abandoning the attack upon the fort, the English now stormed through the streets of the town, losing heavily, but taking so many prisoners that they hardly knew what to do with them. All the time the fort kept firing vigorously, and the enemy, rallying in the houses, surrounded them on every side. From every

---

[1] Here Hacke interposes with a theatrical story of how Sharp, the deposed commander, " took water and washed his hands, saying : ' Gentlemen, I am clear of the blood of this old man.' " There is nothing of the sort in Ringrose's original MS., and it probably never happened, though the action would certainly be characteristic of Sharp.

window and doorway came a hail of missiles.   It was a hopeless situation.   Watling was killed ; and Sharp then took command, and conducted an orderly retreat from the town, leaving behind only their surgeons, who had somehow managed to get gloriously drunk, and could not be found.   And so, being " such a small parcel of our men and the enemy's horse quite round us, we got our disabled men into the middle, and in good order marched down to our canoes and boats, but with heavy hearts to think we should leave so much plate behind us." [1]

This successful retreat did something to restore Sharp's credit ; but it was a sadly disgruntled party which took ship once more, and sailed to the north.   They landed at Hilo again, and stole some wine and figs and sugar by way of revenge.   Embarking again, Cox records more grumbles from those people who were " every day for a new broom."   A shortage of water accentuated this discontent, and by the time they reached the island of Plate, on April 17th, 1681, matters had come to a head.   Dampier, who now suddenly comes into prominence, explains that " a great number of the meaner sort " were for reinstating Sharp in the command, but " the abler and more experienced men, being altogether dissatisfied with Sharp's former conduct, would by no means consent to have him chosen."   Reconciliation was impossible, and it was finally decided that they must part company, by putting the matter to the vote, the majority to retain the ships, and the minority to return overland with their canoes to the western seas.   On a division, the ayes had it, and Sharp, for the last time, took command.   The loyal, deluded Cox of course remained with him.

Dampier thereupon publicly declared his mind, " which I had hitherto kept to myself," and joined the land party.   Wafer, the surgeon (not one of those who

[1] Cox.

had got drunk at Arica), was also in the minority—" I was of Mr. Dampier's side in that matter," he says—so were the two Cooks, Captain Edmund and plain John. Ringrose, however, unable to get over his fear of the " wild Indians " on shore, elected to stay with Sharp. We part from him regretfully.   In 1682 he paid a brief visit to England, in company with his commander, and must then have given his journal into the printer's hands. But long before its publication in 1684, he had sailed as supercargo with Charles Swan, and he never saw England again.

CHAPTER VI

HE ADVENTURES TO AFRICA
AND BACK

OR the third time in the course of this brief narrative, a party of English buccaneers sets out to cross that dangerous and pestiferous isthmus of Darien. Unless you cross by the Panama Canal, it is hardly less dangerous and pestiferous to-day, so that lady travellers who happen to have been there write exciting books on the subject (just as Dampier and Wafer and Ringrose did), emphasizing the fact that they were the first civilized women to visit the place, and laying special stress upon the numbers of alligators in the swamps, the jaguars that prowl through the forests, and those mysterious tribes of white Indians, as to whose existence the best scientific opinion seems to be still in some doubt. The buccaneer chroniclers, by the way, frequently mention white Indians—though whether they really saw whole tribes of them, or were deceived by the appearance of an unusual number of albinos, I cannot say. It is a subject better left to the anthropologists.

On this occasion the travellers numbered forty-four white men who bore arms ; a Spanish Indian, also armed ; two Mosquito Indians, always greatly valued on such occasions for their skill in catching fish or turtles ; and " five slaves taken in the South Seas, who fell to our share." We are to imagine the two Mos-

quitos dressed in European clothes of the period of
Charles II, which must rather have cramped their style
as hunters.   But Dampier tells us that they were so
pro-British that, when serving with Englishmen, they
made a point of putting on English clothes, though their
costume at ordinary times consisted only of a " piece of
linen " tied about their waists.   I quote from Dampier's
journal, which now becomes our chief authority, being
full and clear and reliable, as he always is when he sets
out to describe an adventure at length.

They started about two o'clock in the morning on
April 17th, 1681, being twelve leagues north-west from
the isle of Plate where they had left Captain Sharp.
They travelled in a launch or long-boat, one sound canoe,
and another canoe which had been cut in halves with the
idea of making it into water-barrels, and was now pre-
cariously joined together again.   They had fitted these
vessels with sails, and loaded them with as much flour
as they could carry, and twenty or thirty pounds of
chocolate and sugar to sweeten it withal.   " These things
and a kettle " it was intended that the slaves should
" carry on their backs " after they had landed ; " and
because there were some who designed to go with us
that we knew were not well able to march, we gave out
that if any Man faltered in the Journey over Land he
must expect to be shot to Death ; for we knew that the
Spaniards would soon be after us, and one man falling
into their hands might be the ruin of us all, by giving
an account of our Strength and Condition." [1]

The isle of Plate lies about six hundred miles as the
crow flies from the isthmus of Darien, and the buccaneers
had an unpleasant journey thither, the winds being
mostly contrary, with heavy showers of rain.   On the
18th, they captured a Spanish barque, and took her
along with them.   On the 25th they lost the second

[1] A good example of Dampier's compressed, yet fluent, style.

MOLL'S MAP OF TH

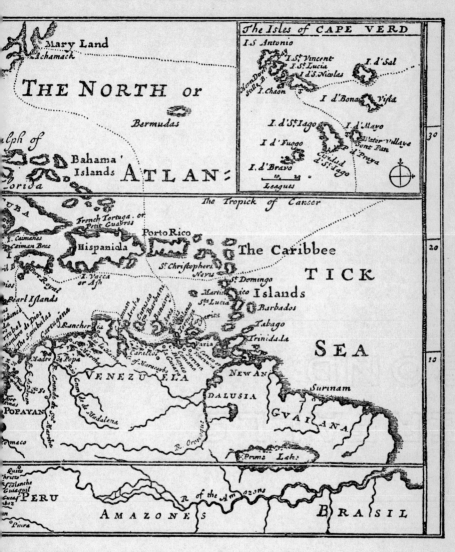

LE PART OF AMERICA

canoe, which was a serious inconvenience, for it was feared that the barque might be unsuitable for river work ; and, on the 30th, they entered the Gulf of San Miguel, and anchored near the mouth of the river, under cover of a large island.   There they got intelligence of a Spanish ship, with a hundred and fifty men on board, waiting for them at the river's mouth, and of two other heavily armed Spaniards which cruised in the Bay, looking for them.   Thereupon Dampier's companions lost their nerve, and though he urged them with all the eloquence at his command to attempt another river called the Congo in their canoes, they insisted upon landing immediately, while they were still unobserved, and sinking all their boats to avoid detection.   So they hurriedly rowed ashore and landed their clothes and provisions, while the Mosquito Indians caught a " plentiful dish of fish," upon which—seated on the beach—they dined.

At this point, Dampier interjects a description of the Mosquito Indians, of whom he held a high opinion. If properly trained and led by Europeans, they make stout soldiers.   " They are in general very civil and kind to the English," and we, on our part, " always humour them, letting them go any whither as they will, and return to their own country in any vessel bound that way, if they please."   They are keen to speak English, and " take the Governor of Jamaica to be one of the greatest Princes in the World."

On the 2nd May, the party began their march, stopping in the evening at a small Indian village to purchase some native food (" fowls and peccary ") for their dinner.   This they ate all together, " having all sorts of our provisions in common, because none should live better than others, or pay dearer for anything than it was worth."   One of these Indians accompanied them next day as far as the house of a countryman who could speak Spanish, and gave them some rough directions

for their journey.   That morning a nameless Englishman deserted from the company, " being tired."

Their average day's march at this time was between
six and eight miles, but no doubt the way was hard.
For another forty-eight hours they struggled on, rations
becoming so short that there was no other topic of
conversation ; and they quite forgot their fear of the
Spaniards.   On the sixth day of the march, an unfortunate accident happened to the surgeon, Wafer.   His
knee was seriously " scorched " by the accidental ignition
of some gunpowder, and marching became a torture to
him.   His companions allowed him a slave to carry his
medicine chest and personal belongings, " being all of
us the more concerned at the accident," says Dampier
frankly, " because liable ourselves every moment to misfortune, and none to look after us but him."

That evening they crossed a river, and then came to
another winding stream which they had to ford several
times, though it was deep.   Dampier, foreseeing such
obstacles, had provided himself with a thick piece of
bamboo, sealed at each end, and swam the river, pushing
it in front of him.   Best of all, he had the forethought
to place his precious journal and other papers inside it,
thus preserving them from the wet.   Two of the company fell behind in the course of this day and never
rejoined.   The rest spent a damp evening ; to add to
their discomfort, it rained " extraordinarily hard," with
much thunder and lightning.   Finally their slaves, taking
advantage of the darkness, decamped in a body, including
the fellow with Wafer's medicine chest.   The unfortunate surgeon could no longer dress his wound, and
found the going heavier than ever.

Next day they had to cross a swollen river, and, in
trying to get a rope to the opposite bank, a man named
Gayny was drowned, being weighed down by a bag
containing three hundred dollars, which was strapped to

his back.   A little later they found his body ; but it is
significant of their condition that they did not even
trouble to take away the gold, " being only in care how
to work our way through an unknown country."   In
the afternoon they reached a pleasanter district, and
marched more at their ease.   Here they bade farewell
to the Spanish Indian, who turned back towards his
home ; and here they met many other Indians who
were kind and helpful.   After a fortnight's rest, they
rose betimes one morning and prepared to resume their
march.

Wafer, however, could go no farther.   He and two
other men, named Hingson and Gopson,[1] who now fell
out from the effects of exhaustion, had therefore to be
left behind, as the surgeon pathetically puts it, " among
the wild Indians in the isthmus of Darien."   It is hardly
necessary to add that the rigorous order about shooting
all laggards was not enforced against them.   On the
contrary, " the company took a very kind leave of us "—
no doubt expecting that it would be the last.   The others
pressed on, accompanied by some friendly Indians.   The
details of each day's journey are carefully recorded in
Dampier's diary, and need not be repeated here.   They
shot monkeys and wild turkeys for their food, and were
greatly assisted by the Indians whom they met.   One
old man who was carrying a load of plantains distributed
the fruit among the hungry buccaneers, and departed
empty-handed, asking no reward but their thanks.   On
the twentieth day, they crossed the Chepo river, climbed
a high mountain, and from its summit, " to our great
comfort," saw the Northern sea.

Two more days brought them to the coast, where
they eagerly inquired of the Indians what ships had been
seen in the neighbourhood.   They were told that there
was a French privateer now lying at La Soundes Key,

---

[1] Sometimes spelt " Gobson," which hardly improves matters.

an island of the Samballas group, about three leagues distant, and on the 24th May they put off in canoes and went on board this French vessel, where they were affably received by the commander, one Captain Tristian. Their Indian guides were still with them, and the buccaneers very properly " resolved to reward them to their hearts' content." They therefore made a levy among themselves of half-a-dollar a man, and with the money purchased all the beads, knives, scissors, looking-glasses and other " toys " that Captain Tristian possessed. The Indians were delighted, and " returned with joy to their friends "—a fortunate circumstance, as it turned out, for Wafer and the others who had been left behind.

Thus ended this toilsome overland march of 110 miles, which, as Dampier remarks, might have been fifty miles shorter and have occupied less than half the time, if they had landed from the South Seas at the proper place.

We now enter upon a new stage in Dampier's association with the buccaneers. He is so reticent about himself, while so informative about everything else, that it is impossible to say whether he was actually advanced in rank, but it is plain that he was now a man of some little weight among them. He seems conscious of his own superiority. Behind his quiet manner there is a complete self-confidence—more, perhaps, than was ever quite justified by the results.

Captain Tristian, soon after the arrival of the Englishmen, weighed anchor, and sailed to Springer's Key, another of the Samballas Islands, where he found a fleet of eight privateers, consisting of four English vessels, commanded by Coxon [1] (whom we have met before),

---

[1] This reappearance of the quarrelsome Coxon seems to have been unaccountably missed even by such careful historians as Mr. Philip Gosse and Mr. Masefield. Mr. Gosse makes him cross the isthmus with Dampier's party, whereas, as we have seen, he did the journey just a year before.

Payne, Wright and Williams ; one Dutchman, under
a Captain Yanky, or Yankes ; and three Frenchmen.
All the other commanders came on board Tristian's ship,
when they heard whom he had with him, and Dampier
says that the English in particular were " overjoyed to
see us." In fact, there was a merry reunion, Coxon
having most of his old company with him ; and we
may be sure that no one was so tactless as to mention
the disappearance of that medicine-chest twelve months
before !

It now appeared that the privateers were contemplating
another march overland against the town of Panama,
and they closely questioned the new arrivals as to their
chances of success, the condition of the rivers that
would have to be crossed, and so forth. What they
heard, says Dampier, " disheartened them quite from
that design." Several other plans were proposed, and
debate ran high.

It seems that these buccaneers had an excellent intelligence department. Whenever they took any prisoners,
they examined them at length, and they made a point
of comparing the different statements thus obtained, so
that they now knew the strength of every Spanish town
upon the coast, the nature of the surrounding country,
and where the " look-outs or sentinels " were placed.

At last it was decided to rendezvous at the small
island of S. Andreas, near Providence Island, with a
view to an expedition against the mainland. On the
way they encountered a gale which scattered the fleet.
Dampier and his companions, much to their disgust,
had been transferred to another French ship, because it
happened to be the only one of the privateers not
already overmanned. They liked their new commander,
Captain Archembo, well enough, but the French seamen
were " the saddest creatures that ever I was among."
When the weather was rough, the " biggest part of

them never stirred out of their hammocks but to eat or ease themselves." When, therefore, Archembo reached the rendezvous, and found only Wright there, with a Spanish *tartane*, which he had just captured, the Englishmen of Dampier's party went to Wright, and told him plainly that, as independent privateers, they refused to remain with Archembo, and would go ashore and build canoes for themselves, unless he (Wright) would take them over. The English captain hesitated, being afraid to offend the French ; but the *tartane* was capable of carrying thirty men, and he at last agreed to put them into it as a prize crew, if they came to him as one ship's company.

So it was concluded, and Captain Wright, with his prize, sailed to Bluefield's River, where the *tartane* was careened, and Dampier went hunting with some Mosquito Indians, whose method of harpooning the manatee seems to have fascinated him. Sailing from there, they fell in with Captain Yanky, who told them that there had been a fleet of Spanish armadilloes in pursuit of the buccaneers, and that Tristian had sailed into the midst of them, mistaking them for his friends, but had got away, somewhat scarred. Payne and Williams had also been chased, so that the privateers were now hopelessly scattered, and Wright and Yanky decided to cruise together on their own account. One evening in August they arrived off La Soundes Key, and fired their guns as a signal to the Indians on the mainland, hoping to get some news of the men whom Dampier's party had left behind four months before. Soon a number of canoes approached, and as the Indians climbed on board, they were delighted to recognize among them Hingson, Gopson, and two other men who had dropped out at an earlier stage of the march.

But where was Wafer ? As a matter of fact, the worthy surgeon had prepared a little surprise for his

friends. He here takes up the story himself. While
the other Englishmen were being welcomed, the Indians
squatted on the deck after their fashion. Wafer, naked
like them, with his body painted and " my nose-piece
hanging over my mouth," sat quietly among them,
" cringing upon my hams," and no doubt hugely enjoying the joke. Suddenly one of the English crew recognized him, exclaiming, " Here 's our doctor ! "   It was
a great moment in the career of Lionel Wafer.

Wafer had a good story to tell. He had won much
credit with the Indians, owing to his skill in blood-
letting ; for this was a cure which the native doctors
also practised, but very clumsily, their method being to
shoot light and specially constructed arrows into the
unfortunate patient's skin, until it bristled like a porcu-
pine's. Wafer soon became physician-in-chief among
them, and found it necessary to conform to many of
their customs, especially in the matter of dress. Finally,
he demanded that he and his companions should be
taken down to the coast, and put on board the first
European ship that came in sight, and so strong was
his influence that the Indians at last consented. The
other Englishmen had not accommodated themselves so
well to the Indian mode of life. Poor Richard Gopson
came on board ill and exhausted, and died a few days
later. Dampier now struck up a close friendship with
Wafer, for whom he had evidently acquired a new respect.
Henceforward in his writings, he frequently refers for
information about the natives to " Mr. Wafer's book " ;
and among his papers are some useful contributions
marked as by " the chyrugeon," or from " M. de la
Wafer's observations which he made when he was left
behinde in the midst of the country amongst the salvage
indians."

Wright and Yanky, pursuing their voyage eastward
along the northern coast of South America, passed by

the famous city of Cartagena, " a place of incredible wealth," [1] and sailing so insolently close to the shore that they had " a fair view " of its great monastery and its churches. Dampier pauses to have a hit at the alleged miraculous powers of Our Lady of Cartagena : " Any Misfortune that befalls the Privateers is attributed to this Lady's doing ; and the Spaniards report that she was aboard that Night the ' Oxford ' Man-of-War was blown up at the Isle of Vacca, near Hispaniola, and that she came home all wet ; as belike she often returns with her cloathes dirty and torn with passing through Woods and bad ways, when she has been out on any Expedition ; deserving doubtless a new Suit for such eminent Pieces of Service." Still steering east, they passed the towns of Santa Marta and La Hacha— the latter once a considerable place, but so often sacked by the buccaneers that the inhabitants had temporarily deserted it. It now lay empty and bleaching in the sun—a reproach to everyone concerned. Turning back, they sighted a Spanish ship and went in pursuit. Wright was the first to come up with the chase, and he engaged her until Yanky joined him, when they boarded her together and made her their prize.

At once a quarrel broke out, both captains claiming the ship. Most of the men, rather surprisingly, took Yanky's side, though Wright had obviously the better claim ; but Dampier explains that Yanky held a commission from the French authorities which gave a semblance of legality to his acts (he might call himself a French privateer) whereas Wright had none, and the men were afraid that if he took the prize into port to dispose of it, they might all be arrested as pirates. Matters were arranged on the basis of a kind of " general

[1] When the French took it, sixteen years later, they obtained over a million of money from the town.

post." Yanky went on board the prize, and Wright took over Yanky's ship, burning his former vessel, which was small and unserviceable. He also sold the *tartane* to a passing Jamaica trader, and added Dampier and the others to his own crew.

They visited the Dutch island of Curaçoa, with the object of selling the cargo of sugar which they had found on the prize ; and here Dampier heard of the disaster which had lately befallen an old ally of his, the French Admiral D'Estrées. He had been sent against the Dutch West Indies in 1678, with a French squadron and one or two French " privateers " ; but ran ashore on the rocks of the island of Aves, and all his ships were lost. Most of the men, however, got to shore, and the privateers, according to the stories told to Dampier, had made themselves very comfortable after their fashion, there being plenty of wine and brandy washed up from the wrecks, or still to be found in their shattered hulls. We get one memorable snapshot : " There were about forty Frenchmen on board in one of the Ships where there was good store of Liquor, till the after part of her broke away and floated over the Riff, and was carry'd away to Sea, with all the Men drinking and singing, who being in drink did not mind the Danger, but were never heard of after-wards." Wright got two guns out of the wrecks that were still there, and careened his ship on the island of Aves, where he remained till February, 1682. The Dutch authorities having refused to buy his sugar, he sold it all to a passing French war-ship. On board the Frenchman there were two officers who seem to have taken a fancy to Dampier, for they " offered me great encouragement in France, if I would go with them." He must have been a noticeable figure in that stupid, riff-raff crew. It probably puzzled the Frenchmen (as it puzzles us to-day) that he should be so obviously out of his element, and in a junior position too, and yet so apparently contented. It astonished them, no doubt, when he quietly refused their offer, giving as his reason that " I ever designed to continue with those of my own nation." But that was Dampier all over. He hated personal explanations. He would have died sooner than admit that he was still pursuing a schoolboy dream of adventure.

In April the buccaneers were at La Tortuga and Blanquila, Dampier taking voluminous notes all the time. He observes the many and rapid changes that took place " in these parts," local industries appearing and disappearing in the course of a month or two ; and whole cities being swallowed up by the jungle, while their names still figured large on the map. In regard to one of them, called Nombre de Dios, he says, " I have lain ashore in the place where that city stood ; but it is all overgrown with wood, so as to leave no sign that any Town hath been there." At Tortuga, where the men were " drunk and quarrelling " all the time, Wright and Yanky finally parted company—or, as Wafer puts it, " Captain Yanky left Mr. Dampier." Wafer went with Yanky, Dampier with Wright.

The remainder of Wright's cruise is of no great interest, apart from Dampier's lively descriptions of the different places they visited. He had, of course, a genius for writing travel notes. In one of the many bays of the northern coast, which he does not name, but which must have been somewhere near Cumana, they captured three small Spanish barques, and having apportioned their spoils, which were now considerable, they divided the company among the ships, each of which shaped its course independently. Dampier and twenty others took one of the prizes, and decided to sail direct for Virginia, where they hoped to dispose of their goods. They had an uneventful voyage, and in July, 1682, arrived safely in the English colony of Virginia, which,

as Dampier remarks, " is so well known to our nation
that I shall say nothing of it."

Of Dampier's life in Virginia we know next to nothing.
He lived there for just over a year, and it is not un-
reasonable to suppose that he would send home for his
wife, since he was now comparatively prosperous.   But
he says nothing of this.   Women played but a very
small part in his life.   With his usual tantalizing
modesty, he declines to " detain the reader with the
story of my own affairs."   All we know is that he had
" trouble," and it is not difficult to guess at the nature
of that.   We are now in the transition stage between
the brave days of the buccaneers and of ordinary common-
or-garden piracy.   The authorities are beginning to
look askance at " privateer " captains who sail the seas
without commissions ; and it will be remembered that
Wright had none.   (It was for this reason that the
Dutch governor of Curaçoa had refused to buy his sugar
from him.)   Awkward questions may have been asked
about the origin of the goods which Dampier had for
sale, and he may have found it necessary to get rid of
them unostentatiously, and at a heavy loss, as seems to
have happened to Wafer and others at a later date.   But
all this is supposition.   At any rate, when he left
Virginia on his next voyage, he was apparently a poor
man once again.   We may, however, hazard the guess
that if it had not been for this money trouble, whatever
it was, he would at this point have severed his connection
with the buccaneers, instead of sailing with them on
another voyage.

Dampier's next voyage took him round the world.
It started in curious circumstances.   In April, 1683,
there arrived in Virginia, where Dampier was living
with only his " troubles" for company, a party of Englishmen who had been with Captain Yanky, and had since
had a remarkable series of adventures.   They were led

G

by John Cook,[1] who, we now learn from Dampier, was a Creole and also a " sensible man." They told Dampier that Cook had been given the command of one of Yanky's prizes, and had sailed in her ; but that while he and Yanky, and some French privateers, including Tristian, were at the island of Vacca, the foreigners had plundered the English of their ship, goods and arms, and turned them ashore.   Tristian, however, in a moment of weakness, had consented to keep eight or ten of them, including Cook and Davis, on his ship ; and these few Englishmen, seizing their opportunity, had turned the tables on the French, recovered their countrymen from the shore, and sailed away in Tristian's own ship ! They made several captures—one of them a French ship—and, transferring themselves to the best of their prizes, they came to Virginia.

It was now proposed, with this new ship, to attempt an ambitious voyage in the South Seas.   The projected expedition was, no doubt, well advertised in Virginia. Dampier and many other old buccaneers who were living thereabouts, including Wafer and Ringrose, willingly consented to join, so that he says the crew soon amounted to seventy men.   Most of these had been with Sharp in 1680, and they must have been about as " tough " a lot as the heart of any buccaneer captain could desire. Dampier was no longer a foremast hand : as will appear later, he occupied some position of authority, probably that of assistant-quartermaster, though he tells us no details himself.   As pilot, they took a certain Mr. Cowley, whose name should be noted, because he kept a journal of the voyage which is our next authority after Dampier's. Although an M.A. of Cambridge University, he is neither a very lively nor a very reliable historian.   He says that the crew numbered only fifty-two, and that

[1] See page 84.   Not to be confused with Edmund Cook, who was put in irons by Watling.

the ship had but eight guns ; whereas Dampier says seventy and eighteen. We do not hesitate to believe Dampier. But Cowley tells us lots of little personal details which Dampier leaves out. Feeling, no doubt, that the presence of an M.A. on a buccaneer's ship required some explanation, he observes that Cook only induced him to join by " pretending to me that I should navigate the ship to a port in the island of Hispaniola," and no farther, and that he was afterwards forced to continue. It is impossible to believe a word of this.

The name of Cook's ship was the " Revenge "— though against whom or what revenge was required, unless Yanky and Tristian, is not very clear. They sailed from Virginia in August, 1683, and without staying for any adventures by the way, they arrived in September at the easternmost of the Cape Verde Islands, where they found the inhabitants to consist of only five men—four Portuguese officers and their servant. " They were all black," says Cowley, " but scorn to be accounted any other than Portuguese, for if any man calls them negroes they will be very angry, saying that they are white Portuguese." Their leader, the Governor, had, according to Dampier, " nothing but a few Rags on his back, and an old Hat not worth three Farthings, which yet I believe he wore but seldom, for fear he might want before he got another, for he told us there had not been a ship in three years before." One of the needy Portuguese gave a lump of ambergris to a buccaneer in exchange for clothes ; but Dampier thinks his shipmate was cheated. " It was of a dark colour and very soft, but of no smell, and possibly 'twas some of their goats' dung."

Here they watered, and here Dampier made his first acquaintance with that graceful bird, the flamingo. He found it very shy. " Yet I have lain obscured in the Evening near a place where they resort, and with two

more in my company have killed 14 of them at once ;
the first shot being made while they were standing on
the ground, the other two as they rose." I am aware
that this confession will damage Dampier's reputation
with modern readers, but, like him, I am determined to
put historical accuracy first. The young flamingoes
were at a serious disadvantage against this kind of
sportsman, being unable to fly "till they are almost
full grown " ; but they run " prodigiously fast." In
Dampier's opinion, " a dish of flamingoes' tongues " is
" fit for a Prince's Table " ; and I should imagine that
few modern gourmets, however wealthy, are in a position
to combat that opinion.

They passed on to another island, where the Governor
sent them a present of local wine (which Dampier found
" like Madeira," but Cowley thought just " bad ") ;
but he would not let them ashore, being afraid that they
might repeat the experiment of the last English visitor,
who had seized the principal men on the island, and
held them to ransom. About this time, the buccaneers
held a consultation to consider whether they should sail
direct for the South Seas in their present ship alone, or
go in search of a second one. They decided to try their
luck at the island of St. Iago ; and there, sure enough,
was a fine Dutch ship in the roads, which they warily
approached. But the Dutchman " strook out her Ports
alow, and presently running out her lower tier of Guns
was ready to receive us ; who by this time being got
something too near him, and seeing so many guns and
men, we thought it more advisable to bear away before
the Wind ; the Hollander at the same time sending
10 shot after us." The above is from Cowley ; Dampier
says nothing of it. After all England and Holland were
at peace ! But it was a rude rebuff.

The buccaneers now took the bold decision to continue their course eastward to Africa to the Guinea

coast, still in search of a better ship. In pursuance of
this design, they presently reached the mouth of the
river Sherbro, south of Sierra Leone, where there was
an English factory ; and here, in the mouth of the
river, they found a new Danish ship of forty guns, which
they immediately boarded in the most barefaced manner,
and " carried her away." Also, says Cowley, " we found
she was very fit for so long a voyage, for she was well
stored with good brandy, water, provisions and other
necessaries." Cowley calls her a " lovely ship." They
named her the " Bachelor's Delight."

At Sherbro, they watered their own ship, too, filling
each cask carefully, " for we intended not to water again
till we came into the South Sea, at the island of Juan
Fernandez." It was important that they should not
have to water on the way, and the reason given for this
by Dampier is interesting. The typical buccaneer crew,
he points out, would always waste a lot of time over
such operations ; and " although these men were more
under command than I had ever seen any Privateers,
yet I could not expect to find them at a Minute's call,
in coming to an Anchor, or weighing Anchor." Notice
that it is Dampier himself who has to find them at " a
minute's call," suggesting, as I have said, that he held
some such post as that of assistant-quartermaster. The
quartermaster was one, Edward Davis, of whom we
shall hear more.

Cowley and the ship's doctor made the preliminary
arrangements for the watering. They went ashore with
an interpreter, and interviewed the nearest native chief,
who was so pleased with a present of a cask of brandy
and some bars of iron and a little cloth, that he not
only " sent his people down to fill our water for us,"
but presented Cowley and the doctor with a black woman
each to keep them company for the night. Cowley,
however, retired on board, " by reason I did not like

her hide." The doctor stayed on shore, and very appropriately caught fever and died. Dampier says that this was a serious inconvenience, since Wafer was now the only surgeon they had. Although they had water, they seem to have run short of meat, for Dampier gives an unattractive recipe for boiled shark—" boiling and squeezing them dry, and then stewing them with Vinegar, Pepper, etc."

So they sailed south-west, back across the Atlantic, for many days, and on the 14th February, St. Valentine's Day, were rounding Cape Horn. Cowley says they " were choosing Valentines, and discoursing on the Intrigues of Woman, when there arose a prodigious storm," which drove them out of their course, " so that we concluding the discoursing of Women at sea was very unlucky." The only thing that vexed Dampier was that they saw so little of the sun that he could not take his usual observations. The value of some of Cowley's observations may be judged from his assertion that the sea was " red as blood," owing to the number of " shrimps " swimming about in it. He also reports that they were surrounded by " an innumerable company of seals," who would lift their heads out of the water and " blaff like a dog." On the 19th they were over-hauled by a ship coming up from the south, which at first they took for a Spaniard ; but it turned out to be Captain Eaton (in the " Nicholas " of London), who came on board and told them of the fine times he had been having on the coast of Brazil with one Captain Swan, whom now he had unfortunately lost. As they were all bound for Juan Fernandez, Captain Eaton kept them company. They sighted the island on the 22nd March, 1684, and Dampier tells us that the first thing they did was to send a boat ashore to look for an unfortunate Mosquito Indian, who had been left there by Watling in 1681.

Now this Indian has almost as good a claim as Alexander Selkirk himself to be regarded as the " original " of Robinson Crusoe.   The truth probably is that they should share the honours.   When Watling drew off the buccaneer fleet from Juan Fernandez,[1] on an alarm of the approach of Spanish warships, the Indian was hunting goats in the woods.   He had with him only a gun, powder and shot, and a knife.   When his ammunition was spent, he contrived to saw the barrel of his gun into small pieces, which he used for harpoons, lances and fish-hooks.   Thus he managed to feed himself.   He lived in a little hut lined with goatskins, and wore skins for his clothing.   As the boat from Cook's ship approached, they saw the castaway waiting for them on the beach.   Another Mosquito Indian, named— rather significantly, I think—Robin, was the first to leap ashore and greet his long-lost compatriot, who had prepared a feast of goat's meat for his rescuers.

Dampier was much interested, and took copious notes, from which it would appear that this was not a bad sort of desert island to be marooned on.   It was (and is) very mountainous—so much so that when the Spaniards, annoyed that the goats they had left on the island should be supplying food for visiting Englishmen, landed fierce dogs to destroy the herds, the goats merely climbed to the mountain tops, and " the dogs it was that died." The valleys are well wooded, being full of cabbage palms,[2] and the great herds of goats wandered free, while " seals swarm as thick about it as if they had no other place in the world to live in."   Fish were equally plentiful.

Cook and Eaton remained at Juan Fernandez for sixteen days, during which time many of the men fell

[1] See pages 81-2.

[2] Dampier says the fruit of the cabbage tree is " as white as milk and as sweet as a nut."

ill (probably from the sudden change of diet). Among them was that rather uninteresting person, Cook himself. He never recovered. They sailed north to the coast of Peru, and there took several prizes. Captain Eaton proved a useful partner, for his ship turned out to be a better sailer than Cook's. At Galapagos Islands they made a little tent on shore for their sick captain ; but the rest does not seem to have done him much good, for when they reached Cape Blanco on the mainland of Mexico he made an end and died. They sent a boat ashore with twelve armed men to dig a grave and bury him ; but the ceremony was interrupted by the appearance of three Spanish Indians, whose inquisitive attitude so alarmed the men that they broke off to pursue and capture two of them, whom they afterwards brought on board. Eaton (in whose ship Dampier was now serving) ascertained from these prisoners that the whole countryside was alert, having been warned of his arrival, but that there was a herd of cattle near at hand, which he might safely steal. Dampier and twenty-three others were sent ashore for the purpose in two boats. They found the cattle scattered, and one boat immediately returned ; but the other was burnt by the Spaniards and its crew rescued with difficulty next morning.

Edward Davis, a man of some character, and of few words, was now made captain in place of Cook, and the buccaneers sailed along the Mexican coast looking for a chance to surprise a town, but always finding the Spaniards too well prepared for them. At last Davis ventured into the Gulf of Amapala with two canoes, and succeeded in capturing a Spanish-speaking Indian, who occupied some kind of official post, for Dampier always refers to him as " the Secretary." This man had " no great kindness for the Spaniards." He willingly agreed to guide the buccaneers to the nearest Indian village, where the inhabitants received them rather doubtfully, but agreed to go with them to the church, where they commonly held their public meetings, and discuss matters there.   It was Davis's pleasant intention to get all the people into the church, and then lock the door, and demand tribute from them ; and the astonishing thing is that, according to Dampier, the " secretary " was in the plot with him.   But just as they approached the church doors, one of Davis's men gave an Indian a push, to hurry him along ; whereupon all the natives immediately took alarm and fled like wild animals. Davis's men fired a futile volley, which killed the wretched secretary, but did no other good.   " Thus," says Dampier, bitterly, " our hopes perished by the indiscretion of one foolish fellow."

After this, they captured several Indian villages, but waxed no fatter thereon.   They met Captain Eaton, but Davis's men would not allow him a fair share of the spoil, and he parted company in disgust. Dampier, who was now with Davis, remarks with his usual fairness that it was all the fault of his own party. But another ally turned up in the person of Captain Swan, in the " Cygnet " of London, Eaton's former consort.   This unfortunate (and corpulent) commander had been forced into buccaneering by his crew.   There is in existence a letter[1] from him, in which he implores his owners in moving terms to intercede for him with the King, " for as soon as I can, I shall deliver myself to the King's justice."   In the meantime, however, he was as forward in the wicked game as any of them.   If at times he repented of his sins, there were other times when he was simply a fat humbug.   With him was a certain Captain Peter Harris (nephew of the Harris who was killed before Panama) in command of a small barque.

The buccaneers, now a considerable force, sailed south

[1] Quoted by Mr. Masefield.

wards, doubling Cape Blanco, and proceeded to attack the town of Payta. They captured the place without the loss of a single man ; but the inhabitants fled with their goods, and after hanging about for some time in the vain hope of a ransom, Swan set fire to the town in a rage, and departed. Their next, and their most important, objective on this cruise was the town of Guayaquil, in the modern republic of Ecuador. They left their ships off Cape Blanco, and made this long journey south in their canoes. But luck was against them once more. On entering the Gulf of Guayaquil, they made first for Santa Clara, where the lighthouse now stands ; then, by a clever surprise attack, they captured the town of Puna and all its inhabitants, so that no one got away to warn the Spaniards in Guayaquil. The island of Puna lies near the mouth of the Gulf, and the buccaneers, after capturing it, waited here quietly till the flood tide, when they launched their canoes and began to row as hard as they could up the Gulf towards the unsuspecting town. But they had made some mis-calculation ; perhaps the canoes were too heavily manned for speed ; at any rate when dawn broke they found themselves still two leagues from Guayaquil, and only one hour of the flood tide left. So they put into a lonely creek, and hid there, waiting for the evening and the next flood tide.

Davis presently became impatient, and attempted an overland march with a party of volunteers ; but they returned in an hour or two, soaked to the skin, having tumbled into innumerable creeks which barred the way to the town. At dusk the canoes crept out again, and were presently in full view of Guayaquil. It must have been a pretty sight, for " we saw lighted torches or candles all the town over "—which much disturbed the buccaneers. Some thought the Spaniards had been warned, some that the lights were there only because it

was the eve of a saint's day. At the urgent request of
Davis, who upbraided Swan and his men with cowardice,
they landed at a point two miles from the town, but
soon found themselves hopelessly lost in the undergrowth. They had an Indian guide, but he escaped.
It afterwards appeared that the rope which held him had
been deliberately cut by one of the buccaneers, who did
not want to go any farther. So they turned back sadly,
and rowed away in their canoes, leaving Guayaquil
behind them. " They did not fire one gun at us, nor
we at them."

At Puna next morning they found that one of their
ships, which had followed them, had captured three
Spanish vessels loaded with negro slaves to the number
of a thousand. Swan and Davis picked twenty or thirty
of the best, and turned the rest ashore. Dampier,
leaning over the side of his canoe and watching this
transaction, indulged in what he calls " golden dreams."
With a thousand such negroes, he reflected, the buccaneers might have reopened the gold mines of Santa
Maria, on the isthmus of Darien, now deserted by the
Spaniards, and with the friendly Indians to help them
and a line of retreat behind them to the northern seas,
they might have defied all the strength that Spain could
bring against them. But these were might-have-beens.

In the meantime the voyage went on with varying
fortunes. They " jogged on," as Dampier puts it, from
island to island, taking prizes. Sometimes there would
be valuable cargoes, sometimes only " a few boxes of
marmalade, and three or four jars of brandy." Dampier
acquired a liking for clams, which he found " very large
and sweet," and he and Mr. Teat, Swan's chief mate,
compared notes on the subject. They had a look at
Panama, but found it better fortified than when Sharp
and Sawkins were there. At Tobago the Spaniards
made an unsuccessful attempt against them with a fire-

ship, a design which they concluded must have emanated from the fertile brain of an English renegade named Bond,[1] then in Panama, " for it is strange to say how grossly ignorant the Spaniards in the West Indies, but especially in the South Seas, are of sea affairs."

Next day they descried, to their astonishment, a fleet of canoes approaching them.   They were at first in some " consternation," but presently discovered the canoes to be full of French and English privateers.   There were cordial greetings.   Davis and Swan gave Gronet, the French captain, one of their prizes to command ; but he turned out a weak and vacillating ally, somewhat after the manner of the Count d'Estrées.   With these new companions they sailed to the Gulf of San Miguel, where they found Captain Townley, an English commander.   With him they consorted, and began to make plans for the capture of the rich Lima fleet, then about due to leave Lima on its way to Panama.   The buccaneers must have been feeling fit for any exploit, for Captain Townley had distributed all his wine and brandy among the fleet, in order to fill the barrels with water, preparatory to the cruise.   Moreover they were now a powerful fleet of ten sail (Harris had been given command of a prize), mounting well over fifty guns, and carrying nine hundred and sixty men, mostly English.

They set sail on the 4th May, 1685, and on the 28th came in touch with the Lima fleet of fourteen sail and much heavier metal than theirs.   A running fight began, and lasted all that day and most of the next.   At the beginning the English were the pursuers, but in the end they were " glad to get away."   Gronet never fired a shot,[2] explaining that his men would not let him.   It

---

[1] The same who had kidnapped the leading inhabitants from one of the Cape Verde Islands (see page 100).   He hailed from Bristol, and was a common pirate who did not deserve the name of buccaneer.

[2] There exists a French account of this engagement, in which Gronet

was a most unsatisfactory termination to " all we had
been projecting for five or six months." However, they
collected their scattered fleet, and approaching the mainland again, got some satisfaction in taking and sacking
the town of Puebla Nueva, where Sawkins had been
killed five years before.

The cruise of this united fleet was brought to a
happier end than at one time seemed likely, by a
successful attack upon the important town of Leon, in
Nicaragua. The buccaneers landed with 520 men, 470
of whom marched towards the town, while Dampier,
with the remainder, was left behind to guard the canoes—
not a very exciting command, perhaps, but one of
some responsibility. The town lies fifty miles inland.
Townley led the way with eighty of the " briskest " men,
and was followed by Swan and Davis, while Captain
Knight, a new addition to their ranks, brought up the
rear. As they entered the town, about three o'clock in
the afternoon, very footsore and weary, Townley's
advance guard was charged by twice its number of
Spanish horse ; but " two or three of their leaders being
knocked down, the rest fled." The Spanish foot, to the
number of five hundred, were drawn up in the principal
square, but did not even wait to meet the buccaneers,
whose only casualties were among the stragglers in the rear.
One of these, an old man of eighty-four [1] who had fought
under Oliver Cromwell, found the twenty-mile march
under the blazing sun too much for him. He fell out,

is described as doing his best to join in. The author, De Lussan (*Journal
of Le Sieur Ravenau de Lussan*, Paris, 1689 : English translation, 1699),
brings a number of general charges against the English buccaneers,
accusing them of sacrilege and firing their pistols at images in the churches.
He himself was so pious a sea-robber that, as Mr. Gosse says, he " never
allowed a Spanish town to be plundered until his crew had attended
Mass in the cathedral." (*My Pirate Library*, by Philip Gosse : London,
1926.)

[1] I think he must hold the age record among the buccaneers.

and was quickly surrounded by the enemy, in the midst of whom he died, fighting gamely to the last, we are told, and refusing quarter. There followed the usual interminable negotiations about a ransom for the town, which ended—again as usual—in the buccaneers setting fire to the place. They marched thence to Realejo, which they sacked and burnt, without encountering any serious opposition. Then they put to sea again, no doubt thoroughly satisfied with themselves.

It was at this point that Swan and Davis (who had never got on very well since the affair at Guayaquil) finally decided to separate, and a new series of adventures began for William Dampier.

CHAPTER VII

AND CIRCUMNAVIGATES
THE GLOBE

HEN Davis and Swan parted company on the twenty-fifth day of August, 1685, William Dampier came to the prompt decision to desert Davis, with whom he had served so long ; and he therefore left him on that day, and went on board Swan's ship, the " Cygnet."

It is to be noted that Dampier had a particular liking for Davis.[1] He always refers to him with respect ; and, so far as I know, this is the only one of all his buccaneer comrades with whom he maintained friendly relations

[1] Davis, as a matter of fact, was an exceptionally able man. Mr. Philip Gosse has pointed out (in *The Pirates' Who's Who*) that he " commanded his gang of ruffians in the Pacific for nearly four years," a record unequalled by any other buccaneer or pirate captain, with the exception of the redoubtable Bartholomew Roberts. In the *Calendar of State Papers* there exists a letter from Governor Bellomont, of the Bermudas (the same who hounded poor Captain Kidd to his death), stating that he had in custody a " pirate who goes by the name of Capt. Davies, that came passenger with Kidd from Madagascar." Bellomont adds, " I suppose him to be that Capt. Davies that Dampierc (*sic*) and Wafer speak of, in their printed relations or voyages, for an extraordinarily stout man ; but let him be as stout as he will, here he is a prisoner, and shall be forthcoming upon the order I receive from England concerning Kidd." This letter is dated October 24th, 1699. We know from Dampier's references that Edward Davis was living quietly in England only two or three years before this date ; and we also know that he was going strong again in 1702. So I conclude that the Governor was mistaken.

in England after they had both taken to a more respectable way of life.   But Davis was determined to return to the coast of Peru, whereas Swan had much more ambitious ideas in his head.   Dampier explains that his decision to leave Davis " was not from any dislike to my old Captain [who seems to have borne him no grudge for it] but to get some knowledge of the northern parts of this Continent of Mexico.   And I knew that Capt. Swan determined to coast it as far North as he thought convenient, and then pass over for the East Indies ; which was a way very agreeable to my inclinations."

Let us try to see Dampier as he was at this time.   He was in his thirty-fifth year, a hard, well-seasoned sailor, and a man of parts withal, among a crowd of thoughtless swashbuckling adventurers.   Instead of wasting his time on wine and women, he had known how to use his eyes and his natural intelligence ; and it is probable that not one of them—certainly not the official pilot, William Ambrosia Cowley—was so well equipped to navigate a ship through those waters.

Cowley, who frequently mentions how he " ordered the quartermaster " to do this and that, probably never realized that the self-contained, quiet young man who was the quartermaster's assistant was already a better hydrographer and " artist " (the usual word in those days for navigator) than he was himself.   Yet his single allusion to " Mr. Dampier " in his journal is noticeably respectful.   A comparison between the characters of these two men is instructive.   Cowley's claim that he was, as he puts it, " a jackdaw among the rooks " from the point of view of honesty, is as unjustifiable as his boast that they could not have navigated the " Revenge " without him.   When Cook's ship was between Sierra Leone and Sherbro he was put under arrest—he says because the buccaneers were afraid that he intended to leave them when they got ashore.   He adds that they would undoubtedly have hanged him " had they had another man to carry their ship to the south sea." This is palpably absurd. Dampier, or even Davis himself, could have done it. Dampier could " shoot " the sun as well as Cowley could, and was already doing it regularly and accurately, as we see from his journal. Moreover, he had far more intelligence in making the appropriate deductions from his observations, and (as we shall discover) far more honesty when it came to putting them before the public.

Cowley was quite irresponsible. When the " Bachelor's Delight " reaches the South Seas, in its voyage from Africa, he begins naming islands right and left. Most of these islands were in the Galapagos group, and, of course, were already named. But Cowley calls them after King Charles II, the Duke of York, the Duke of Albemarle, Lord Culpeper, Sir John Marborough, and others. " And between York and Albemarle's island lieth a small one, which my Fancy led me to call Cowley's Inchanted Island." A conceited ass ! As for " Pepys Island," named after Samuel, the diarist, which he " discovered " a little earlier as they passed the Falklands, it simply did not exist.

Smyth has gone very fully into this matter, and I am indebted to him for the following explanation of Cowley's blunder. In his manuscript journal, now in the British Museum, Cowley merely states that they espied an island in latitude 47° 40'. But on his return to England, desiring to publish his manuscript, he selected as editor a gentleman we have met before—William Hacke. Hacke, deceived by the latitude, thought—or pretended to think—that this must be a new discovery, and therefore a good opportunity of paying a compliment to Pepys, who was Secretary of the Admiralty. Deliberately cutting out the forty minutes of latitude in order to carry his " discovery " farther away from any known land, he—or he and Cowley—dished up the entry from Cowley's journal for the public thus : " We held our course S.W. till we came into the lat. of 47 deg. when we saw land ; the same being an island not before known, lying to the westward of us. It was not inhabited [how on earth could he know that ?] and I gave it the name of Pepys Island." [1] So much for Cowley.[2] While he blundered along in this fashion, scattering new names like largess over the map, his assistant quartermaster was quietly noting everything—giving the ship's position with unfailing accuracy almost every day, observing the winds and the tides, identifying every island and investigating it himself if possible, or questioning the inhabitants. Already he must have been incomparably the most knowledgeable hydrographer in the South Seas.

[1] This imaginary Pepys Island persisted in the maps for years. The great Captain Cook was one of the first to declare publicly that it did not exist.

[2] To finish with William Ambrosia :—He sailed with neither Swan nor Davis. Already, before their separation, he had transferred himself to Eaton's ship as navigator. We do not hear that his former messmates on the " Bachelor's Delight " found any difficulty in navigating that ship without him. Eaton had sailed for the East in August, and we have Cowley's record of that voyage. Whether or not Cowley was a buccaneer *malgré lui*, he soon became a pirate at heart, like his new commander. For instance, at the island of Guana, at their starting east, they had some dispute with the Indians, and shot a large number of them without any of their own men being hurt. Also, says Cowley, " we took four of these infidels prisoners and brought them on board, binding their Hands behind them ; but they had not been long there when three of them leaped overboard into the Sea, swimming away from the Ship with their Hands tied behind them : However, we sent the Boat after them, and found a strong Man at the first Blow could not penetrate their skins with a Cutlace ; one of them had received in my judgment 40 shots in his body before he died ; and the last of the three that was killed had swam a good English mile first, not only with his Hands behind him, but also with his Arms pinioned." A very interesting observation, which tells us even more about the mind of William Ambrosia than about the thickness of the poor Indians' skulls.

Dampier was now appointed pilot, or navigating officer, on the " Cygnet," Swan's ship. He does not say so himself, but it is plain from what followed. He was very much in Swan's confidence, in fact his right-hand man. The intention to sail to the Eastern Seas was at first a carefully guarded secret between the two of them. Moreover, Dampier was looked up to by the whole ship's company as a recognized expert in all matters connected with the sea. He even admits it himself. The passage in question—which I take from his manuscript, where it is much fuller than in his book—runs as follows :

" It was first mentioned here [at the Maria Islands, off the coast of Mexico, according to the book ; at Cape Corrientes, according to the manuscript] of going to East India, but many opposed it. Captain Swan and Josiah Teat [he of the clams] who came out of England Swan's chief mate, were very earnest for it, and though I was such, for I left Davis for the same purpose, yet had still a mind to make farther discoveries, and my advice and counsell was ever accepted by the Company, as much as any one man's ; and indeed it was ever a designe between Captain Swan and myself to promote it and use our utmost endeavour to persuade the unthinking Rabble to it ; and although we had discoursed of such a voyage a long time before, yet never till now proposed it. The chiefest objection that the adverse party had against it was want of provision. . . ."

This is the sole and only reference that this least boastful of men ever makes to the esteem in which he was held by his fellow-buccaneers. And even now he changes his mind before the book is published, and cuts the passage out ! In the book, indeed, he leaves us to conclude that he personally had nothing to do with the decision. " Captain Swan," he says, without any reference to himself, " here proposed to go into the East Indies : Many were well pleased with the voyage, but some thought, such was their Ignorance, that he would carry them out of the World ; for about two thirds of our Men did not think there was any such way to be found ; but at last he gained their Consents."

The whole incident is illuminating in the light it throws on Dampier's character. There is no sign yet of that famous temper of his, no vacillation or indecision such as his enemies later accused him of. But there is a high spirit of adventure, and a full measure of that eager, unselfish curiosity which has been the mark of every great explorer since the world began. Few English discoverers—I think none at all—have been more conscious than Dampier that their work was greater than themselves.

But before they sailed for the East there was to be one further misfortune—as though to prove to them that there were no more easy plums to be picked in the West. Swan was still cruising off the coast of Mexico— at first in company with Townley, later by himself—not gaining much booty, nor increasing his popularity with the inhabitants,[1] when he decided to seize the town of Santa Pecaque on the mainland, about a hundred miles north of Cape Corrientes, with the object of replenishing his stock of provisions—for he had always that Eastern voyage in mind. But this flabby commander—flabby in both senses of the word—was already showing that weakness as a disciplinarian which was to be his ruin later on. Once comfortably established in Santa Pecaque, his men got out of hand, and refused to

---

[1] Dampier records that on one occasion a friendly Spaniard on horseback was in the act of drinking a health to the buccaneers when " one of our men snatched up his gun, and let drive at him, and killed his horse." In fact they behaved like bullies.

move from the neighbourhood of the wine-cellars until all the provisions had been carried down to the canoes. Swan was therefore compelled, against his better judgment, to send off a party with a long string of horses carrying the goods. Presently those in the town heard the sound of heavy firing ; but they still refused to budge, until riderless horses with blood-stained saddles came galloping in, bearing plain proof of disaster. Then they marched out, and found the baggage train scattered and all their comrades dead, " and so cut and mangled that we scarce knew one man." They lay, says Dampier, " all along the path as they were killed, one and one, not two abreast anywhere, by which it was easy to guess that their own folly ruined them, for they had as many horses as men, and therefore every man led his horse, which made a great distance between the foremost and the hindermost, and the Spaniards had the advantage to destroy them singly."

They lost fifty men here, and among the dead was that unfortunate gentleman, Mr. Basil Ringrose—" my ingenious friend," says Dampier, recording the incident with a rare touch of feeling. Ringrose had transferred to the " Cygnet " with Dampier, and was employed by Swan as " Cape-Merchant or Supercargo." Dampier must have felt the loss of Ringrose keenly ; for Wafer had gone with Davis, and with the doubtful exception of Captain Swan, there was no other kindred spirit on board.

Quite discouraged by this reverse, the buccaneers re-embarked, and drifted down the coast to the Maria Islands, where Dampier, who had been suffering for some time with dropsy, effected a cure by burying himself up to the neck in the hot sand, and remaining there for half an hour—after which he " did sweat exceedingly." It was here that Swan and Dampier opened up their project of a voyage to the East, as recorded above, and they must have found the men in a receptive mood. The astonishing fact emerges that no one knew the exact distance to the Ladrones, their first port of call. In the Spanish maps, the distance from Cape Corrientes was given as between 2300 and 2400 leagues, whereas the English made less than two thousand. As they had only sixty days' provisions on board, caclulating at the rate of half a pint of maize daily for each man—and they had practically nothing else but maize—it will be allowed that the "Rabble," as Dampier calls them,[1] showed a very commendable spirit in falling in with Swan's proposal. What seems to have clinched the argument was the captain's promise to cruise among the Philippines in an attempt to intercept the valuable "Manila ship" (which they had already been looking for in vain) when it arrived there from America.

So they set sail across the Pacific on the 31st March, 1686. They were two ships in company, Captain Swan's ship the "Cygnet," and a small barque commanded by Teat. "We were 150 Men, 100 aboard of the Ship and 50 aboard the Bark, besides Slaves "— of which there cannot have been many. They had " a fresh Trade-wind " and very fair weather, so that Dampier " made many good observations of the Sun." But the men were troublesome, and early insisted on an increase in their rations. Dampier, for his part, thought the short allowance suited him, " for I found that my strength increased and my dropsy wore off." One man was caught stealing food, and was condemned to receive three blows from a rope's end from every person on the ship. "Captain Swan began first, and struck with a good Will ; whose example was followed by all of us." They saw no fish of any sort, but " a great number of boobies." When they had covered a distance which,

[1] See page 115.

according to the English reckoning, should have brought Guam Island under their bows, the men began to murmur against the captain for bringing them on the voyage. But he soothed them with fair promises ; and, sure enough, a few days later, Teat, who was ahead, sighted land. At four o'clock on the 20th May they cast anchor " to our great joy " at the island of Guam.

They had then just three days' rations left. Dampier afterwards discovered that the men, in their desperation, had formed a plot, which was " first to kill Captain Swan and eat him when the Victuals was gone, and after him all of us who were accessory in promoting the undertaking this Voyage." On hearing of this, Swan remarked, " Ah, Dampier, you would have made them but a poor Meal ! "—for the pilot, as he explains, " was as lean as the Captain was lusty and fleshy." At the end of his account in his journal of this fifty-two days' voyage, Dampier appends a table, showing the vessels' daily course, the position at the beginning and end of each day, with a note on the winds. He adds that he would have given a further set of figures to show the variation of the needle, but that it " was very small in this course."

The hungry sailors found at Guam rice, cocoanuts and bread-fruit in abundance, and no doubt did themselves well. Dampier's description of the bread-fruit, so familiar to the modern traveller, was probably the first to reach England. Another novelty in those days was the drink called *arack*, of which the buccaneers partook freely. Dampier liked it well enough, but he remarks that " it must have a dash of brandy to hearten it," being not strong enough " to make good punch of itself." It was not until dusk that the " Cygnet " came in close to the shore, and the Spaniards in the fort evidently mistook her for a vessel of their own nationality. One of their priests, coming on board under that impression, was promptly seized, and through him negotiations were opened with the Governor, who consented to supply them with pork, in addition to the vegetarian fare mentioned above.

The " Indians " of Guam, who were very hostile to the Spaniards, tried to persuade the buccaneers to attack the fort, but Swan would have nothing to do with it. On the contrary, he cultivated friendly relations with the Governor, and, at the latter's request, made him a present of an " English dog," which they had on board. The animal was evidently a sort of ship's pet, for Dampier tells us that the gift went " much against the grain of many of the Men, who had a great value for that Dog." At the same time, this friendly Governor sent out swift canoes to warn all Spanish ships of the presence of the buccaneers—we can hardly blame him for that. The truth is that the Spaniards of these islands, as in other parts of the world, would willingly have traded with the English if their dog-in-the-manger Government would have permitted it ; and the local governors, here as elsewhere, would often wink at such commerce, providing their own perquisites were assured.

From Guam Captain Swan sailed to Mindanao, the southernmost of the Philippine Islands, there to do a little trading on his own account and—as his men hoped—to keep an eye cocked for the Manila ship. Their reception at Mindanao town, where they arrived on the 18th July, was almost overwhelmingly friendly : so much so that they quite settled down in the place, and lived there for a period of six months. A good many of them died there, too, as shall be told presently. Mindanao was at this time independent of Spain ; but Manila was only just across the way, and the Sultan of Mindanao no doubt felt that his position would be considerably strengthened against that dangerous neighbour if a large party of Englishmen were settled in his country.

He did his best to encourage them to stay. Dampier, for his part, regrets that they did not forthwith abandon their "roving life" and establish a permanent trading "factory" in this hospitable land. He thought there was money to be made ; and he points out that they had among them carpenters, bricklayers, shoemakers, tailors, etc., so that they would have been very well able to look after themselves.

In the meantime, he was very greatly interested in the Mindanayans. He was constantly ashore with his note-book, observing the manners and customs of the people, and the plant and animal life of the island. He interposes a little essay on the plantain, which he " takes to be the king of all Fruit, not except the Coco itself." The clove, the nutmeg, and the betel-nut came under his eye, as also the durian, which he says " sends forth an excellent scent "—a point on which not everyone will agree with him. On the whole he liked the people. The women were free with strangers, but without losing their self-respect. They " walk stately " and they wash themselves twice a day, night and morning, a habit which astonishes our seventeenth-century Englishman. He adopted the practice himself after a bit, and believed that it cured him of an attack of dysentery. On the other hand, the houses were insanitary, and the living-rooms gave forth " a prodigious stink." Another nasty habit of the Mindanayans was that of poisoning those who offended them, " even upon small occasions." Dampier adds : " Nor did our Men want for giving offence, through their general Rogueries, and sometimes by dallying too familiarly with their Women, even before their Faces." Some of the buccaneers died from the effect of these slow poisons long after they had left the island.

The Englishmen found a staunch friend at the Sultan's court in the person of Raja Laut, the commander-in-chief of the army. This powerful minister entertained Swan at his palace, advised him on the conduct of his men in their intercourse with the people, and invited parties of them to join in processions through the streets on occasions of public rejoicing. In fact he sought to show them honour in every possible way. There were difficulties even with him. On one occasion the ship's cobbler presented him with a pair of English shoes, which turned out to contain hogs' bristles, to the horror of this pious Moslem. Another time some of the English were giving an exhibition of dancing in their national manner, when Raja Laut's attention was attracted by the agility of a certain John Thacker, who " was a seaman bred," says Dampier, and had " learnt to dance in the musick-houses about Wapping."

Now Thacker had been with Captain Harris in the South Seas, and had laid out some of his ill-gotten gains in the purchase of an unusually fine suit of clothes. The Raja—or the " General," as Dampier always calls him—therefore turned to one of the other sailors, and innocently enquired whether Thacker were not a person of noble extraction. The man thus addressed saw an opening for a good joke at their host's expense, and proceeded to pitch him such a yarn that Raja Laut began to treat the astonished Thacker with the deference due to a great nobleman. Unfortunately Captain Swan got to hear of it, and in a great rage gave the " nobleman " a sound drubbing—nor could he ever endure him afterwards, though, as Dampier remarks, " the poor fellow knew nothing of the matter."

Swan, as a matter of fact, was getting spoilt. He had become a swaggering bully. When he sat down to table, his " two Trumpeters sounded all the time that he was at dinner "—almost as though he were in a modern London restaurant ! His weight must have gone up prodigiously. He took to punishing his men in public, with the natives looking on.   Even Teat, his second-in-command, was publicly flogged.   Teat never forgave him.   Finally, he began to quarrel with Raja Laut—and all this without showing the slightest intention of departing from the island, or of taking any steps at all about the Manila ship.   His men were growing restive : two or three of them deserted, and fled into the interior ; the others held meetings of protest on the ship in Swan's absence.   When they were not doing that they drank too much.   This disgusted Dampier, who, as we have noted, " did ever abhor drunkenness."   At the same time he admits that the Mindanayans were so hospitable that an Englishman " could hardly pass the Streets, but we were even hal'd by Force into their Houses, to be treated by them." Christmas Day came round with a great banquet on board, when Swan was confidently expected to speak his mind and indicate some scheme of future operations. But he ate his dinner and went wheezily ashore again, without saying a word of his intentions.

No one knew better than Dampier that the fat man had not the slightest intention of going after the Manila ship.   Apart from being very comfortable where he was, he was sick of buccaneering and of buccaneers, and was only longing to be rid of it all, and go home to England, and there throw himself upon the mercy of the Government.   Yet, as he said rather pathetically to Dampier on one occasion, " there is no Prince on Earth is able to wipe off the stain of such Actions."   Undoubtedly the poor fellow had a conscience.   We have no record of Dampier's reply.   In the meantime, however, if Swan was sick of the buccaneers, they were becoming equally sick of him.   While he was disporting himself on shore, some of them had been reading his journal, which was left on the ship, and there found themselves most bitterly blamed, in such a manner as could hardly fail to make things exceedingly uncomfortable for them should the journal ever get to England.   There was more grumbling at this, and the injured Teat, aided by one John Read, of Bristol, seized the opportunity to fan the flames into open mutiny.

There is no doubt that they would have sailed away forthwith, leaving Swan and Dampier and many others on shore, but for the accident that there happened to be no surgeon on board at the time.   To remedy this, they sent a message to the town pretending that one of them was ill, and after some delay Herman Coppinger, the assistant surgeon, and a friend of Dampier's, prepared to go on board.   By pure chance, Dampier went with him.   This was in the evening ; but when they reached the ship and discovered the trick that had been put upon them, they seem to have gone quietly to bed, without making the slightest attempt to warn their Captain.   In the morning, however, Read and Teat put out into the harbour, and there stayed and fired a gun, as a signal to all who might wish to join them.   At the request of one or other of Swan's friends, they remained until 2 p.m., expecting to hear from him.   But he made no sign, and that afternoon the " Cygnet " sailed away, leaving her commander and thirty-six other Englishmen stranded in Mindanao.

It was a shabby trick—for even supposing that Swan was indifferent how he left the buccaneers so long as he left them, it would be a wild presumption to assume that all the other thirty-six mariners were within hearing at the time, or in a condition to make up their minds about their futures.   Yet we must not suppose that they were all unwilling to remain.   " The main division," says Dampier shrewdly, " was between those that had Money and those that had none. . . . For they that had money lived ashore and did not care for leaving Mindanao ; whilst those that were poor lived aboard, and urged Captain Swan to go to sea." Dampier was among the poor ones.

There is, however, good evidence that his passive acquiescence in the desertion of Swan weighed on Dampier's conscience. Perhaps some instinct warned him that a time would come when he himself would have trouble with his men. He was now on a pirate ship rather than a buccaneer. Read took command, with Teat as master and Henry More as quartermaster. Dampier was distrusted at first ; but later he seems to have been made merchants' representative, or supercargo.

I think it unnecessary to follow this singularly unremunerative voyage in detail. After cruising unsuccessfully in the Gulf of Siam, they sailed north to the Pescadores Islands, between Formosa and the mainland of China, where the Governor sent them a present of the " fattest and kindliest Beef that I did ever taste in any foreign country," and the men " licked their lips " over a new kind of strong liquor distilled locally from wheat. From there to " Bashi Island," which the crew, characteristically, named after a kind of beer which the inhabitants made (and the islands bear the name to this day). Here they obtained meat, for the natives would exchange " a good fat goat for an old iron hoop," and here they remained from the 6th August to the 3rd October, 1687, eating and drinking their fill, but getting no richer. Passing southward down the eastern side of the Philippines, with the idea of making for the Spice Islands, they reached Mindanayan territory once more ; and here Dampier's conscience quite got the upper hand. While Read and Teat and others were on shore, he made an eloquent appeal to the remainder of the crew, and got them to agree to sail round the island to Mindanao town, and take Swan off. But one man slipped away, and warned the leaders, who came on board and " presently dissuaded the men from any such design." They seem to have borne no ill-will to Dampier for his action ; but he and Coppinger had long ago made up their minds to leave " this mad crew " at the first opportunity.

Many months later Dampier heard of the fate of Swan. He served with distinction in Raja Laut's army, and the latter appeared to be grateful, but would never listen to any of Swan's requests to be allowed to return to England. The point is that Swan had with him £5000 in gold, the property of the owners of the " Cygnet," and Raja Laut knew it. Some of Swan's men died in Mindanao, and some got away on Dutch ships. Finally he and his head surgeon secured a small canoe, and had just put off secretly from the shore in an endeavour to reach a Dutch sloop which lay in the roads, when they were overtaken by a party of natives who upset their canoe, after seizing the money, and killed them both as they struggled in the water. Almost certainly Raja Laut was the villain of the piece.

In pursuance of their resolution to go for the Spice Islands, Read and Teat sailed next to the Celebes, and here occurred one of the most puzzling incidents in the whole of Dampier's career. On December 27th, in the most disappointingly casual way imaginable, they decided to have a look at Australia—"*terra Australia incognita*"— just " to see what that country would afford us." This is less than we should have expected of our explorer. At the moment, evidently, he saw nothing in the project more than another probably futile attempt on the part of Read and Teat to " get rich quick." He does, however, remark with some show of interest that " it is not yet determined whether it (Australia, or New Holland, as it was called on contemporary maps) is an Island or a Main Continent " ; adding that he personally is con- vinced that " it joins neither to Asia, Africa nor America " —a pretty safe guess in the case of the last two !

As supercargo, Dampier can have had very little to do with laying the course, but as usual he kept his eyes open, and his notes are very full. The voyage was uneventful. On the 14th January, 1688, they made their landfall in the latitude of 16° 50′. Mr. Clark Russell[1] thinks this may have meant Bathurst, or Melville Island, which would make Dampier's note of the latitude grossly incorrect. Mr. Masefield favours King Sound, or, alternatively, Collier Bay. I see no reason to doubt the wisdom of the mapmakers, who have named the country round King Sound "Dampier Land," and the group of islands at its mouth—there was "an abundance of islands," says Dampier—the "Buccaneer Archipelago."

They were not unduly impressed by their first glimpse of Australia. The land was barren, and there was nothing of interest to be seen except some strange tracks upon the sand like those of "a great mastiff dog," possibly made by dingoes. They cast anchor, however, and established themselves on shore, and, eventually, got in touch with some of the aborigines. Here we get Dampier at his most amusing best. His description of the people is unflattering. Even the "Hodmadods" (Hottentots), though "a nasty people," are "gentlemen to these." The buccaneers completely failed to make these people understand them, gesticulate as they would. The black men merely "grinned like so many monkeys."

But what impressed Dampier most was that even the offer of European clothes and little pieces of finery made no impression on their minds—a point on which they would seem to have been inferior even to monkeys ! It was the same with the ship, though they could never have seen anything like it in their lives. Nearly all of them suffered from "bad eyes," which made it easy to

[1] *Op. cit.*

approach and catch them ; and the buccaneers, seeking to establish good relations, caught two or three of them and took them on board, where they were treated to such dainties as the ship's larder could boast. But they merely gobbled up any food within reach, without lifting their eyes from it, or displaying the faintest interest in their strange surroundings. Dampier took the trouble to find out all about their methods of catching fish, and describes them in detail ; but adds the surprising statement that they possessed " no instruments " for hunting bird or beast. Apparently he never saw a boomerang.

At the beginning of March, they prepared to depart, and Dampier chose this moment to put in a plea to be allowed to leave the company, asking them to set him ashore at the nearest English factory. In reply, Read threatened to maroon him, and he therefore said no more, but waited quietly for an opportunity to desert. After all, no one was making a penny out of this absurdly pointless voyage. At Bashi Islands they had been offered gold rings for sale at derisive prices, but Dampier had no money to buy anything then. As supercargo, he could have used some of the iron which was stacked in the hold ; but this was really the property of the owners, and his conscience prevented him.

After leaving Australia, their first port of call was an island near Sumatra, and here Read used a characteristic method of stopping desertions. He deliberately ill-treated the natives, in order that his crew might become unpopular and be afraid to go ashore. Another result must have been to prevent any trading operations ! From Sumatra they sailed to the Nicobar Islands, and here at last Dampier broke away, and put a final end to his career as a buccaneer.

It was a blazing hot day, and the tar all blistering in the seams of the ship's deck as she swung at anchor, and the Nicobar beach looked empty and inhospitable

enough—for the people had all fled at the approach of
the buccaneers—when Dampier approached the skipper
with an innocent request to be allowed to land. A surly
nod, and " I soon got up my chest and bedding and
immediately got some to row me ashore, for fear lest
his mind should change again." The canoe danced
lightly across the waves, piled high with Dampier's
belongings, those melancholy, obstinate eyes of his
turning often back towards the ship to mark whether
the manner of his departure, with all his goods about
him, had been noted. Arriving on the beach, his shipmates helped him ashore, and he carried up his things
to one of the deserted houses, intending to settle down
there for the night.

But it was not to be so easy. An hour later, Teat
arrived with an armed party, and compelled him with
threats to return to the ship. There he found everything in an uproar. Three more men—Coppinger,
Robert Hall and one Ambrose, whose surname we never
got—encouraged by Dampier's example, had announced
their intention of joining him on shore. The morale of
the buccaneers had gone to pieces, and the crew openly
sympathized with the deserters. Daunted by the clamour,
Read at last agreed to everything except the loss of his
surgeon, whom he swore he would keep. Coppinger
thereupon sprang into Dampier's canoe, and, snatching
up a gun, threatened to shoot anyone who should detain
him. But several of them jumped in after him, and
dragged him back to the ship. Dampier, Hall and
Ambrose were allowed to go ; " and one of the men
that rowed us ashore stole an Axe and gave it to us,
knowing it was a good Commodity with the Indians."

It was already dark when they landed in the little
bay ; so they lit candles, and Dampier, " being the
oldest Stander in our new Country," conducted the
others across the white beach into one of the empty

I

houses.   There they slung their hammocks.   " It was a fine clear Moonlight Night," he says, with an unconsciously dramatic touch, " in which we were left ashore " ; and they " walked on the sandy Bay to watch when the Ship would weigh and be gone, not thinking ourselves secure in our new-gotten Liberty till then."   At last they saw her white sails move out from the bay, and fade into the darkness.

" Then we returned to our Chamber, and so to sleep. This was the sixth of May."

Only twenty-four hours earlier, had they but known it, King James II had published his Declaration of Indulgence which was to lose him his throne ; and as Dampier and his friends stood alone on the beach at Nicobar, watching the departure of their ship, Dutch William was sitting down to prepare his plans for the invasion of England.

CHAPTER VIII

HE MAKES A NAME IN ENGLAND

IT was a curiously assorted group of mixed nationality whom we left in the last chapter standing on the beach at Nicobar. Soon after Dampier, Hall, and Ambrose had reached the shore, another boat came after them, bringing — by the Captain's orders — four Malays of Achin who had been captured by the buccaneers in a native boat off Sumatra, and an unfortunate Portuguese whom they had taken out of a Siamese junk in the Gulf of Siam, and had been carrying about with them ever since, employing him as an interpreter. They were now in a part of the world where Portuguese was not spoken, and the interpreter and the Malayan prisoners were, from Read's point of view, just so many extra mouths to feed. He was no doubt glad to shift the responsibility on to Dampier's shoulders. The three English deserters, for their part, found the Malays extremely useful in helping them to get food. Dampier evidently did not like the " mongrel Portuguese," as he calls him—indeed, he despised the whole nation, " than whom are not a more despicable People now in all the Eastern Nations."

The first thing to do was to establish friendly relations with the natives. Dampier felt quite easy on this score. Speaking from an already wide experience, he expresses the opinion that " there are no people in the World so barbarous as to kill a single Person that falls accidentally into their Hands, or comes to live among them ; except they have been injured by some Outrage or Violence committed against them." He also expresses a disbelief in the existence of cannibalism, which, as we now know unfortunately, did more credit to his heart than to his head. However, it had never come within his own experience, and in such a situation as he then was in, his ignorance was bliss. He was to require all his tact the next morning when the native landlord turned up, and was not a little astonished to find his house full of strangers. They pacified him with the present of an axe, in return for which he gave them his canoe.

The possession of this canoe filled them with joy. Already they saw themselves safe and sound at the English factory at Achin in Sumatra, 150 miles away by sea across the Indian Ocean. In the enthusiasm of the moment, they even launched the crazy vessel straight away, and tumbled into it with all their things, intending to make for the southernmost point of the island, and wait there "till the monsoon shifted." A hundred yards from the shore the canoe capsized, leaving them to swim for their lives, dragging with them their chests and clothing. Everything was wet, and they remained on the beach for three days drying themselves and their belongings with the aid of a fire which they lit. Dampier specifically says that their papers had to be dried, and we get a picture of him anxiously holding the leaves of his precious journal close to the flames.

When we consider that the gunwales of this canoe were not more than three inches above the water, it is amazing that they should have contemplated any sea voyage in it—much less a trip to Achin ! But the Malays now fitted it with "outlagers," or outriggers, such as may be seen on many native canoes to-day, and these had the effect of steadying the little craft, and preventing it from taking in too much water. So they sailed safely to the south of the island, and waited there, according to plan. The natives in this part were very hostile, which gave Dampier an opportunity of trying his theories upon them. He would walk smilingly towards them, while they shook their weapons at him and howled with rage ; then, suddenly turning on his heel, he would present his back while he fired his musket towards the sea, " so that they might see the shot graze on the water." Thus he would indicate at once the sharpness of his claws and his desire not to use them unless compelled. The result was that they were presently able to trade with the inhabitants, and purchase cocoanuts and native bread for their impending voyage.

On the 15th May, 1688, Dampier and his seven companions set out from Nicobar on one of the most remarkable canoe voyages of which we have any record. Before leaving the " Cygnet," Dampier had studied the ship's chart of the East Indies, and taken some notes in his pocket-book which were of good service now. He had also brought away his pocket compass. He says that Hall was the only one of his companions who had the least idea of the peril of their present undertaking, and that the responsibility for the lives of the other six, who trusted them wholeheartedly, weighed heavily upon these two. He and Hall took it in turns to steer. On the second day out, they found, to their keen disappointment, that the current had carried them back, so that they were again in sight of Nicobar. On the third day the wind freshened, and soon the sky was full of clouds and it blew a gale. That day, for the first time, Dampier was unable to take his usual observations of the sun ; but he kept up the entries in his diary both then and throughout this voyage. Having given his directions to Hall, and ordered the sail to be furled, he lay down to sleep.

A few hours later they waked him. The wind was

blowing harder, and the sea " roaring in a white Foam about us." There was " a dark Night coming on and no Land in sight to shelter us, and our little Ark in danger to be swallowed by every Wave." Worst of all, " none of us thought ourselves prepared for another World." There is the authentic Robinson Crusoe touch in Dampier's reflections upon this occasion. Indeed, it is clear that the passage I am about to quote must have caught the eye of that great journalist, Daniel Defoe. I do not find Dampier in the same repentant mood anywhere in the long history of his wanderings. He writes :

" I have been in many imminent Dangers before now, some of which I have already related, but the worst of them all was but a Play-game in comparison with this. . . . Other Dangers came not upon me with such a leisurely and dreadful Solemnity. A sudden Skirmish or Engagement or so was nothing when one's Blood was up, and pushed forward with eager Expectations. But here I had a ling'ring view of approaching Death, and little or no hopes of escaping it ; and I must confess that my Courage which I had hitherto kept up failed me here ; and I made very sad Reflections on my former Life, and looked back with Horrour and Detestation on Actions which before I disliked, but now I trembled at the remembrance of. I had long before this repented me of that roving Course of Life, but never with such concern as now. I did also call to mind the many miraculous Acts of God's Providence towards me in the whole Course of my Life, of which kind I believe few Men have met with the like. For all these I returned Thanks in a peculiar Manner, and thus once more desired God's Assistance, and composed my Mind as well as I could in the Hope of it, and as the event shew'd, I was not disappointed of my Hopes."

There is a simple dignity and natural eloquence in that passage which Defoe himself could hardly have equalled.

About midnight the wind abated, and they set their small mat-sail ; but at two o'clock it blew up again, and thunder and lightning followed with a heavy fall of rain, so that they were soaked to the skin and in " a starveling plight." Dampier or Hall steered, while the others baled for their lives. Only the outriggers prevented their " little ark " from sinking. By noon on the following day they came in sight of land, and early next morning on their fifth day out from Nicobar they got into a small harbour (apparently Passir) on the island of Sumatra, about a hundred miles east of Achin. They were so exhausted that it was all they could do to stagger into the nearest fishing village—where their Malays were fortunately " well acquainted "—and throw themselves down on the first beds that were offered. Here they lay for a fortnight, all the Europeans of the party racked with fever which they could not shake off. Dampier tried to bleed himself with his pen-knife, but the blade was too blunt. Natives would come to the door of their hut and stand in groups staring at them. At last a local notable sent them on by canoe to Achin, where the merchants of the English factory were much interested in their story, placed a room at their disposal, and left them to recover their health. In the case of two of them, it was too late. The Portuguese died within three days, and Ambrose a little later. Hall was almost given up, but eventually recovered. As for Dampier, his illness left him with a kind of chronic dysentery, which handicapped him for many months. Only an insatiable traveller would have defied it, as he did, instead of taking the first available passage home to England.

It is also true that only a penniless adventurer, as he was, would have thought it necessary to get another job

almost at once. Having refused the offer of a trip to
Persia, Dampier next signed on with a Captain Weldon,
to go with him on a voyage to Tonquin, this being
the month of July, 1688. Weldon promised that at
Tonquin he would buy a sloop and put Dampier in
command of her to trade on the coast of Cochin China ;
and this no doubt was an attractive prospect. Moreover,
he might hope that the sea-voyage would restore his
health, and that of his friend, Hall, who accompanied
him, though in a very weak condition. The journey
that followed is described in Dampier's *Voyage to Tonquin* ;
and it may be said at once that, in spite of his continued
illness, his journal is nowhere more full and accurate
and entertaining than it is at this time. The journey
which he made in the country now called French Indo-
China, entirely unaccompanied, ignorant of the language,
and suffering all the time from his wasting disease,
constituted a remarkable feat of endurance, and the liveli-
ness of his descriptions shows that nothing could damp
his spirits when there were strange sights to be seen.
They sailed about twenty miles up the Tonquin river,
and anchored. This was the spot normally resorted to
by English trading vessels, and Dampier tells us that
" a little town " had sprung up there in a month's
time.

Cachao, or Cha-cho, another hundred miles up the
river, was the capital of Tonquin, and there was an
English factory there. Dampier visited this factory,
travelling in the " country boats," and enjoying the
" delightful prospect of a large level fruitful country."
He stayed there seven or eight days, and gives us an
account of the place almost as full as in the case of
Mindanao. Returning to the ship, he " lay on board
for a great while and sickly for the most part ; yet not
so much but that I took a boat and went ashoar one
where or other almost every day." And thus " I took

as particular notice as I could of the country." Let us take a few of his observations at random.

Of the local cooking—which must have been a subject of painful interest to him in view of the nature of his malady—he says : " They have many Sorts of Dishes that would turn the Stomach of a Stranger." He does not appear to have encountered the edible bird's nest, but he refers with something like a shudder to a dish consisting mainly of raw pork. He greatly admired the lacquer-work, but remarks that their joiners or cabinet-makers were bunglers compared with ours. A certain Captain Pool was the first to take the wise step of bringing out joiners from England to make " fashionable commodities "—cabinets, desks and so on—for the natives to lacquer afterwards. The Tonquinese earthenware was not such a marketable article as it had been before the superiority of the " China ware " became known in Europe.

It is rather surprising to find Dampier complaining of the ill-paved streets in Cachao. " In the wet season," he says, " they are very dirty ; and in the dry time there are many stagnant Ponds, and some ditches full of black stinking mud in and about the city." Yet seventeenth-century London had nothing " on " Cachao in this respect.[1] The Tonquinese, he found, made excellent servants, like the Chinese ; but, like them, too, were slaves to " the Reigning Vice among the Eastern Nations "—gaming. " Neither the awe of their Masters,

[1] Only a proportion of the London streets were paved. All were very muddy and bestrewn with " base, ill-favoured rubbish," so that passers-by were " forced to stop their noses " according to a contemporary authority. The Strand was so bad that merchants and others often had to leave their coaches stuck there in the mire and complete the journey to the City by the river. Pepys nearly broke his leg crossing London Bridge one night, through putting his foot into a large hole in the roadway. English roads in general have never been so bad, before or since, as in this half-century following the Civil War. And those of Somerset (Dampier's native county) had a specially evil reputation !

nor anything else is sufficient to restrain them till they have lost all they have, even their very Cloathes." Here we are confronted by the unchanging East. It is hardly an exaggeration to say that if Dampier were to start on his travels again to-day he might wander over that particular part of the world without noticing any change, provided he kept away from the ports and the occasional railway lines.

After five or six weeks of spasmodic sight-seeing, with the ship as his base, he became " weary of lying still and impatient of seeing something that might further gratify my curiosity." So he hired a Tonquinese guide for one dollar, and started up the river again, this time on foot in order to see as much as possible of the surrounding country. In his pocket he had just two dollars ! His fever, "which I brought from Achin," had left him, but the dysentery was worse than ever, owing to his having foolishly eaten fruit.

His guide could not speak a word of English nor he of Tonquinese. On the whole, it was an adventurous undertaking, even for an ex-buccaneer. They did not stick to the tow-path, but struck out boldly across country. The people, as a rule, were remarkably kind and courteous to Dampier, who must have seemed a far stranger figure to them than even the modern tourist does. At every village they came to, this ill-assorted pair were given lodgings for the night ; and after supper—usually of rice and eggs or a roasted yam— Dampier, if the evening was not too hot, " took a ramble about the Village to see what was worth taking notice of." It was generally dark before he returned to his rough couch. " My guide," he says, " carried my sea-gown, which was my covering in the night, and my pillow was a log of wood." He can hardly have been unaware of the risk he ran—or, if he was, it was abruptly borne in upon him a few days later.

They were wandering across some fields on the third day of their journey when they observed a large crowd of natives assembled round a small wooden tower. There were stalls loaded with fruit and meat—Dampier estimates that there must have been " fifty or sixty hogs cut up "—and a busy air of coming and going, which suggested to Dampier that this must be a market. The only thing that puzzled him was the tower, and when they reached the crowd he elbowed his way through to have a look at it. " I went round the tower and viewed it. . . . I saw no door to enter in : it seemed very slightly built with thin boards." It was, as a matter of fact, a funeral pyre, and the whole scene—the crowd, the stalls and the food—were but part of the ceremonial connected with the decease of a local notable, who was now about to be cremated, along with a handsome supply of provisions for use in the other world. Dampier was quite unaware of this. Leaving the tower, he turned towards the stalls. It was now " between four and five o'clock in the afternoon," and he was wanting his " supper " ; so he walked up to the meat stalls, and taking hold of a quarter of pork made signs for a piece to be cut off for him. Instantly Bedlam broke loose. The crowd set upon him. " They assaulted me on all sides, buffeting me and rending my Cloathes, and one of them snatched away my Hat." The guide, who had no doubt been vainly trying to explain the situation, now plunged in to the rescue. He dragged Dampier out of the crowd, and dusted him down, and even succeeded in recovering his hat for him. Then, after profuse apologies to the angry mourners, he led our hero away in a somewhat chastened mood.

On the fifth day they reached Hean, and here Dampier dismissed his guide, and went on alone by river boat. He sat on the deck among the native passengers, feeling very lonely and very ill again. They were a jovial enough party, " but I was mute for want of a person I could converse with." Finally he reached Cachao, and, after some difficulty, found his way to an English merchant's house, where he was hospitably entertained. He learnt, however, that Weldon had no intention of purchasing the sloop which was to have been given to him, and he therefore returned to the ship and went back to Achin with her when she sailed. He had undoubtedly enjoyed his trip to Tonquin, and probably thought it well worth the discomfort he had endured. But his continued ill-health had become a question that could no longer be trifled with, and he therefore settled down quietly to live at Achin for a time, not seeking any work, and dieting himself on " salt fish broyled and boiled rice, mixed with *tire* (or sour milk)." The only excitement during this period was a civil commotion among the natives, some of whom wanted to get rid of their Queen. The European residents, warned by the authorities, packed up their valuables and rowed out to the ships in the harbour, where they spent the night. Dampier, who was still wretchedly ill, lay on his back in one of the small boats, unable to sleep. As he stared up at the sky, he noted that there was an eclipse of the moon ; but he was too ill even to make a note of the date in his diary.

When he was able to get about again, Dampier sailed from Achin as mate of a trading ship, with a crew of Moors under him. On their way to Malacca, they spoke a Danish ship, and he found his old friend, Herman Coppinger, on board. The surgeon had at last succeeded in eluding the buccaneers, but he had not yet found a means of getting back to England. In Malacca, Dampier's captain sold opium and other things. On the way back, they had an amusing adventure at one of the Dutch islands. It should be interjected here that the Dutch had now become quite polite and helpful towards English traders. Dampier, in one of his rare allusions to politics, opines that " the news of our Revolution [that of 1688] in England had sweetened them ; for they often drank the King's health with us very heartily."

The Governor of this particular island had invited the English skipper and his passengers (including a lady) to supper, and had sent out his men in boats to secure a supply of fish for the occasion. He had also provided punch, concocted from brandy, lime-juice and sugar. Dampier, who had already dined with the Governor, was left in charge of the ship, and was astonished to hear a wild commotion on shore just when the festivities should have been at their height.

What had happened was that in the middle of supper, one of the Governor's soldiers had burst in upon the company crying out, " The Malayans ! "   The Governor instantly sprang out of the window, followed by his officers. " Everyone of them," says Dampier, " took the nearest way, some out of the Windows, others out of the Doors, leaving the three Guests by themselves." The latter, when they had recovered from their astonish-ment—for they had not understood a word that was said—followed their hosts at their best speed, and pre-sently found them all taking refuge in the fort. It then appeared that one of the Governor's fishing-boats had been attacked by Malays and several of the fishers killed. Dampier, on the ship, was not greatly alarmed, for it was raining, and he knew from experience that the Malays never undertook military operations in bad weather. In this case he was right. It is plain, however, from his rather malicious description of the behaviour of the Dutchmen, that he hugely enjoyed the whole incident.

Returning to Achin again, he met another member of Read's crew, who gave him a sad account of their fate. Some of them had joined the great Mogul, and were last heard of plundering villages in the south of India, and " fleeing when they were pursued "—in fact behaving like brigands. Others took shore service under a native prince in Madagascar. Read deserted his ship, and got a passage to New York ; Teat joined the Mogul ; and the " Cygnet " herself, with a crew of strangers on board, was lost in the Red Sea on the way home to England.

Dampier made several other trading voyages : one to Fort St. George—he gives us an interesting description of Madras in the year 1690—and another to Bencoolen, in Sumatra, where there was an English factory, and where the Governor offered him the post of chief gunner at the fort, with the duty of advising on the rebuilding of the fortifications. That Dampier should have been looked upon as an expert in military architecture seems to reflect unfavourably upon the intelligence of the Governor himself and his officers. However, he accepted the post, and remained there for some months. He staked out a new bastion " with the curtain belonging to it." He began, and had almost finished a second, but found that " the Governor would not gratify me for my pains, so in the night I had the stakes out of the ground, and put them to seek a new method, for I knew none of them did understand how to do it." [1] Obviously no man could have been with the buccaneers for close on ten years without acquiring a rough knowledge of how to build fortifications—and especially of how to do it quickly—but that neither the Governor nor his officers should have been able to carry on in his absence, not even with one of his models before them, is an astonishing fact.

About this time he had purchased a half-share in the possession of an unfortunate native chief, the " Prince

[1] Dampier's marginal note in the manuscript of his journal.

Jeoly " or the " Painted Prince," as he calls him.   He
had first seen Jeoly at Mindanao, where he was being
offered for sale to European visitors.   He was a prisoner
of war from one of the islands, and his attraction in
the eyes of Dampier and Moody (the other part-owner)
was that his body was covered with tattoo marks of an
unusually elaborate pattern, which, it was thought, might
be exhibited in England with considerable profit to the
showmen.   This unfortunate black was now at Bencoolen
with Dampier.   So was his mother ; but she died, and
Dampier buried her under the walls of the fort.   He
then addressed himself to the task of consoling her son,
whose grief was such that he nearly followed her to the
grave—a calamity which Dampier was determined to
avert at all costs.   Nor must we exclude the possibility
that he may have become attached to his " painted
prince "—" whom I might have made a great deal of
money by."

Dampier soon got tired of Bencoolen, and especially
of the Governor "whose humours were brutish and
barbarous."   Also " I began to long after my native
country, after so tedious a ramble from it."   Accordingly
on the 2nd January, 1691, he applied for permission
to return to England, a homeward-bound ship, the
" Defence " (Captain Heath), having just then arrived
in harbour.   The Governor refused to let him go ; so
he sent Jeoly on board, and himself slipped out at midnight, " creeping through one of the portholes of the
fort," and getting off to the ship without being missed.
Next morning the vessel sailed, and Dampier entered
upon the last stage of his first circumnavigation of the
globe.

It was an unpleasant voyage.   There was some
mysterious disease on board which proved fatal to no
fewer than thirty of the ship's company before they
reached the Cape.   Dampier thinks it was due to the

water, and adds that the food was also very bad. However, Captain Heath struggled on, with barely enough men to work the ship, and he was able to get some additional hands at the Cape. After that they called at St. Helena (then in the possession of the English East India Company), where they stayed for some days, and where the appearance of Jeoly caused a mild sensation among the inhabitants. On July 2nd, in company with two other ships, they resumed their voyage to England, and on September 18th they were off the coast of England and cast anchor in the Downs. Dampier had been away for twelve years, and we will presume that poor Judith, "from the household of the Duke of Grafton," was glad to see him back again.

He landed in England penniless. All his boyhood's dreams of buccaneers loaded with booty, the spoils of fair cities in West and East, had vanished into thin air. He owned nothing but the clothes he stood up in. In his hurried flight from Bencoolen, he had left behind him all his "books, drafts and instruments, clothes and bedding and wages." He had not brought back so much as a parrot—only the faded, sea-stained, scarcely legible sheets of his journal, tucked away in an inner pocket ; and a half-share in this wretched, shivering blackamoor. The fate of Jeoly is easily foreseen. Dampier was soon compelled to sell his interest in him for ready money. Removed from the care of one who at any rate understood something of his requirements, the unlucky prince was carted about England in the cold autumn weather, until he finally caught smallpox at Oxford and died. Mr. Masefield has unearthed a folio broadsheet of the date 1691-92, which contains the following vivid description of Jeoly :

" This famous Painted Prince is the just wonder of the Age, his whole Body (except Face, Hands and Feet) is curiously and most exquisitely *painted* or *stained* full of Variety of Invention, with prodigious Art and Skill perform'd. In so much, that the antient and noble Mystery of Painting or Staining upon Humane Bodies seems to be comprised in this one stately Piece.

" The Pictures and those other engraven Figures painted from him, and now dispersed abroad, serve only to describe as much as they can of the Fore-parts of this inimitable Piece of workmanship. The more admirable Back Parts afford us a Lively Representation of one quarter part of the World upon and betwixt his shoulders, where the Arcktick and Tropick Circles center in the North Pole on his Neck.

" This admirable Person is about the age of Thirty, graceful and well proportioned in all his Limbs. . . . He is exposed to publick view every day (during his stay in Town) from the 16th day of this instant June, at his Lodgings at the Blew Boar's Head in Fleet Street, near Water Lane : where he will continue for some time, if his health will permit.

" But if any Persons of Quality, Gentlemen or Ladies, do desire to see this noble Person at their own Houses, or any other convenient place, in or about this City of London : they are desired to send timely notice, and he will be ready to wait upon them in a Coach or Chair, any time they please to appoint, if in the day time.

" VIVANT REX and REGINA "

There is a curious portrait of Jeoly, engraved by Savage, with a narrative of his adventures attached, also a smaller one, copied from the above, with a purely fictitious life-history. Dampier always threw cold water on these romantic stories about his captive. All that was really known of him, he explained, was contained in the brief references in the *Voyages*.

K

Nothing is known of Dampier's movements during the next five years. No doubt he went to live with his own people in the West Country—not at East Coker, but at his brother's farm in Dorsetshire, or on the small estate which he himself now possessed in that county. The family seem to have been fairly prosperous—there is an allusion in a letter to "our ryefields" and other property—and they were probably inclined at first to look upon Dampier as a poor relation of rather doubtful antecedents.

Brother George, the farmer, was a man of enterprising mind, very different from the ordinary bucolic type. Indeed he seems to have had a keener eye for the main chance than William ever displayed. About this time he blossomed out as the inventor of a patent medicine, known as "Dampier's powder," which he claimed to be an infallible cure for hydrophobia. It was made of Jew's-ear and pepper. At the moment, William Dampier could be of little assistance in promoting the sale of this interesting remedy ; but five years later, when he had become acquainted with the President of the Royal Society and other prominent people, we find George's medicine inserted in the 237th number of the Philosophical Transactions. There is a grateful letter from George to William (who was in London), dated "Exmouth, Feb. 2nd, 1697-8," in which he thanks him for having shown "my letter and medicine for the bite of a mad dog" to a number of gentlemen, and magnanimously agrees that "for the good of others I am free that those worthy and incomparable ingenious gentlemen may use their pleasure about it." I am afraid that this association can have done brother William little good in the end.

It has been assumed [1] that Dampier made at least one

---

[1] *E.g.* by Mr. Masefield and Sir Albert Gray.

voyage on a merchant ship during this period of five years after his return from the East. If he did so—and we should expect it of his restless spirit—it is surprising, to put it mildly, that so conscientious a diarist should have left no kind of record behind. Yet the evidence is at first sight irresistible. Towards the end of his *New Voyage*, in his brief account of the journey home from Bencoolen, he remarks incidentally that on one occasion he felt just such a wind from the shore as he had also encountered " *as I lay at anchor at the Groin in July 1694.*" Now " The Groin " was, of course, the old name for Corunna. That sounds clear enough : he was at Corunna in 1694—three years after his home-coming from the East.

But it is a curious coincidence that, in the manu-script, the copyist has made a mistake in the date of his departure from Bencoolen, which is given as " January 25th, 1694," instead of 1691. Dampier has added some of his marginal notes just here, but they do not correct this mistake, which evidently escaped his attention. The next date given in the manuscript (that of the departure from St. Helena) is correct. The passage about Corunna would come in between these two dates ; but it does not, as a fact, appear in the manuscript, having been interposed later with several other pages of additional matter, for the purposes of the published book. It is, therefore, a feasible theory that some copyist may have added the year to the date of the Corunna incident, copying it from the wrong date which he would see just above in the manuscript. Against this is the fact that the other mistake (in the date of the departure from Bencoolen) was put right in the published book. But I find it hard to believe that Dampier, whose voyages have been described more fully than those of any other man of his time, both by himself and by his enemies, succeeded in sandwiching in this mysterious anonymous trip, as to which we have not a single other word from **any** source whatever.[1]

I think that he just stayed quietly at home, resting himself, until the spring of the year 1697. But he would have to spend a good deal of time in London, consulting his publisher, James Knapton. His book was now on the stocks. The journal which he had taken so much trouble to preserve, sealing it up in a piece of hollow bamboo as he swam the rivers of the Darien Peninsula, smuggling it out of the Bencoolen Fort when all his other papers were left behind, drying it over the fire on the beach at Nicobar, sitting up at night on pirate ships and trading vessels to fill in the day's entry, was now to be turned into money at last.

Probably he did not expect to make much out of it. Of the two acquisitions which he brought home with him from the East—all that he had to show for twelve years' endeavour—there is no doubt that he believed Jeoly to be a far more valuable property than the journal. Knapton must have known better. He did not hurry with the printing, but that may be explained by the fact, which Dampier himself admits, that the manuscript was submitted to a number of the author's friends for their suggestions and corrections, before it was sent to the press. Dampier's enemies, at a later date, even suggested that he did not write the book himself, and at the beginning of his next book, the *Voyage to New Holland*, he goes out of his way to reply to this absurd charge, arguing that " the best and most eminent authors are not ashamed " to have their work " revised and corrected by friends."

---

[1] It is possible that he might have been at Corunna in 1691, as he returned from the East; for he mentions that his ship was temporarily separated from her consorts in the Bay of Biscay by a storm, and Corunna would be a convenient refuge from the weather.

There was no need for such excuses : Dampier was always the world's worst controversialist. A comparison between the original manuscript in the Sloane Collection [1] and the published book completely disposes of the charge. It shows that Dampier himself did all the revising and the correcting. The manuscript, as we have seen, is covered with his marginal notes, most of which, though not all, are incorporated in the book. The other new matter in the book consists of natural history notes from all parts of the world and some other details of fact (such as the reference to Corunna) which no one but Dampier himself could have added. It is plain that his friends made no *additions* to the book : they can only have advised as to what should be included or omitted. It is also perfectly plain to any discerning reader that the whole is written in Dampier's own very individual style.

But though his friends, whoever they were, cannot have helped him much, a good deal of time would be lost in passing the manuscript round among them, and so the publication of the book was delayed till 1697. When it did appear, it was an instantaneous success, and ran into three editions within a few months. Dampier woke up to find himself famous. He had dedicated his great work to Charles Montague, the President of the Royal Society ; but he evidently did not know his patron personally at the time, for with his usual modesty he apologized for " the boldness of a stranger " in venturing to lay the book before him. It is unlikely that he had any acquaintance among prominent people at this stage.

But with the appearance of his book the scene changed like magic, and the Dorsetshire farm can have seen very little of him after this. Charles Montague took him up, and it was, no doubt, on his recommendation that

[1] No. 3236.

in August, 1697, Dampier was given a post as a " land-carriage man " in the Customs. The salary attached to this post was only £8, 15s. a quarter, but that was a sum not altogether contemptible in those days, and, what was more valuable from Dampier's point of view, he was able to arrange for it to be paid to his wife during his subsequent long absences from England. Thus the long-neglected Judith was provided for. He was beginning to be taken notice of in official circles, too. In July, 1698, he was ordered to appear before the Council of Trade and Plantations to be " examined as to the design of the Scotch East India Company to make a settlement on the Isthmus of Darien " under William Paterson. Lionel Wafer was another witness, and the two men were able to give the Council first-hand descriptions of the country it was proposed to colonize. Dampier, as we know, had " golden dreams " in his head about the fortunes that might be made out of the gold mines of Darien, if worked by slave labour ; but apart from that it seems unlikely that the evidence of himself and Wafer can have given the Council much encouragement to persist with the scheme.

Other leading men in the scientific world who now became Dampier's friends were Sir Robert Southwell [1] and Sir Hans Sloane [2] ; and I think it must have been about this time that the latter ordered the explorer's portrait to be painted by Thomas Murray. It hangs in the National Portrait Gallery, and, as I have said, tells us more about Dampier the man than could be obtained from any bare record of his private life at the time. As to that, we have only one piece of evidence of import-

[1] Diplomatist and man of letters ; President of the Royal Society from 1690 to 1695.

[2] The distinguished collector, patron of men of science and founder of the British Museum. He became Secretary of the Royal Society in 1693, and succeeded Sir Isaac Newton as its President in 1727.

ance—the invaluable entry in Evelyn's *Diary*, under date August 6th, 1698.   I quote it in full :

" I dined with Mr. Pepys, where was Captain Dampier, who had been a famous buccaneer, had brought hither the painted prince Job,[1] and printed a relation of his very strange adventures and his observations.   He was now going abroad again by the King's encouragement, who furnished a ship of 290 tons.   He seemed a more modest man than one would imagine by relation of the crew he had assorted with.   He brought a map of his observations of the course of the winds in the South Seas, and assured us that the maps hitherto extant were all false as to the Pacific Sea, which he makes on the South of the line, that on the North end running by the coast of Peru being extremely tempestuous."

Evelyn did not forget this meeting.   In his *Numismata : a Discourse of Medals*, which was published in the following year (1699), he makes the very proper suggestion that among those " famous and illustrious persons " whose heads might well appear upon medals specially struck to commemorate their " most signal works and actions " there should be included, under the heading of " Great Travellers," the name of Captain William Dampier.   He rather spoils it, however, by adding " and the rest of the Buccaneers."   Still worse, he thinks there might be a medal struck in memory of that pathetic, but slightly ridiculous figure, Prince Jeoly. As to Dampier's criticism of the maps, it may be remarked parenthetically that the word " Pacific " was then used in a literal sense ; and Dampier was undoubtedly right when he said that it was too flattering a description of some parts of the South Seas.

The new voyage, which Dampier was about to under-

[1] Jeoly.

take " by the King's encouragement," was, of course, that of the " Roebuck," to be described in the next chapter.   It is to be observed that he had been given this important appointment in the year following the publication of his book.   It was, in fact, the book—not the voyages themselves—that had " made " him.   He might have wandered about the world for the rest of his life, filling his journal with observations of the highest importance for the future of exploration, without attracting any particular attention, if the great success of his book had not forced him upon the notice of those in authority.   He had won fame not as a traveller, but as a travel-writer.

Some perception of this may have come to him ; for he instantly fell in with Knapton's suggestion that he should produce another volume.   Before the " Roebuck " was ready to sail in January, 1699, his *Supplement to the Voyage Round the World*, together with the *Voyage to Campeachy* and the *Discourse on the Trade Winds* (constituting the second volume of his *Voyages*), was already in the printer's hands.   Unfortunately the printers had not done with it when he sailed ; for he wrote from the Downs to Lord Orford, First Lord of the Admiralty, apologizing for not being able to send him a copy, and explaining that " the gentleman that I employed to compile an Index [it is the weakest feature of the book] has occasioned the delay."   I say " unfortunately," because Dampier would have been gratified if he could have witnessed the reception given to this book.   It probably did even more for his reputation among educated and " ingenious " people than his first volume had done.

Still, we find him now a man of reputation, his talents widely recognized, his name familiar in every coffee-house, and his authority as a geographer and hydrographer accepted as it deserved to be.   He is at last reaping the reward of all that conscientious note-taking from the West Indies to Cochin China, and of all the trouble he took to preserve his notes when written. In a sense, indeed, this is the apex of his career, though his greatest voyage of discovery—that of the " Roebuck " to Australia—is yet to come. He is full of confidence. He feels that he knows the oceans of the world as no other living Englishman knows them. Since he left that little grammar-school in Somerset on his career of adventure, he has, with much labour, taught himself everything that an explorer ought to know. He is now forty-seven, and the time has come to prove it.

Alas ! there is just one thing he has forgotten to learn—the habit of command. He does not yet realize that his long association with the buccaneers in a subordinate position (though that was by his own choice), his long acquiescence in their slipshod ways and their occasional brutal punishments in place of a proper system of discipline, have bred in him unconsciously a certain attitude of mind in regard to these matters, which will prove more or less of a handicap for the rest of his life, and will be one (though only one among many) of the causes which, as we shall see in the next chapter, placed the greatest prize of all just beyond his reach.

CHAPTER IX

HE EXPLORES AUSTRALIA AND
NEW GUINEA

HENEVER you hear Dampier described as a failure or a might-have-been ; damned with faint praise in the *Dictionary of National Biography* ; or denied even his right to a place in the roll of " Men of Action "—he who had gone abroad in his 'teens, fought in the Royal Navy, served with the buccaneers, and three times circumnavigated the globe !—whenever you hear this kind of criticism, you will know that what the critic has in mind is the voyage of H.M.S. " Roebuck " to Australia. Dampier's bitterest enemy cannot say that, as an explorer, he missed any other chance in the whole of his career. But he might have discovered Australia ; he might have anticipated Cook ; and the simple fact is that he did not. How far it was his own fault, or the fault of the Admiralty, or the fault of his cantankerous lieutenant and backboneless crew is quite beside the point. An explorer is judged on the additions he makes to the map ; and while Dampier's discoveries in Australia were important, were sensational, in the year 1700, and still rank as memorable achievements, they did not solve the great problem which was waiting to be solved—they did not disclose the Continent of Australia. It was touch-and-go ; it might almost be said that a mere

accident prevented him ; but accidents are the stuff of which history is made.

In this chapter we shall see what in fact he did accomplish, and shall be able to judge for ourselves of the importance of a voyage of discovery which was undoubtedly the greatest made by any Englishman for over half a century ; and of the fairness of describing it as a " failure " in the light of our much more recently acquired knowledge of the things it just missed. We have noted Dampier's rather disappointing attitude towards Australia, or New Holland, when he visited it with Read's buccaneers ; but he was then in uncongenial company, whose only object was to make money, and the place itself and its inhabitants had impressed him unfavourably. In the seclusion of his home in Dorsetshire his ideas widened, and he began to see that Read had missed a great opportunity. The position and extent of the *Terra Australis Incognita* was a common subject of conversation in England at that time. A translation of Tasman's journal, in which the gallant Dutchman described his discovery of Tasmania, was published in London in 1694. From passages in his letters it is clear that Dampier realized as well as anyone that Australia was probably a continent, and the more he thought the matter over, the more plainly he saw that here was the great opening for exploration. He also, with prophetic insight, considered Australia " a country likely to contain gold." He therefore put up a proposal [1] to the Admiralty to the effect that one of the King's ships should be fitted out to explore the coast of New Holland. In this memorandum he observes that, apart from Australia, " there are several places which might probably be visited with good advantage " ; but adds that " there is no larger tract of land hitherto

[1] Probably in response to the request of Lord Orford, the First Lord, to whom Charles Montague had introduced him.

undiscovered than the Terra Australis, if that vast space surrounding the South Pole, and extending so far into the warmer climate be a continued land, as a great deal of it is known to be."

Yet he still envisaged a voyage to Madagascar, and from thence " directly to the Northernmost part of New Holland "—in other words, to that same North-western corner of the continent where he had already landed. Perhaps he was still hankering after " warm voyages," still remembering with a shudder the deadly cold of that early trip of his to Newfoundland, when he had sworn that he would never sail so far from the Equator again. At any rate, better, wider ideas prevailed, and in the spring of 1698, when he had been definitely commissioned to undertake the voyage, he made up his mind to sail round the Horn, and so fall in with Australia on the east coast, and follow the coast northward along it till he came to New Guinea. Had he done so, it is hardly conceivable that he should have failed to realize the extent of his discovery. Even with his crazy ship and his half-hearted crew he must have got in before Cook, and remade the map.

But delay followed delay, and the sailing in September turned out to be as wild a dream as the gold mines of Darien. He was continually being called up to London to advise the Government. The Council of Trade and Plantations wanted to know[1] whether he had heard of any proposals or bribes offered to Lionel Wafer by the Scotch East India Company. He replied (in July, 1698) that he had not, and added that Wafer would be incapable of ".doing the Scotch East India Company any great service." On September 27th, on the principle of setting a thief to catch a thief, he was called in again to advise about fitting out a squadron against the pirates

[1] *Calendar of State Papers. Colonial Series. (America and the West Indies.)*

" to the East of the Cape of Good Hope."   Again he is
asked on the 26th how long a ship might be " running
from England to Madagascar at this time of year."   He
replies at length, giving three and a half months as the
best possible time.

But these were minor delays.   The real trouble was
with the ship, the crew, the stores, and so forth.   As
early as March 25th—so pleased was Lord Orford with
the idea of this voyage of exploration—Dampier had
been appointed to command the " Jolly Prize," " when
fitted out " ; but at the beginning of July he reported
that the " Jolly Prize " was " altogether unfit for the
designed voyage."   After a considerable pause, he was
given another vessel, the " Roebuck," a King's ship
carrying twelve guns and a crew of fifty men and boys,
and provisioned for twenty months.   She was a fifth-
rater, almost certainly of two decks, and had previously
been a fireship.   She was then at Deptford, and did
not leave till October 6th ; and on the 13th, as she lay
at Tilbury, she got into collision with the " Isabella
Pink " and damaged her head and sprit topmast.

She finally anchored in the Downs on the 22nd and
Dampier went down there to see to her fitting-out.   He
was disappointed at the smallness of his crew, and says
so in one of his letters to Lord Orford.   The following
officers were engaged : Jacob Hughes, master ; George
Fisher, lieutenant ; Philip Paine, gunner ; R. Chadwick
and John Knight, mates.   The doctor and the captain's
clerk were " two Scotch dogs," [1] named William
Borthwick and James Brand.   Further delays took place
over the appointment of a boatswain, and when Dampier
at last engaged a suitable man, there were violent
quarrels, as we shall see, between the bo'sun and the
lieutenant.

[1] Lieut. Fisher's name for them, as stated by John Rumbold in evidence
before the court-martial.

About November 21st Dampier wrote to Lord Orford, setting forth " what I would propose to have put into my instructions "—which shows that he really drew up the instructions himself. He explains that it is now too late in the year to go round the Horn,[1] and he would therefore have to sail *via* the Cape of Good Hope. He asks that a small gratuity or even a " promise of somewhat at our return " may be offered to his men to keep them cheerful, and inspire them with " a generous resolution of hazarding their persons." He hopes their lordships will not think him " too bold " in asking for all this ; he is still " much a stranger to his Majesty's service," and may have erred in etiquette.

On November 30th came his formal instructions from the Admiralty, directing him to proceed to the Cape, " and from thence to stretch away towards New Holland." They gave him permission " to steer any other course " if he saw fit ; but reminded him that the expedition was an expensive one, and that he must " take a special care " to use his best endeavour to make some discovery of value. He is only to bring home natives (as he had suggested) " provided they shall be willing to come along." A vague promise is made to the men " that such of them as shall behave themselves well and cheer-fully perform their duty in this affaire, which 'tis hoped may tend to the advantage of the nation, shall at their return receive all fitting reward and encouragement."

So the idea of an early start in September and a voyage round Cape Horn was already abandoned. And already the internal squabbles which were to act as a powerful brake on the expedition, and in which George Fisher was the leading spirit, had made their appearance on board. Fisher's complaints may be studied in detail in the evidence which he gave before the court-martial,

[1] So late a start would mean that he would be rounding the " Cape of Storms " in the very depth of the winter.

Bow and Forebody

Scale of Feet

Sheer Draught

Stern

After Body

A FIFTH-RATER OF 1864

which was held after Dampier returned to England.   It will be more convenient here to take them chronologically, mentioning each " incident " as it occurred in the course of the voyage.   Fisher was obviously looking for trouble from the day he joined the ship ;   for in giving his evidence he is so particular in his dates that we can only conclude that he must have kept a note-book for the purpose.   To mention each of his complaints may seem like giving undue prominence to petty grievances ;   but they have an historical value in the light which they throw, not only on Dampier, but on life on shipboard at the end of the seventeenth century.

Obviously the root of the trouble between Dampier and Fisher was the captain's somewhat shady past. Dampier was an ex-buccaneer, Fisher a regular officer of the King's Navy.   It is true that he only joined as a volunteer in 1689 (he served with some distinction in William's fleet at the relief of Londonderry), but, as so often happens in these cases, he was more forward to assert the dignity of the service than any grey-haired martinet.   The first " incident " occurred on November 1st.   The flagship of Sir Clowdisley Shovell [1] had appeared in the Downs, and it behoved all the King's ships there to mind their p's and q's.   Fisher was called on board the flagship, and there found Dampier, who, according to his story, took him aside, and said that while he (Fisher) had been ashore " there was like to have been a mutiny on board the ' Roebuck,' for that James Grigson and T. Knight had been drinking with the Boatswaine in his cabin, and was overheard by the Master to swear that when they came to Sea they would heave the Master overboard and run away with the King's ship."   Dampier is alleged to have added

[1] Appointed Admiral of the Blue, 1696.   He was also Comptroller of Victualling at this time.   In 1705 he was made commander-in-chief of the Fleet.

that he " did not like the Boatswaine " and to have " demanded Fisher's advice in the case."

It would not be unnatural that he, who in his own words was still " much a stranger to his Majesty's service," should have discussed the matter with a regular officer. If so, his confidence was ill-rewarded. Fisher says he merely advised Dampier to tell the Admiral about it, and he complains that Dampier did nothing of the kind—which again we can well understand. On November 5th Captain Jumper and Captain Cleasbie, Sir Clowdisley Shovell's secretary, came on board the " Roebuck " " to see if our crew were seamen "—in other words to inspect. Fisher, as they arrived, " commanded the Boatswaine to order the Pinnace astern out of their way, but he answered with an Oath that he would not obey his commands when the Captain was on board." So that Jumper and Cleasbie had to climb over the pinnace to get on board the " Roebuck "—a very undignified proceeding. Fisher complained to Dampier of the bo'sun's conduct, and he did it, characteristically enough, in the presence of the two visiting captains. Dampier, according to him, was " told by them that he ought to see that Fisher should be protected in his commands." They also " reprimanded the Boatswaine "—a piece of interference which I imagine no captain would tolerate nowadays.

All this, it should be noted, is taken from Fisher's own account of events. Dampier, who had obviously forgotten all dates and details, replied at the court-martial only in the vaguest terms. He was, as I have said, the world's worst controversialist. His idea of an answer to this rigmarole was to tell the court-martial that " when the ship lay in the Downs," Fisher, in conversation with the gunner, said, " Damn him for an old rogue, he minds nothing "—meaning Dampier. He also says that on some other unspecified date, Fisher

was heard by the doctor, the purser and Brand (one of the
" Scotch dogs") to speak disrespectfully of the Lords of
the Admiralty, and "was reproved for it by the Captain."
It is hard to say which story is the less convincing.

But in the Master's Log, kept by Hughes, there is a
reference which throws new light on the incident.[1]
Evidently there was some kind of " trial" or inquiry
into the quarrel between Fisher and the boatswain ; for
on November 21, " the order came " that " our lieutenant
and boatswain and a woman " should be transferred to
another ship, the " Messenger," and on the following
day " they went for Chatham in order for a tryall."   So
there was a woman in the case !   Fisher, in his evidence
before the court-martial, might not be anxious to recall
this aspect of the dispute ; but it is extraordinary that
the other side did not do so.   Hughes, who kept the log,
was actually a witness for Dampier.   In fact, Dampier's
defence seems to have been grossly mismanaged.

To return to Fisher's version, on November 12th he
" moved the Captain to punish James Grigson, still
finding him a refractory and dangerous fellow " ; and
Dampier reluctantly agreed that Grigson should be
" made fast to the gangway."   After an hour of this,
he was, in Fisher's words, " set loose without any punish-
ment," whereupon Fisher complained to Dampier that
this was " an ill example."   We can understand that
about this time the easy-going Captain felt his affection
for his lieutenant sensibly cooling.   To have done with
this particular grievance of Fisher's, on December 6th
he went on board the flagship, and after telling his
troubles to a group of officers, actually appealed to the
crew for volunteers to replace Grigson and Knight.
Dampier, of course, refused to accept them.   The
wonder is that he did not immediately turn Fisher out
of his ship, and it would have been better for his reputa-

[1] The Master's Log of the " Roebuck " is in the Public Record Office.

tion (having already missed the great opportunity of his lifetime through these delays) if he had done so, and had waited for a new lieutenant.

However, such delays as these, vexatious as they were, could not continue for ever. Very early on the morning of Saturday, January 14th, the " Roebuck " sailed from the Downs with a fair wind, loaded with her twenty-months' provisions. At noon they were off Dungeness. Next morning they found themselves, with a number of other English ships, " nearer to the French coast than we expected." The master, Hughes, was " somewhat troubled at this discovery " ; but Dampier explains that it was a very common mistake in those days, and " fatal to many ships." The occasion of it, he says, " is not allowing for the change of the Variations since the making of the Charts, which Captain Hally [1] has observed to be very considerable." Dampier was familiar with Halley's work, and explained the situation to Hughes. On the 19th they sighted Cape Finisterre, and on the 28th " Lancerota " (Lanzerote) of the Canary Islands.

On that day there was more trouble with Fisher. His own account is that he was " walking on the Deck with the Captaine and the Captaine's Clerk " when " 3 Drops of Blood fell from his Nose on his hand." He immediately fainted ! Being taken to his cabin and bled, he felt a bit better, and in the middle of the night summoned the chief mate, and asked him about the vessel's course. To his horror he discovered that they were heading straight for the island of " Algoranca " (Alegranze), and that the Captain was apparently unaware of the fact, since no look-out was being kept. He instantly advised that they should shorten sail. Dampier's own account mentions simply that they sighted Alegranze, as expected, and that he took " sights " of the island at two different

[1] E. Halley (1656-1742), astronomer, discoverer of Halley's Comet, author of the *General Chart of the Variations*.

bearings and distances. He had, of course, already forgotten more about navigation than Fisher would ever know. At the court-martial he added one other incident of this day—namely that the Lieutenant had insisted on going to sleep with all his bedding in the pinnace, which "lay on the boomes," and that when Dampier spoke to him about it, reminding him that it was against orders, he "bent his fist and held it to his nose and said he did not care a —— for him."

On January 30th they put into Santa Cruz, Teneriffe, "to take in some wine and brandy for my voyage," says Dampier. The Captain went ashore, and saw the Spanish Governor, and was invited to dine with him next day. On the following morning he started out, accompanied by the doctor and the purser (but not the lieutenant), on a typical tourist trip to Laguna, the principal town, which was some miles inland, so that there was only just time to get back for the Governor's dinner-party. It was a hot and dusty journey, and longer than they expected. But there were "publick houses scattering by the way-side, where we got some wine," and perhaps that kept them back. At any rate, their thirst was unquenched, for when they reached Laguna they were "glad to refresh themselves with a little wine in a sorry Tipling-house." In the course of some characteristic notes upon the island's resources, Dampier remarks that "the true Malmsey Wine grows on this island ; and this here is said to be the best of its kind in the World." There is "also Canary Wine, and Verdona, or Green-wine." As I have said, they were due to dine with the Governor of Santa Cruz ; "but staying so long at Laguna I came but time enough to sup with him." However he was "a civil discreet man," and perhaps he did not ask too many questions about the cause of their delay. The Governor visited the "Roebuck" next morning in return ; "but he was presently sea-sick, and so much out of order that he could scarce eat or drink anything, but went quickly ashore again."

There were other English ships in harbour besides the " Roebuck," and the commander of one of these, Captain Travers, of the " Experiment " galley, came to visit Dampier on the day the " Roebuck " arrived. His visit was the occasion of yet another scene with Fisher. Travers asked for beer—apparently it was the first word he uttered as he stepped on board—and Dampier told Fisher to see about it. But the purser (who was responsible for the beer) happened to meet the man who was going to break in the butt, and understanding that it was by Fisher's orders " threatened to break his head " instead. Again Fisher complained to his Captain, and again in the presence of the other Captain, who tactlessly " seconded him," and according to his account said to Dampier, " If you suffer your Lieutenant to be thus used it may be of ill consequence in your voyage." Again Dampier does nothing. Next day, however, he heard that Fisher had been thrashing a midshipman named Barnaby (a youth he had already been accused of bullying), and indignantly rebuked him. As Fisher left his captain, he swears that Dampier's clerk, his special enemy, " whispered Fisher to cane Barnaby, which if he had done, Fisher perceiving their intent was to draw and run him through in the scuffle "—a singularly unconvincing story of a murder plot. But Fisher now believed his life to be in danger. He told the court-martial that, before leaving Santa Cruz, Dampier took on board a Spanish assassin, whom he had hired for the express purpose of murdering his subordinate, but set him ashore again when he saw that Fisher's suspicions were aroused. It is astonishing to think of Sir Clowdisley Shovell and the other members of the Court listening gravely to stuff like this.

From Santa Cruz they set a course for the island of Mayo, of the Cape Verde group, which Dampier knew of old, getting into harbour there on February 11th. Here Dampier laid his plans for the remainder of the voyage. Before attempting to round the Cape, he " thought it requisite to touch once more at a cultivated place in these seas, where my men might be refreshed." He had no hardy crew of buccaneers with him, as on the occasion of his last visit to the island of Mayo. With these new men, he aimed at " inuring them gradually and by intervals to the fatigues that were to be expected in the remainder of the voyage, which was to be in a part of the world they were altogether strangers to."   He decided upon Pernambuco in Brazil as a suitable port of call, and left St. Iago, in the Cape Verde Islands, for that destination on February 22nd.   Fisher alleges that in getting to St. Iago from Mayo the Captain completely lost his way, and that he (Fisher), " Hearing the men cry out Land ! " rushed on deck and asked Dampier what he meant to do.   " He answered (as if crying) he did not know what the master designed." Whereupon Fisher, knowing the master to be drunk at the moment, took charge of the helm, and with great address managed to save the ship !   The Master's Log, however, makes it a perfectly normal landfall.

They had now a month's voyage ahead of them to the coast of Brazil, and it was not to be a pleasant one. The " atmosphere " on board grew worse and worse. Dampier says that " the ignorance and obstinacy of some under me," who would never trust his ability as a pilot, " occasioned me a great deal of trouble."   They all thought " we should never be able to weather Cape St. Augustin," and became discontented and surly, though Dampier assured them that the " calms and shiftings of wind " which were the cause of their fear were but to be expected in crossing the Line.   His assurances that

all was well were doubted.   " They would not believe it
till they found it so."

Meantime Fisher describes a little scene among the
officers in the cabin, which seems hardly to have been
worth the attention of a court-martial, but undoubtedly
gives the modern reader a delightfully intimate picture
of their lives—a glimpse right into the heart of the
period.   One afternoon as the ship slips gently southward, Fisher gets a message from the Captain, asking
him civilly whether he would like to " clubb for a bowl
of punch."   He agrees, and they assemble in the cabin
round the flowing bowl.   Tongues are loosened.   The
Captain is no drunkard, but after all he has sailed with
the buccaneers ; and presently, amid the general chatter,
he is heard saying something to the effect that " had he
commanded one of the King's ships in the late Warr,
all French men he took in Privateers he would have
tyed back to back and thrown overboard, adding all the
King's Captaines were fools they did not do it."

Fisher professes to have been horrified.   To the
Captain's face he said it was " a very cruell thought,"
and even the doctor (Scotch dog though he was) declared
it to be " barbarously intended."   But Dampier retorted
that " it would have made a quick end of the war." [1]
Fisher then introduced the somewhat delicate topic of
pirates, beginning to say that " if all nations would give
no protection to Pirates, but hang them as soon as
taken, it would be of good service."   The Captain cut
in with a demand to know " what he meant by Pirates ? "
to which the lieutenant answered cautiously, " Such as
Everye (Avery) [2] and his men."   Whereupon Dampier,
no doubt a little elevated by the punch, " swore if he

[1] There is something very modern about this discussion after all.

[2] The celebrated freebooter, known as the " Grand Pirate," whose
exploits in Madagascar are introduced by Defoe into the story of *Captain
Singleton.*

meet with any of them he would not hurt them, not a hair of their heads." If he could have seen Fisher copying it all down in his note-book a few moments later, he might have been less free with his talk. The note-book must have been getting almost full by now, for Fisher records many more disputes—quarrels between himself and the purser, and so forth.

" It was the tenth day of March, about the time of the Equinox, when we crossed the Equator," says Dampier. He gives his usual full notes of the winds, and of " a great swell out of the S.E.," and of " small uncertain gales " with rain ; and remarks that he was troubled by the carelessness of his men in lying down in their hammocks in their wet clothes. On such occasions he would give them a dram of brandy, and order them to change their clothes. They always took the brandy, but they seldom or never changed. Apart from this there was a " refractoriness of some under me " and " discontents and backwardness of some of my men " which in the end led him to drop the idea of Pernambuco, and make for Bahia de Todos os Santos instead. For at Pernambuco ships had to anchor two or three leagues from the shore, whereas at Bahia the civil authorities were near at hand to help him in the event of mutiny.

Mutiny was now a real possibility ; the Fisher comedy had passed from the stage of farce to that of melodrama. Once again the *casus belli* was a barrel of beer. On the very day that they crossed the Equator, the cook came to Fisher and complained that " it was three in the afternoon and they had no beer." Thereupon Fisher, on his own responsibility, ordered the cooper to broach a new cask, without informing either captain or purser. Dampier summoned Fisher and the cooper to the quarter-deck. He fairly lost his temper. According to Fisher, he first thrashed' the cooper, and then fell upon the

lieutenant with his cane, and " caned him to the forecastle and confined him to the cabin." According to
Dampier, Fisher, when spoken to, " called the Captain
names softly, and urged the Captain to strike him, then
he loudly called him a great many ill names, as old
Rogue, old Dog, old Cheat, and endeavoured to stir up
the seamen to a mutiny, by telling them that the Captain
knew not whither he was going, that he was no artist,
that he knew nothing, but was a mere theaf, and when
he would not be silent was at last confined to his cabin."
From his cabin, Fisher continued to shout abuse, bawling
out that he knew the Captain intended to run away
with the ship and " turn pirate "—until they put him
in irons.

The situation was a grave one. They were a fortnight
out from St. Iago, and could not expect to sight their
Brazilian port for another two weeks. Dampier's
officers, " such as I could trust," advised him to sleep
on the quarter-deck for safety ; and on the 18th he had
all the small arms brought up there and the gun-room
door locked. He also ordered the arrest of three men
suspected of being ringleaders in the trouble. One of
them gave evidence implicating Fisher, but not to any
serious extent, and Dampier's next move in the matter
must be put down less to any immediate fear of mutiny
than to a determination to get Fisher off the ship at all
costs. On the 23rd they sighted Brazil, and coasted
southwards to Bahia de Todos os Santos, which they
reached at midnight of the 24th. A Portuguese vessel
piloted them in, and when they anchored, although it
was so late, the Portuguese skipper came on board the
" Roebuck " to welcome them. " Indeed," says Dampier
(who seems to have modified his old opinion [1] of the
Portuguese), " I found much respect, not only from this
gentleman, but from all of that nation, both here and

----

[1] Which he had formed in the East.

in other places, who were ready to serve me on all occasions."

On the following day, Dampier got in touch with the Portuguese Governor, and on the 28th he sent Fisher ashore. He says that Fisher himself clamoured for this to be done, desiring to return to England *via* Portugal. Fisher says that he was amazed at it ; further, that he was sent ashore in irons like a malefactor, and thrown into the common jail among a lot of " negroes and mulattos," and that Dampier, in spite of his urgent messages, did nothing to get his condition improved before the ship sailed.[1] Here we say good-bye to this troublesome person—for the moment. His Captain's treatment of him at Bahia was the one really serious charge put forward at the court-martial—and the only one that seems to have the ring of truth.

In the meantime Dampier was calmly using his month's stay at the Portuguese port to write a wonderfully full account of the place and of the surrounding country. He enumerates the principal public buildings in the town, describes the domestic architecture, the strength of the garrison and the shipping in the harbour. There were thirty " great ships " from different parts of Europe, but the " Roebuck " was the first English ship for eleven or twelve years. He gives us some street scenes. The wealthy merchants (one of them was an Englishman, Mr. Cock) were carried about in hammocks, slung on stout bamboo which negro slaves bore upon their shoulders. There were so many slaves that Dampier says " they make up the greater part or bulk of the inhabitants." They " will easily be engaged to do any sort of mischief," and rather specialized in murdering sailors, so that Dampier was very chary in

[1] He was kept in jail at Bahia till July 4th and was then sent to Lisbon on a Portuguese ship. At Lisbon the authorities released him and he crossed to England in December 1699.

giving his men shore leave. He describes the cotton-fields and other forms of agriculture, and then comes to a list of animals and birds—a favourite subject of his—illustrating his remarks with some delightfully life-like drawings. There is a particularly spirited description of the great snakes, especially of the anaconda, which lives in pools and " flourishes its tail " out of the water to lasso passers-by. Dampier met an Irishman in Bahia who told him that his father had been caught in this way, and dragged head first into the pool to be swallowed by the monster.

Dampier also used the opportunity of his month's stay in Bahia " to allay in some measure the ferment that had been raised among my men." He found their heads still " filled with strange notions of Southerly winds that were now setting in (and there had been already some flurries of them) which, as they surmised, would hinder any further attempts of going on to the southward . . . though I told them they were to look for them." Some of the officers were just as bad, and " very listless to the getting things in a readiness for our departure."

But at last it was done. The beer barrels—cause of so many disputes, but now void of beer—were sent ashore and filled with water. Oranges, rum and sugar were taken on board, and on the 23rd April the " Roe-buck " weighed anchor and put to sea. The weather was fair, in spite of those occasional " flurries " from the South. In a few weeks they began to meet westerly winds, " which did not leave us till a little before we made the Cape "—yet without apparently convincing the malcontents that their Captain knew what he was about. Dampier could never be quite certain of his position on this voyage, for he " had not a good glass in the ship, beside the half-watch or two-hour glasses." The " half-minute glasses," used at the heaving of the log, were equally unreliable. As Dampier remarks—

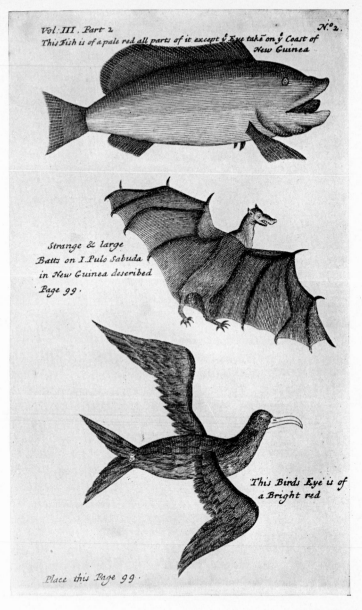

Vol: III. Part 2   *N.º 2.*

This Fish is of a pale red all parts of it except y̆ Eye take on y̆ Coast of New Guinea

Strange & large Batts on I. Pulo Sabuda in New Guinea described Page 99.

This Birds Eye is of a Bright red

Place this Page 99.

A PAGE ILLUSTRATION FROM DAMPIER'S "A NEW VOYAGE ROUND THE WORLD"

mildly enough in the circumstances—" a ship ought to have its glasses very exact." Especially, he might have added, when it has been fitted out by the Admiralty for an important voyage of exploration in uncharted seas ! But in those days sailors were accustomed to seek their bunks at night with so little idea of where they would find themselves in the morning that to us the marvel is that there were not even more wrecks than actually occurred.

Dampier says that " another thing that stumbled me there was the Variation." This is one of his favourite topics, and the occasion of some of his best and most helpful work as a writer on navigation. He found the variation at the Cape more than it was thirty leagues east of it, whereas it should have been less. " These things, I confess, did puzzle me "—indeed were " most shocking to me." " Neither was I fully satisfied as to the exactness of the taking of the Variation at Sea : for in a great sea, which we often met with, the compass will traverse with the motion of the ship ; besides the Ship may and will deviate somewhat in steering, even by the best helmsmen." To make the nature of his troubles clearer, he appends an elaborate table of variations, with dates—observing modestly that he considers himself incompetent to advance theories of his own, and therefore merely states the facts, for Halley and others to make use of.

They sighted the Cape, and left it below the horizon on June 6th. On that evening the Captain stood on his quarter-deck admiring the sunset. " As the Sun drew near the horizon, the clouds were gilded very prettily to the eye, though at the same time my mind dreaded the consequences of it." At midnight they had " a pale whitish glare in the N.W."—another bad sign— and at 2 a.m. it was blowing a gale. But the " Roe- buck," though a crazy craft, " steered incomparably well," and on the 19th the gale abated. On the 25th they saw a large number of fish and birds, which made them think they must be near land, and on the 30th more of them, so that at midnight they sounded, and " had forty-five fathoms, coarse sand and small white shells." Next day they saw Australia, and coasted along it, looking for a nice sheltered bay.[1] On August 6th, in the morning, Dampier spotted a promising opening in the land, and nosed his way in, the ship's boat going ahead with the lead, and sounding. Dampier called the mouth of this great sound (for such it turned out to be) " Shark's Bay," on account of the number of sharks they saw in the water. It has retained the name to this day—and I understand that the bathing is still regarded as dangerous !

He appears to have anchored in the bay now named after him, to the north-east of the Peron Peninsula. He went ashore with some of his men, " with pickaxes and shovels," to dig for water, but found none. This was a vexation, for their barrels were nearly empty. Otherwise the appearance of the land was attractive, with many fragrant trees and shrubs, and " some very small flowers growing on the ground that were sweet and beautiful, and for the most part unlike any I had seen elsewhere." Among the animals he noted " a sort of raccoons, different from those of the West Indies, chiefly as to their legs, for these have very short fore-legs, but go jumping upon them as the others do (and like them are very good meat)." This has been taken as an early description of the kangaroo, but as Mr. Masefield suggests, it is more likely to refer to the kangaroo-rat, which is fairly common in those parts. The shore was lined thick with " very strange and beautiful shells," of which Dampier immediately made a collection, but subse-

---

[1] Hughes, the master, could perceive " neither trees nor bushes " on the land, which " promises very barren."

quently lost it. They caught turtle ; and sharks, too,
which "our men eat very savourily."   In one shark's
stomach they found the head of a hippopotamus—and
that too they ate ! On August 11th they ventured
farther into the bay, narrowly avoiding many shoals,
and still without any luck in the matter of fresh
water.

Two days later Dampier gave it up.   Leaving Shark's
Bay, he began to feel his way northward along the
coast.   Had he turned south at this point, two or three
days' sail would have brought him to the site of the
modern Port Gregory, and another two days to Perth
and Fremantle.   It is a tantalizing reflection ; but we
have to remember that his instructions were to go north.
He doubted, too, whether his "heartless" men would
have been able to stand the "winter weather" which
they must have met with in the south ; and he, for his
own part, confesses that he "was not for spending my
time more than was necessary in the higher latitudes,
as knowing that the land there could not be so well
worth the discovering as the parts that lay nearer the
Line and more directly under the Sun."   Here is the
"warm voyage" complex again.   That early trip to
Newfoundland had a lot to answer for.

On the 21st they found themselves among a group of
islands which must have been those now called the
Dampier Archipelago.   Our navigator here hazards the
guess that "from what he saw of the tides" there might
be a passage hereabouts right through New Holland to
the South Seas, and adds that he thought seriously of
attempting it after his return from New Guinea, whither
he was now bound, according to plan.   He was only
drawing a bow at a venture, of course ; but this theory
of Australian geography had its supporters in Europe
for many years afterwards.   At the moment it was not
practical politics to pursue the matter.   There was an

instant and urgent need of water. The sun blazed down upon them ; " the rocks looked of a rusty yellow colour and I despaired of getting water on any of them." Again he went personally on shore with the shovel and pick party. No good ! On the 23rd he left the islands, still with " fair clear weather," and continued his search along the mainland. Hughes notes " an abundance of small flies which annoyed our people very much in tickling their faces and buzzing about their ears."

A week later, while ten or eleven men were on shore, digging for water under the supervision of their commander, groups of blacks appeared, and began to make hostile demonstrations. At last Dampier took two men with him, and, leaving the rest digging (with their weapons close at hand), walked casually along the beach. His idea was to lure the blacks to follow him, so that he might seize one of them, and endeavour through him to establish friendly relations and get some information about water. Nothing, in fact, could be more eloquent of the courage of English seamen of those days and of the contempt in which they held the " native." Dampier's device succeeded. The farther he got from the rest of his men, the more the aborigines crowded upon him, and the more truculent became their demeanour. When they were quite close, Dampier and his two companions suddenly dashed at them. He observes " We could easily outrun them " : I rather wonder if that would be true to-day.

The blacks fled. But as Dampier was just about to grasp his quarry, he glanced over his shoulder, and saw that a number of the fugitives had turned at bay, and were fiercely assailing one of his companions with their " wooden lances." The young sailor, who was thus attacked, defended himself with his cutlass, but the blacks were all round him. Dampier, coming up, began firing his musket over their heads to frighten them. It

did, at first, but seeing that no harm was done, they
" soon learnt to despise it, tossing up their hands and
crying ' Pooh ! Pooh ! Pooh ! ' " To save his fol-
lower, who was wounded in the face by a lance, Dampier
then shot one of them down ; whereupon the rest drew
off, and the Englishmen retired to their main body,
Dampier very gloomy, and " sorry for what had happened." He observes once again that the Australian
aborigines " have the most unpleasant looks and the
worst features of any people that ever I saw, though I
have seen great variety of savages." In fact, he finds
them " the same blinking creatures " described in
Chapter VII.

So the unfruitful search went on. They found " a
little brackish water "—no more. They also met the
dingo—" 2 or 3 beasts like hungry wolves, lean like so
many skeletons, being nothing but Skin and Bone." It
was now the beginning of September, and the men were
" growing scorbutic " for lack of water and fresh food.
They were in the modern slang term " fed up " with
Australia. " If it were not," says Dampier, " for that
sort of pleasure which results from the Discovery even
of the barrenest spot upon the Globe, this coast of New
Holland would not have charmed me much." It is
clear that he fully intended to come back and have
another shot at it ; he explains that he " thought to
come round by the south of Terra Australis in my return
back which would be in the Summer season there."
But in the meantime he could not see his men die of
thirst. He therefore drew off from the land, and set
his course for the island of Timor. And so he bade
farewell to Australia.

The curious thing is that, though there was every
practical reason for his decision, he seems to have been
dimly aware that he was making a mistake. He hung
about the coast as though reluctant to leave. He

writes : " This large and hitherto almost unknown tract of land is situated so very advantageously in the richest climates of the world . . . that *in coasting round it, which I designed by this voyage if possible*, I could not but hope to meet with some fruitful lands, Continent or Island, or both." Alas, though he did not know it, it was now too late. But this much, at least, may be said, that he had already left his mark upon the map. Nothing more was discovered of the western and north-western coasts of Australia until a hundred years after Dampier's death.

I do not propose to describe the rest of his voyage in detail. There is no controversy about it ; we have no record but his own, and the Master's Log. He steered for the island of Timor, on his way to New Guinea, where he expected to make some important discoveries— and he was not disappointed. After a rather doubtful reception from the Dutch authorities at Fort Concordia on Timor [1] (they had recently suffered at the hands of a French privateer, and mistook the " Roebuck " for one of the same kidney), he " jogged on " from island to island, taking in fresh food and water, which soon restored his men to health. Returning to Timor, he repaired his ship's sides, which, owing to the " ignorance and waste " of his carpenter were in a deplorable state for want of pitch. On the 4th and 5th of November, they fired a number of guns " in honour of King William and in memory of the Deliverance from the Powder Plot "—which so much alarmed the Dutch in Fort Concordia that they sent to find out what it was all about. Everything was explained, and Anglo-Dutch relations now became pleasanter. Dampier even dined with the Governor. But he knew that the Dutch in their hearts were " enemies to all Europeans but such as are under

[1] The date of the arrival at Timor (September 22nd) is given only in the Master's Log, which is very useful about here.

their own Government," and he was glad to get away north again towards New Guinea.

On January 1st, 1700, the southern coast of New Guinea came in sight—a " pleasant prospect " with " tall flourishing trees " and " very green." They began to coast round the island towards the west, with the intention of investigating its northern shores. Dampier was particularly anxious to get in touch with the natives ; but though two large canoes came off, and there was much futile shouting and making of signs between the two parties, neither could make the other understand, and the natives presently returned to the beach. Dampier himself followed them in a boat, and though he could see hundreds of them " lying in ambush behind the bushes," he approached close enough to throw some " knives and other toys " ashore. This did the trick. The natives emerged from their hiding-places, casting aside their weapons, and soon the deck of the " Roebuck " was like a market-place, " roots and fruits " being bartered for " toys " and brandy. Rounding the north-western end of New Guinea, Dampier picked out one of the most attractive looking islands of the Waiang group, and went ashore there, and named it after King William, solemnly drinking his Majesty's health.

He then turned east along the northern coast of New Guinea, naming Little Providence and other islands—in fact the map is very largely his about here. The natives were more " difficult " than ever. At one place they began to stone the ship, using powerful slings for the purpose, so that Dampier, generally so patient with them, was provoked into firing a shot which wounded several. At Antony Caen's island, " the bays were covered with men going along as we sailed." Many tried to swim off to the ship, but were left astern. Others followed in dug-outs. Yet only three were brave enough to come on board ! Hughes describes the

M

natives as "lusty, raw-boned men," with their bodies painted in "several colours" ; but "the chiefest thing I admired was their having large holes through their noses, having through them crabs' claws, white shells and painted shells, which made them look very gashly."

Steering over to the mainland again, Dampier at first supposed himself to be still off the coast of New Guinea, as all the maps of those days indicated. In reality he had discovered the large island of New Britain. He describes St. George's Channel, which divides New Britain in two, as a " bay " ; but it has kept the name of St. George, which he gave it, ever since. The natives continued shy. They would accept the hatchets and looking-glasses offered to them by the Englishmen, and then fail to return with the cocoanuts or pork which were to be given in exchange. When the English approached their villages they fled to the jungle, so Dampier coolly appropriated a number of their fishing nets as a " recompense " for his " toys." Then he very foolishly allowed some of his men to go ashore without him, and of course there was a row, and several natives injured, and " images " (gods) stolen from their shrines, and a dozen or more fine fat pigs brought on board. Dampier, still anxious to be friends, immediately sent a canoe to the beach with six knives, six looking-glasses, a bunch of beads and four glass bottles, which his men spread out " to the best advantage," and then came away. He meant it well, but how shall a man be repaid for the loss of his gods !

The " Roebuck " was now approaching Dampier Strait, which divides New Britain from New Guinea. Its discovery was the most important achievement of the voyage. Dampier soon realized this, and was vexed that a sudden indisposition kept him so much to his cabin. However, he was able to look around him, and to name the great island to the north Nova Britannia

(New Britain), and another smaller one after Sir George Rook, who was one of the Lords of the Admiralty, and had served with him nearly thirty years before as a lieutenant on the " Royal Prince " in the Dutch War.

One night as he lay in his cabin, the chief mate roused him to come on deck and see a " burning hill " on an island near at hand.[1] " All night," says Dampier, " it vomited Fire and Smoke very amazingly, and at every Belch we heard a dreadful noise like Thunder, and saw a Flame of Fire, the most terrifying that ever I saw . . . and then might be seen a great Stream of Fire, running down to the foot of the island, even to the shore."   Ill as he was, he had not lost his gift of description.

The morale of the " Roebuck's " crew was now better than it had ever been, and as far as his men were concerned, Dampier might have sailed on to the S.E. until he came to those farther shores of Australia, which to-day are crowded with flourishing cities and attracting their thousands of immigrants from Europe every year.   But the poor old " Roebuck " herself was in such a condition that, if he had done so, he would never have lived to tell the tale.   It was necessary to get back to some port where her leaking sides could be repaired. He returned, therefore, by the way he had come, all round the coast of New Guinea, and set his course across the Banda Sea.   It was an uneventful voyage.   Off Ceram Island, they spoke a Dutch sloop, on board of which there was a Malayan merchant, who told them that about six months previously the Governor of Bencoolen (Dampier's old enemy) had " either died or was killed," and that an English skipper of one of the ships then in harbour had succeeded to his post.   They

---

[1] Mr. Masefield suggests that it may have been the small volcano on Ritter Island in Dampier Strait, which is still active.   Hughes gives its position, but he is not sufficiently accurate in these matters to enable us to say with certainty which island he means.

put into port at Batavia, and lay there till the 17th October, 1700, refitting for the long voyage home.

That voyage was like a nightmare. The ship could hardly be kept afloat. Dampier even forgets to give us his usual description of the places visited—an eloquent testimony to his state of mind. They were at the Cape on the 30th December, at St. Helena on the 2nd February, and on the 22nd February were off the island of Ascension, where " we sprung a leak which increased so that the chain pump could not keep the ship free." With the help of the hand pump, however, they managed to get into harbour where they could look for the leak. Dampier blames the carpenter's mate, whose efforts only seemed to make matters worse. All hands were called to the pumps, and, heartened with " some drams to comfort them," they worked magnificently. But the water still increased. They had to give it up. They warped in close to the land, and made a raft " to carry the men's chests and bedding ashore." They also landed some bags of rice and water ; but Dampier complains that many of his books and papers were lost.

He says little of the sinking of the " Roebuck," but it must have been a dismal sight for them as they sat on this bleak, uninhabited island, watching the old ship settle down to her undignified grave in three fathoms of water. Did Dampier's dreams sink with her—with this first important command of his ? I think not. He does not give the impression of having cared about command for its own sake—but only for the greater mobility it gave him as an explorer. In his heart he probably cursed the " Roebuck," as he watched her sink, because she had not carried him further. But there is no word in his diary to suggest that he felt himself in any way to blame for what had happened. He was not disillusioned, only angry—and rather hungry—like his crew.

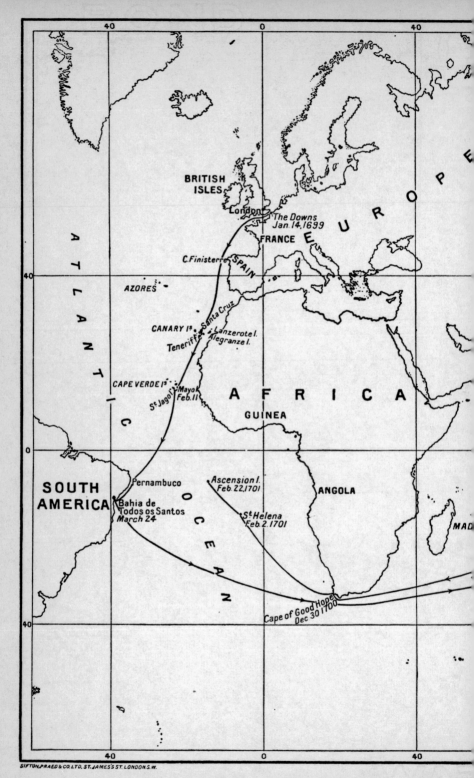

The Downs
Jan. 14, 1699

C. Finisterre

AZORES

CANARY Is. Santa Cruz
Teneriffe Lanzerote I.
Alegranze I.

CAPE VERDE Is.
St. Jago I. Mayo I.
Feb. 11

GUINEA

Pernambuco
Bahia de
Todos os Santos
March 24

Ascension I.
Feb. 22, 1701

St. Helena
Feb. 2, 1701

ANGOLA

Cape of Good Hope
Dec. 30 1700

BRITISH
ISLES

London

FRANCE

SPAIN

EUROPE

AFRICA

SOUTH
AMERICA

ATLANTIC

OCEAN

SIFTON, PRAED & CO. LTD. ST. JAMES'S ST. LONDON S.W.

MAP ILLUSTRATING THE

A

S

I

A

40

INDIA

CHINA

JAPAN

Ceylon

PHILIPPINE
ISLANDS

Sumatra

Borneo

Waiang Is

New Britain

S! George's. Chan.

0

DIAN

Batavia

Banda Sea

New
Guinea

Dampier Str.
Apr 26.1700

June 30,1700   JAVA

Timor

Port Concordia
Sep

Dampier Land

Dampier Arch°

CEAN

Dampier Bay
SharksBay
Aug.6.1699

AUSTRALIA

NEW
ZEALAND

40

F H.M.S. 'ROEBUCK'

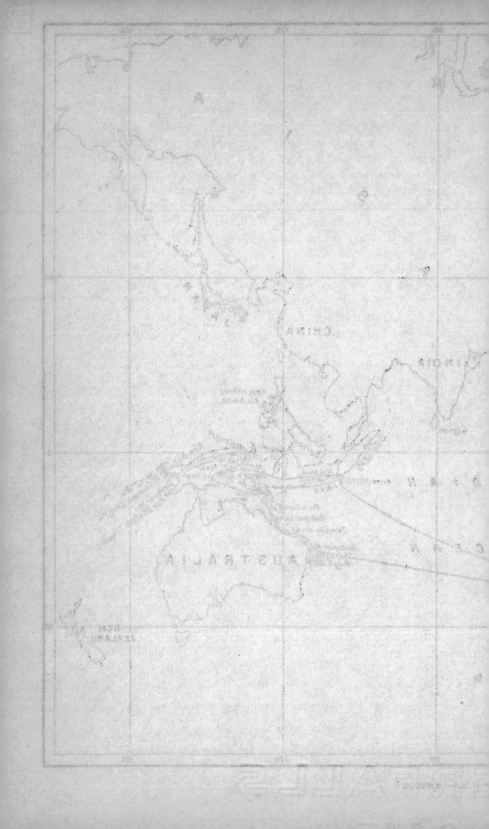

However, they found turtles to eat, which many a stay-at-home Englishman might envy them—and places in the hollow rocks where they could shelter from the weather. And on the 3rd April, after five weeks of this Robinson Crusoe existence, four ships came into harbour, and took them off. These were three men of war, the " Anglesey," the " Hastings " and the " Lizard," and one East Indiaman, the " Canterbury." Dampier at first went on board the " Anglesey," with most of his men ; but on the 8th May the King's ships bore away for Barbadoes, " and I being desirous to get to England as soon as possible took my passage in the ship ' Canterbury,' accompanied with my Master, Purser, Gunner and three of my superior officers." He probably had some inkling that trouble was brewing at home.

CHAPTER X

HE IS COURT-MARTIALLED BUT GETS ANOTHER COMMAND

THERE is no incident in Dampier's career that throws a more vivid light upon his character, and upon the whole manner of life on shipboard in those times, than the court-martial which followed upon his return to England after the loss of the " Roebuck." And the fact that his principal biographer, Rear-Admiral Smyth, moved by some strange obstinacy, denied that any such court-martial had ever taken place (whereas the minutes and all relevant documents are available at the Public Record Office), while that very readable short biography by Mr. Clark Russell in the " English Men of Action " series simply ignores it, is one of the principal reasons why a new biography of Dampier was due to be written.

Enemies had been busy in England for some time, while Dampier and his company were exploring the coasts of New Holland, straightening out the map of New Guinea, and being shipwrecked on Ascension Island. In those days they did not prepare public receptions for returning explorers who had lost their ships. They prepared courts-martial instead. And Lieutenant Fisher, who had been in England since December, 1699, had seen that the case for the prosecution] was well worked up. Dampier had, in fact, to face a whole series of inquiries. In regard to the first, which was simply the ordinary and inevitable investigation into the loss of one of the King's ships, the " Roebuck," Fisher's evidence, happily for Dampier, had no relevance, since he was not present at the time. The Court had before it the evidence of Dampier himself, of Hughes, the master, of the boatswain's mate, of two of the seamen, and of the unfortunate carpenter's mate (whom everyone blamed). Dampier mentions that he had no carpenter on board except this man, Penton ; and Hughes confirms Dampier's account, quoted in the last chapter, adding that he heard the captain say that he " never was in any ship where we cutt for leakes, but I am no carpenter, therefore desire you that understand it to use your utmost endeavour to stop it." It is obvious that this cutting away of timber to get at the leak accelerated the inrush of water. Penton in his evidence merely says that " we sprung a grate leak," and could not stop it. This inquiry was held on the 29th September, 1701. No verdict is recorded, but the evidence is all one way, and we may safely presume that Dampier was honourably acquitted.

But Lieutenant Fisher had not allowed the grass to grow under his feet. He must have written a dozen or more letters to the Lords of the Admiralty, beginning with his first petition while still a prisoner at Bahia, continuing from on board ship, from Lisbon, where he was first landed on his way home, and from different addresses in England, almost up to the date of the trial. Dampier, for his part, had taken the precaution, while in harbour at Bahia, of forwarding to the Admiralty six separate versions of his quarrel with Fisher, written by supporters of his—Hughes, Chadwick, Rumbold, John Knight, Paine the gunner and Watson the carpenter. He also put in a formal petition addressed to him at Bahia, over the signatures of the master, the gunner, the carpenter and the boatswain, expressing their " unanimous opinion " that " it is not safe or expedient to carry him (Fisher) on your designed voyage," as he would certainly endeavour to stir up a mutiny.

After his return to England, Fisher induced the widow of the boatswain, Norwood, who had died at Barbadoes, following the escape from Ascension Island, to petition the Admiralty, claiming that her husband's death was due to the severity of his treatment by Dampier, who had kept him in confinement on board ship for a period of four months. It will be remarked that Fisher himself had been the first to quarrel with Norwood. On the evidence of the " Roebuck's " surgeon, who said that the illness which eventually killed the boatswain had been present in his system long before his imprisonment, and moreover that he had been at liberty no less than ten months and in moderately good health before it reappeared and made an end of him, the Court acquitted Dampier on this charge. Dampier complained that he never heard of it until just before the court-martial met.

Another old enemy of Fisher's was the seaman Grigson [1] (or Gregson). This man deserted the " Roebuck " at Bahia, after a quarrel with the purser, and, going to see Fisher in prison, the latter induced him to write a letter to the Admiralty, in which he pleaded that, though a deserter, he should have his wages paid to him on account of the behaviour of the captain and officers of the " Roebuck." According to him, the master was quite incompetent, and, more often than not, drunk ; while Dampier is represented as little better than an imbecile, who never knew within fifty leagues where they were, nor ventured to take charge of the ship in the master's absence. When Grigson complained to him of the master, he " seemed to tacke no notis of itt."

[1] See page 159. Hughes calls him a " midshipman."

Grigson adds : " I believe it was through ignorance, for I have known him some years and did always think I should find him to be a very ignorant man." The court-martial ignored Grigson's charges ; and the extraordinary thing is that Fisher, although he had got this letter out of him, and though they were comrades in distress at Bahia and came home together, pursued the man with implacable animosity, petitioning the Admiralty again and again to have him arrested, and trumping up new charges, as that he had offered to turn Roman Catholic at Bahia, and spoken " traitorous and villainous words " against King William III, and so forth. The Admiralty seems to have ignored these charges, too.

After all, there was only one serious point in the whole case, and this must have been very clear in the minds of Sir Clowdisley Shovell, the President of the court-martial, Vice-Admiral Hopson and the rest, when they went on board H.M.S. " Royall Souveraine " at Spithead on June 8th, 1702. The point was this : was Dampier justified in his treatment of Fisher at Bahia ? Fisher may have been a poisonous fellow, it may have been true that no voyage of exploration could have succeeded with him on board ; but the question was whether he had done anything which justified his captain in thrusting a commissioned officer into a dirty Portuguese jail, and leaving him there (as it appeared) without any means of subsistence for himself and the two sailors with him, while the ship sailed away. Judged by the buccaneers' code, no doubt, Dampier had treated his lieutenant very lightly ; under Sawkins or Read, Fisher would have been left, not in a jail, but on the beach of the nearest desert island, to starve at his leisure. But this was one of the King's ships. Fisher held the King's commission ; he was a gentleman, and had been an enthusiastic Whig volunteer ; and I cannot help thinking that the members of the court-martial were unconsciously influenced in their decision by the difference in the records of the two men.   Here is their verdict :

" The Court . . . is of opinion that Captain William Dampier has been guilty of very Hard and Cruel Usage towards Lieutenant Fisher, in beating him aboard ye sd. ship, and confining him in Irons a considerable time, and afterwards imprisoning him on shore in a strange country, and itt is resolved that itt does not appear to the Court by ye evidence that there has been any grounds for this ill usage of him, and that the sd. Captain Dampier falls under ye 33rd Article for these his irregular proceedings, and that the Court does adjudge that Hee be fined all his pay to the Chest at Chatham . . . and itt is farther the opinion of ye Court that the said Captain Dampier is not a fitt person to be employ'd as Commdr. of any of Her Majesty's ships."

Well, there it is.   Sir Clowdisley Shovell saw the witnesses ; I did not.   But I have read the evidence carefully, and can only say that Fisher must have been a very good witness indeed (which you would never suspect from the rambling, irresponsible, abusive tone of his letters) and Dampier a very bad one—which again you would not guess from the clear incisive style of his books.   But, as I have said before, he was always a poor controversialist.   One thing is certain, that the morale of the " Roebuck's " crew improved from the moment Fisher left, and that Dampier's important discoveries in Australia and New Guinea would never have been made if his enemy had remained on board.

The verdict did Dampier no harm.   Whether because there was some doubt in official circles as to the justice of the decision, or for some other reason which we do not know, he was reinstated in a new command with quite startling promptitude.   Just ten months after Sir

Clowdisley Shovell and the other officers had pronounced him unfit to command any of Her Majesty's ships, we read in the *London Gazette*[1] that "Captain William Dampier, being prepared to depart on another voyage to the West Indies, had the honour to kiss Her Majesty's hand, being introduced by His Royal Highness, the Lord High Admiral."[2]

This almost looks like an official snub for the members of the court-martial. In one respect, however, the situation had changed very much in Dampier's favour. The War of the Spanish Succession had broken out, in which France and Spain were our enemies, and, in every port on the southern coast, English privateers were being fitted out to prey upon French and Spanish commerce. In these circumstances, the services of a man like Dampier could hardly be refused. The allegation of his enemies that he was incapable of navigating a ship can never have been taken seriously. The court-martial, as we have seen, ignored them. On the contrary, there was no officer afloat better acquainted with those seas in which the rich commerce of Spain lay open to attack. So that when the owners of the privateer, "St. George," of twenty-six guns and carrying a crew of 120 men, then lying in the Downs, wished to appoint Dampier as her commander, official approval was promptly forthcoming.

It must have been a busy scene in the Downs, and we can well believe that many of Dampier's old companions, many hard-bitten ex-buccaneers, were on the look-out for a job—and getting it without much difficulty too. Lying next to the St. George was another privateer, the "Fame" (Captain John Pulling), and it was intended that the two ships should sail in company to the West Indies. They were well supplied with " warlike stores "

[1] *London Gazette*, No. 3906.
[2] Prince George of Denmark.

and victualled for nine months, and "had commissions from H.R.H. the Lord High Admiral to proceed in warlike manner against the French and Spaniards." They also obtained an official "protection" against the naval press-gangs, then busy in all the ports.[1] On board the "St. George" was a steward named William Funnell, to whom we are indebted for the only description of this voyage which we possess.

Dampier, for some reason, had ceased to keep a journal. It is true he lost all his papers in the course of this voyage, but apparently there was no diary among them. His record of the "Roebuck" adventure was the last that he ever wrote. William Funnell is an amusing enough writer, and so far as his facts can be checked he seems to be fairly reliable, except where his captain is concerned. He disliked Dampier, and always tries to represent his conduct in the worst possible light. That is a disadvantage, of course ; but we have Dampier's hurriedly written *Vindication*, which he produced after he had seen Funnell's book, and a further *Answer to the Vindication*, by one John Welbe, a midshipman, who takes Funnell's side. Between the three of them, we get a fairly clear idea of the chief incidents of the voyage. But Dampier's dramatic little touches, Dampier's natural eloquence and his powers of observation are sadly missing.

The "St. George" left the Downs unaccompanied, after all. There had been a disagreement between the owners and those of the "Fame," and Pulling had gone off on his own account.[2] Funnell gives us a foretaste of his defects as an historian by alleging that Pulling's

---

[1] *Acts of the Privy Council : Colonial Series.*

[2] He went to Bermuda, and there (in August, 1703) caused a mild sensation by getting his ship blown up in harbour, owing to "the carelessness of one of the Purser's servants," who was "drawing brandy in the Lazaretto" with a lighted candle in his hand, and so started a fire.

departure was the result of a personal quarrel with
Dampier. As a matter of fact, Dampier was up in
London at the time.[1] Funnell says that the plan was
to proceed first to the River Plate, and seize " two or
three Spanish galleons," and " if by that expedition we
go to the value of £600,000 "—an incredible sum—
" then to return again without proceeding further."
They must have expected these galleons to be literally
made of gold ! The truth seems to be that Dampier
had a roving commission to do very much as he liked,
and that nothing was definitely decided upon. They
sailed on April 30th, 1703, and anchored off Kinsale
on the 18th May. Here they were joined by the
" Cinque Ports " galley, a small ship of about 90 tons,
carrying sixteen guns, and a crew of sixty-three men,
commanded by Captain Charles Pickering.

They sailed to Madeira, and thence to the Cape Verde
Islands, sighting St. Iago on October 7th. Funnell
seems to have been unfortunate in his relations with the
inhabitants, whose characteristics he describes with much
bitterness. The natives here, he says, were formerly
Portuguese, banished thither for " murthers, thefts and
other villainies." They " are now mostly black " by
intermarriage with women slaves, but " though they
have changed their colour, they have retained their vices."

[1] Moreover, before his death, he showed himself a good friend of
Pulling's (or Pullein's) by procuring for his son, Henry Pulling, the
appointment of chief adviser to Lord Orford " in settling the South Sea
Company." On April 30th, 1715 (a month after Dampier's death),
Thomas Pulling was petitioning the Privy Council, complaining that
whereas the previous holder of this post had been fourteen years in
office and " procured himself a very good estate," his son Henry, who
had succeeded " on the recommendation of Mr. Dampier, the famous
voyager," was to be superseded almost as soon as he had established
himself " at vast expense," and long before he had had time to feather
his nest in the approved eighteenth-century manner. *Acts of the Privy
Council : Colonial Series* (unbound papers).

" They will take your Hat off your Head at noonday, although you be in the midst of company."

Here broke out the first of those inevitable quarrels, which must, unfortunately, be recognized as a normal feature of life on ships commanded by Dampier—as indeed on most ships at this time.[1]   Once again the central figure was the lieutenant, this time an officer named Huxford.   We may accept Dampier's statement that Huxford and Morgan (who was purser and owner's agent) went ashore and fought a duel, whereupon the local Portuguese Governor clapped Huxford under arrest. Later he came on board again, and then, according to Funnell and Welbe, Dampier thrust him on shore with his chest and clothes and servant, and sailed away, leaving him to perish miserably, " partly from hunger." Welbe tells how the unfortunate lieutenant begged not to be turned ashore " among a parcel of banditties and negroes," saying that " he would be contented to lie in the longboat and go before the mast, rather than go ashore among a parcel of Heathen."   Dampier's excuses are unconvincing.   It is plain that in spite of his painful experience at the court-martial, he was unable to break himself of the buccaneer's trick of marooning troublesome men.

On November 2nd the " St. George " and the " Cinque Ports " crossed the Equator, and three weeks later anchored off Isla Grande, a small Brazilian island near the modern town of Rio de Janeiro.   Funnell attempts to fix the position of this island, but his observations are hopelessly at fault.   He also essays a few natural history notes, which are in amusing contrast with the careful records his captain had formerly kept.   Of the boobies he writes : " They are so silly that when they are weary

[1] It would be easy to multiply examples of ships of the period worse disciplined than Dampier's ; but I do not want to excuse his chief failing by showing how common it was among lesser men.

of flying they will, if you hold out your hand, come and sit upon it : from thence I conjecture that they are called boobies."

Here Captain Pickering, of the " Cinque Ports," died, and his lieutenant, Thomas Stradling, succeeded to the command.   Here also there may have been a quarrel between Dampier and his new lieutenant, Huxford's successor, which resulted in the latter's going ashore, taking eight of the crew with him ; but we have only Funnell's vague account of this incident, to which neither Dampier nor Welbe refers.   I cannot help doubting whether it ever happened.   They steered south for Cape Horn, and on the way one of the men died, and hiς things were put up for auction.   The prices are interesting : " A chest value five shillings was sold for £3 ; a pair of shoes value four shillings and sixpence sold for 31 shillings ; half a pound of thread value 2 shillings sold for 17 shillings and sixpence."   They rounded the Horn, and on February 7th sighted the island of Juan Fernandez (which Funnell pretends that Dampier was unable to recognize).   Here they found the " Cinque Ports " already at anchor.

The three weeks' stay at this island was a happy time for William Funnell.   He enjoyed himself among the " sea-Lyons," of which there were many on the island. The ordinary way of killing these unfortunate creatures was " to clap a pistol just to his mouth as it stood open, and fire down his throat."   But " if we had a mind to have some sport with him, which we call Lyon-baiting," a party of sailors armed with half pikes would " prick him to death, which commonly would be a sport for two or three hours before we should conquer him."   So with this " sport " on shore, and with the watering and refitting of their ships, they passed their time at Juan Fernandez.   But Stradling, as though to show that Dampier was not the only " cruel " captain in those parts, had got into such trouble with his crew that no fewer than forty-two of them—that is, more than half— had gone ashore and refused to re-embark. Dampier, from the " St. George," succeeded in making up this quarrel. Funnell, who seldom has a good word for him, remarks that " by the endeavours of Captain Dampier they were again reconciled."

On February 29th, they sighted a French ship, and went in pursuit. She was a powerful vessel of thirty guns, and though the " St. George " and the " Cinque Ports " " fought her very close broadside and broadside for seven hours," they had made little impression upon her when " a small gale " sprang up and enabled her to sheer off. Dampier would not pursue, thinking it a safer game to wait for some fat Spanish galleon ; but in the meantime they had left most of their boats behind at Juan Fernandez, and this rather cramped their activities. Returning to the island to recover them, they saw two large French ships in harbour, and discreetly " stood away for the coast of Peru." Any reader who has followed me through the story of Dampier's cruises in those waters with the buccaneers will appreciate that, without their boats, our privateers were like birds with broken wings. They could capture ships at sea, but they could do no " cutting out," and they could not land armed parties to seize the Spanish coast towns. Off Arica, for instance, which they visited next, and which Dampier knew of old, the best they could do was to hang about outside the harbour, hoping to catch some ship coming out. They chased two of these, but finding them to be Frenchmen (one was the same they had fought off Juan Fernandez) Dampier desisted, though Funnell says his crew were burning for a fight. He stood along the shore to the northward, and presently took a Spanish ship of 150 tons, out of which he removed " a little of everything," and then let her go, " alleging that if he kept her it would be a hind'rance to his greater designs." It seems a reasonable enough explanation, quite in line with the policy of the older " privateers " ; and Dampier adds that he did not, as a matter of fact, possess an officer who was capable of taking charge of a prize—they were " pyrating fellows, rather than true sailors."

Dampier now prepared an ambitious plan of campaign against Santa Maria, the scene of his earlier " golden dreams," it being " the first place they send all their gold to, which they dig out of mines not far from Santa Maria." On their way thither, they captured two small Spanish ships, the first of which they kept. On the second was a Guernsey man, who had been taken prisoner in the Bay of Campeachy, where he was cutting log-wood, and imprisoned in Mexico for two years. He was overjoyed at his rescue. They arrived at the mouth of the river at eight o'clock at night, " having dark rainy weather, with much thunder and lightning, so that we were all very wet and had a most uncomfortable night, for we were forced to lie in all the rain, having no shelter in our little Bark." From which it is clear that they made the expedition against Santa Maria in the Spanish prize they had just captured, leaving the " St. George " and the " Cinque Ports " to cruise off the mouth of the river. At daylight an Indian canoe came near and hailed them, whereupon, says Funnell, " our captain ordered them to be fired at, which was done accordingly." It seems a particularly idiotic order for Dampier to have given, for of course the canoe immediately paddled away to warn the people of Santa Maria. He himself says that he was " very uneasy and troubled " at this gun having been fired, contrary to his orders. One feels that he would have done better with this crew if he had brought that famous cane of his into action more often.

N

Two launches were sent up the river at once, and the barque followed. It was still very dark, but the men in the launches heard dogs barking near the bank, and following this sound they landed, and captured the small town of Schuchadero, which they found deserted by its inhabitants. The barque, missing them in the darkness, went on up the river as far as Santa Maria, but discovered the mistake and returned. In an Indian canoe they found a packet of letters addressed by the Governor of Panama to the Governor of Santa Maria, warning him of an impending attack by 250 " English from Jamaica," and stating that he had sent 400 soldiers to his assistance, with reinforcements to follow. Obviously no time was to be lost, and next day (April 30th) Dampier and Stradling led a party up the river in their launches and one or two captured canoes to attack Santa Maria. They found the Spaniards waiting for them, and blundered into no fewer than three ambuscades. At this point Dampier was for giving up the expedition, pointing out that the Spaniards must have removed everything of value from the town. Apparently Stradling agreed with him, for they returned down the river to their ships, where provisions were now so short that " five green plantains were boiled for every six men." The attempt had been a fiasco.

At twelve o'clock that night, however, as they lay huddled in their hammocks, trying to forget their troubles, the luck suddenly changed. A tall ship appeared off the mouth of the river—she was, in fact, a Spanish " great ship " of 550 tons—and approaching noiselessly through the mist, dropped anchor just beside the English privateers, whose nationality she had not suspected. Rousing themselves at the sight of this easy prey, the privateers were into their boats and over the sides of the Spaniard before the astonished dons had realized what was happening. She was " deeply laden with flour, sugar, brandy, wine, and thirty tons of marmalade of quinces," not to mention salt, linen and woollen cloth : so that now they might put out to sea with a good heart in search of further adventure. Funnell complains that this rich prize was never properly "rummaged," and in particular asserts that there were 80,000 dollars hidden somewhere in her hold ; but Dampier, who had interviewed her captain, says he had "evident proof that she landed her money at Truxillo." He must have known more about it than Funnell did ; but it is fair to add that the latter had now been promoted from the rank of steward, and was put on board this new prize with Alexander Selkirk, the mate of the "Cinque Ports." In his *Vindication* Dampier complained that his enemies had suggested that he might have obtained ransom for this ship. He becomes almost incoherent in his rage at this suggestion, referring to his critics among the crew as "a parcel of fellows who were perpetually drunk " ; and we, who can remember his adventures among the buccaneers, and how Sharp and Cook and the rest were continually hanging about Spanish harbours, waiting for ransoms that never came—a fire-ship in the middle of the night was a more likely answer—can understand his wrath.

At Tobago, which they next visited, Dampier and Stradling decided to part. There is again a conflict of evidence : Funnell asserting that the two captains quarrelled, which Dampier indignantly denies. What is certain is that, after leaving Dampier, Stradling sailed south to the island of Juan Fernandez, where he had left five members of his crew, and stores and ammunition. He found them all gone, having been picked up by some French ships. But before leaving there he had a bitter quarrel with his mate, Alexander Selkirk, who insisted on being left alone on the island, rather than sail another day with Stradling. And thereby hangs one of the most famous tales in English literature, for Selkirk, as everybody knows, was the " original " of *Robinson Crusoe*.

Dampier's unhappy voyage continued, the discipline of his crew going steadily from bad to worse. On the 7th June they captured a small ship, and got news from her that the Spaniards had fitted out two men-of-war, one of 32 guns, the other of 36, to cruise in the Bay of Guayaquil in search of the English privateers. And on the 21st they came up with one of these warships and fought with her all day, expending an immense amount of powder and shot, but neither giving nor receiving any serious damage. Funnell boasts that the English fired about 560 shots, to the Spaniards' " 110 or 115," upon which Dampier comments sarcastically that " I do verily believe not 60 ever hit her," and he adds that such waste of ammunition was more than he could stand, so that in the end " I was forced to command 'em to forbear firing." They lay to all night, no doubt squabbling and blaming each other for the failure, and in the morning found that the Spaniard had sailed away. Seeing a Spanish village on shore, Dampier sent in a boat to collect wood and provisions, but " upon one shot fired at 'em they all came running aboard frighted." " And these," he goes on in the same bitter tone, " are the Mighty Bravoes that are fit to set people by the Ears at home, and make Scandal as rife with me as 'tis with them." He accuses Bellhash, the master, Clippington, the mate, Bath, the gunner, and others of being always " on the watch to overset the voyage," of cheating the owners, and so forth. In fact, he was as tired of his crew as they were of him. With such an " atmosphere " on board, no voyage could be expected to succeed.

The next move was to the Gulf of Nicoya, where Dampier intended to careen his ship, and repair her bottom. Dampier and the carpenter went among the islands in a canoe, looking for a suitable place, and when they returned to the ship in the evening they brought two turtles with them.   Then, says Funnell, " we went to work, cutting up the turtles, boiling, roasting, frying, baking and stewing, according as each one thought fit." The life of these privateersmen was no doubt full of hardships, but they were at any rate in a position to include real turtle soup in almost every meal !   Having chosen their place, they got the " St. George " in among the islands to a comfortable little anchorage which Dampier had found, " within a stone's cast of the shore all round."   They secured the ship by means of the anchor, and a cable round a tree at the water's edge, and proceeded to make themselves at home.   They set up tents on shore for the cooper and the sailmaker to work in, and others to contain their provisions, which they had removed from the hold of the ship before getting to work at her leaks ;   and those of the men who were not otherwise employed " went ashore often with the Sain (or fishing net) and caught store of fish."   When they came to look at the " St. George," they found her condition deplorable.   To put it vulgarly, Dampier had once again been sold a pup.   Her timbers were even rottener than those of the " Roebuck " ;   her bottom was " eaten like a honeycomb " ;   Funnell asserts that the " firm plank was no thicker than a sixpence," so that in places " we could thrust our thumbs quite through with ease."   These are obvious exaggerations, but they indicate the kind of gossip that was going on among the crew.   Owing to their failure at the native village mentioned above, they were without suitable timber to repair the ship, and the carpenter was forced to " stop the leaks as well as he could with nails and oakum."

Now Dampier had fitted out one of his small Spanish prizes as a long-boat, and on her he had placed all his ammunition and a part of his provisions while the " St.

George " was being repaired. Here was an obvious opportunity for intending mutineers. Dampier's mate, Clippington, a man of surly and cantankerous temper, had long been dissatisfied, and he seems to have come to the conclusion that it would not be safe to put to sea again in the " St. George." He therefore collected twenty-one other malcontents, and, suddenly boarding the prize, he seized her, and sailed away, taking with him the ammunition and provisions. Dampier and Funnell are agreed about the main facts here, except that the latter tries to excuse Clippington, by saying that he later put some of the ammunition ashore, " that we might not be quite destitute." Welbe tells a very improbable story, to the effect that Dampier formally authorized Clippington's proceedings, saying that he and his friends " might take the barque and go where they pleased, and he would give them arms." This is a palpable falsehood ; for if Dampier in a fit of madness had given Clippington leave to take the arms away, why should the latter have come back again and restored some, as he does in Funnell's story ? Obviously he had a twinge of conscience. And obviously Welbe is a witness who will say almost anything. Clippington, in the " Dragon," afterwards made an adventurous voyage to the East Indies, and, returning to England in 1706, he sailed in company with the well-known privateer commander, Shelvocke, who gives him an extremely bad character. He died about twenty years later, being then in a state of destitution.

Finding himself thus deserted by a considerable portion of his crew, Dampier determined upon one last desperate effort to achieve the kind of success that would restore the morale of the remainder, and send them home to England comparatively rich men. He decided to go for the Manila ship. Accordingly they cruised to the west, having " very dirty squally weather," and on the

9th October they took a small Spanish barque, whose
captain was a Spaniard named Christian Martin, who
had been brought up in London and was actually
cruising in the West Indies with Captain Eaton when
he deserted and entered the service of Spain.   This
man was very useful to Dampier in his search
(we may safely disregard Welbe's allegation that at
this point Dampier deliberately attempted to desert
those of his crew who were in the captured barque) ;
and on the 6th December they at last came in
sight of the Manila ship.   The galleon, with her big
eighteen and twenty-four pounders, could have sunk the
" St. George " with one broadside ; but the privateers
attacked her without hesitation, and the Spaniards, with
their usual incompetence, failed to bring most of their
guns to bear.   Funnell says that Captain Martin advised
Dampier to board at once, and indeed it seemed to be
their only chance ; but Dampier, unfortunately, hesitated, and, while the question was still being debated,
the " St. George " received a shot between wind and
water, whereupon " the signal was made to stand off
from the enemy."   Funnell states these facts without
comment, but Welbe flatly accuses Dampier of cowardice.
When he was urged to " clap her on board," all he
could say was " Where is the canoe ?   Where is the
canoe ? " and he " was for getting into the boat to save
his life."   Dampier blames his crew again, asserting
that the " very man at the helm contradicted my orders,
edg'd her away to leeward once more : at which I
offered to shoot him through the head."   Upon which
the obvious comment is that no really efficient commander (Woodes Rogers, for instance) would ever have
been found arguing the point with the man at the helm.

If the men of the " St. George " had been feeling
discouraged before, they were now in a state of gloom
which must sooner or later lead to mutiny.   The end of

it was that the " St. George " parted company with the
barque, upon which were no fewer than thirty-three of
the men (Funnell and Welbe among them) who were
determined to sail in her for India.   Now, according to
Dampier, guns and provisions for the barque were taken
from him by force.   He says that Bellhash, the master,
" took him by the throat, the rest standing by, and swore
he would dash his brains out if he said a word."   Even
Morgan, the owners' agent, was against him.   A certain
Toby Thomas, one of the officers, and a man whose
personality seems to have irritated Dampier to madness,
approached him at this juncture, and said, " Poor
Dampier, thy case is like King James's, everybody has
left thee."   " That buffoon ! " exclaims Dampier,
shrilly—he can never mention his name without a sneer—
that " never-to-be-forgotten noble Captain Thomas ! "
Funnell and Welbe swear that Dampier agreed to the
departure of the barque, which, as it took four of his
guns, with small arms and ammunition and a large part
of his provisions, seems extremely unlikely.   He did,
however, get rid of Welbe, who, from now on, transfers
his attentions to Morgan, libelling him thoughtfully and
comprehensively in a series of letters to Lord Townshend,
which Mr. Masefield has unearthed.

Thirty-five men departed in the barque, leaving
Dampier with twenty-eight followers and twenty-eight
guns on his crazy craft.   Yet the very shipwreck of his
plans seems to have inspired him with new courage.
While the barque and its mutinous crew set sail for the
East, the " St. George " returned to the coast of South
America, and there they landed and took the town of
Puna, which they ransacked.   It was perhaps the most
successful exploit of the whole voyage ; but in the
absence of Funnell we get no detailed description.   After
the sack of Puna, they put to sea, and presently captured
a Spanish ship, to which they transferred themselves,

leaving the poor old " St. George " a drifting, leaking derelict, to sink at her leisure.   Their subsequent adventures are obscure, but it is known that they sailed in their prize to the Dutch East Indies, where, as Dampier had lost his commission at Puna, they were all arrested and thrown into prison.   How long they remained there is uncertain, but they were eventually released, and Dampier returned to England.

He returned, as usual, not a penny richer than he was when he left.   I say this advisedly, for some years later an action was begun in the Chancery Division against Dampier, Stradling and several other defendants, merchants of Bristol, accusing them of misappropriating the proceeds of this voyage.[1]   Morgan, the owners' agent, is also aimed at, though not " joined " in the action. It is alleged that, on leaving Dampier, he took with him half the booty, sold it at a high profit in Batavia, and on his return to England produced only £600, saying he could get no more.   As for Dampier, the story is that, after his return to England, he and others met " at the Young Devill Tavern, near Temple Bar," and at various private houses, and there conspired together to make a division of the spoil and to use the money to fit out a " second expedition "—Woodes Rogers's.   The " inwardness " of all this is that the plaintiff (a woman) was the heir-at-law of one of those who put money into the unsuccessful " St. George " venture, and now hoped to recoup her estate by claiming a share in that of Woodes Rogers, which was very profitable.   The action was apparently dropped.   Dampier never put a penny into the Woodes Rogers voyage.   He was too late to do so, even if he had possessed the means.   And we happen to know that at the very first port of call he had

---

[1] See Dr. B. M. H. Rogers's account in the *Mariner's Mirror*, 1924, of " some MS. papers lent to me by Mr. F. H. Goldney of Cosham, Wilts."   I shall have occasion to refer to these papers again.

to borrow money in order to provide himself with clothes.[1]

But Dampier, when he landed in England, " broke " once more, found himself in a pleasant enough atmosphere. In spite of the failure of his voyage, and the evidence it afforded of those weaknesses of temperament which always prevented him from being a really successful leader of men, his great reputation as a navigator was unimpaired. His friends stood by him. He was called to London, and presented to the Queen, that he might give her an account of his adventures. And when he had relieved his feelings by writing his *Vindication* in reply to Funnell's book, he found that there was still no lack of openings for him at sea. Englishmen who had twice circumnavigated the globe were rare in those days.

It is at this point, I am well aware, that I shall be expected to. explain what effect these events had upon Dampier's psychology. What, in short, were his " reactions " ? It is a fact that he never held another command, and, so far as we know, never asked for one. Is there significance in that ? Was he beginning to doubt himself at last ? That would be tragedy. Dampier himself was the least introspective of men ; but it is safe to answer for him that he never cared a fig for command—only for exploration and adventure. There is one sign, and one only, that his spirit may be failing him a little ; and that is that he no longer keeps a diary. But his courage and confidence are obviously undiminished. As long as he can continue to get about the world, and continue to enjoy the confidence of his scientific friends in London who appreciate what he is trying to do, he will snap his fingers at the rest.

[1] See page 237.

CHAPTER XI

HE MAKES HIS LAST VOYAGE

F all Dampier's voyages, it is probable that this next one, upon which he was about to set out, was, as Sir Albert Gray suggests, the happiest to himself.

He was now a man of fifty-six, a dark, attractive, brooding figure, the friend of leading scientists, the life-long associate of desperate adventurers—a man with a great and well-established reputation, but one of a kind quite peculiar to himself. He had written the best travel-book in the English language since Hakluyt ; but when it came to travelling, he had too often managed just to miss his goal. Merchant adventurers, as Dampier's critics have suggested, may have begun about this time to look a little askance at him, as an unlucky commander. Yet, in some respects, and those not precisely what we should have expected, his reputation evidently stood higher than ever. The continued support of his scientific friends, Sir Robert Southwell, Sir Hans Sloane and the rest, and the Royal favour which this implied, may have been due to better recognition of his value as a writer on hydrography. His admirable *Discourse on Winds*, it will be remembered, had not left the printers' hands when he sailed from England in the " Roebuck." In his absence it had been read and appreciated, and we can imagine people like Sloane and Southwell, and even

Wren and Newton, pointing out to their friends in the coffee-houses that no other living Englishman was capable of producing this detailed account of the conditions that explorers might expect in so many different parts of the world. They would have been interested, too, in his discoveries on the coast of New Guinea. To us, who know what he so narrowly missed on the adjoining continent of Australia, the voyage of the " Roebuck " may seem a failure ; but to his contemporaries it represented a tremendous advance upon the geographical knowledge of their time ; and geographers were prepared to render due acknowledgment to its author, without troubling themselves about his squabbles with his crews.

In the Spanish West Indies, on the other hand, it was his reputation as a fighting man that had become formidable. He had spent so much time there that every local Spaniard was familiar with his name. Contemporary critics are agreed—whether they like Dampier or not—that his name had become a terror in those waters, unequalled since the days of Morgan and L'Olonois. It may seem absurd to us who know how little of the bloodthirsty swashbuckler there was in his character. It may have seemed absurd to many of his contemporaries, who had sailed with him. But in the history of Woodes Rogers's voyages—not a word of which was written by Dampier himself—we shall find evidence again and again of the fear which he inspired all along the Spanish Main. And it is not to be supposed that the merchant adventurers of England were so ill-informed as to be unaware of this fact. They might hesitate to trust their ships in his unlucky hands, but they would want the help, if they could get it, of his unique knowledge and reputation.

Dampier cannot have been many months in England before he heard of the projected voyage of two Bristol

privateers, under that very able commander, Captain
Woodes Rogers. One of Dampier's biographers (Dr.
Harris)[1] has suggested that the voyage was his own idea.
Writing only thirty years after Dampier's death, when
we might expect a reasonable degree of accuracy in
these matters, Harris says : " He [Dampier] addressed
himself to the Merchants of Bristol, who are justly
reputed the most active and pushing people in this
Nation. They heard his proposals with patience,
examined them with attention, and at last saw so much
of probability in what he offered and such likelihood of
his proving a good pilot, tho' he had been but an unlucky
Captain, that they determined to fit out two ships at
his instance." I wish I could adopt this view of what
happened. Unfortunately we know that the voyage had
already been decided upon, the ship selected, and the
command given to Woodes Rogers before Dampier
returned to England from the East. Woodes Rogers
was a member of a well-known Bristol family. The
merchants who made themselves responsible for the
undertaking were his friends, and to those of them who
were still alive on his return to England, he dedicated
his lively narrative,[2] which is our principal authority for
the events of the voyage. Woodes Rogers had pro-
pounded a definite scheme, and got it accepted, before
Dampier appeared in the matter at all. What Harris
may have had in mind was a passage in another account
of this voyage (the only other one we possess) written
by Captain Edward Cooke, who was second-in-command
on the " Duchess," under Woodes Rogers. Cooke,
speaking of the origin of the voyage, refers to Dampier's
recent failure to take the " Manila or Acapulco ship,"

[1] Dr. John Harris, D.D., F.R.S, author of *A Complete Collection of
Voyages and Travels.* London : 1744.
[2] *A Cruising Voyage Round the World.* By Captain Woodes Rogers.
London, 1712.

and adds : " But the said Captain Dampier never gave
over the project till he had prevailed with some able
persons at Bristol to venture upon an undertaking which
might turn to a prodigious advantage." The truth
seems to be that what Dampier did was to advise the
captain and owners as to the objectives to be aimed at,
the general direction and strategy of the voyage. That
was his sole share in the preliminary organization. It
must have occupied a good deal of his time ; and, as
he was only in England eight or nine months, it probably
accounts for the hurried, clumsy style of his *Vindication*,
which he then wrote in reply to Funnell, whose book
had just appeared.

As to the post which Woodes Rogers offered him—
that of pilot—there is no reason to suppose that he felt
in any way degraded by having to accept it. Woodes
Rogers was his friend (for it may be presumed that this
is the " Captain Rogers " several times referred to in
Dampier's writings), and it was no uncommon thing at
that time for one who had held chief command to sail
afterwards in a minor capacity. There were altogether
five captains on these two ships, three on the " Duke,"
and two on the " Duchess." The composition of the
crews is interesting. They had more than double the
number of officers usual in privateers, and Woodes
Rogers explains that he arranged this on purpose " to
prevent mutinies, which often happen in long voyages,
and that we might have a large provision for a succession
of officers in each ship, in case of mortality." Here is
Woodes Rogers's list of the officers of the " Duke " :

" Woodes Rogers, Captain, a Mariner ; Thomas Dover,
a Doctor of Physick, second Captain, President of our
Council, and Captain of the Marines ; Carleton Vanbrugh, Merchant, now our Owner's Agent ; Robert
Fry, a Mariner, chief Lieutenant ; Charles Pope, second

Lieutenant ; Thomas Glendall, third Lieutenant ; John
Bridge, Master ; William Dampier, Pilot for the South
Seas, who had already been three times there and twice
round the world ; Alexander Vaughan, chief mate ;
Lanc. Appleby, second mate ; John Babet, rated third
mate, but design'd Surgeon, if occasion ; he had been
Captain Dampier's doctor, in his last unfortunate Voyage
round the World ; Samuel Hopkins, being Dr. Dover's
Kinsman, and an Apothecary, was both an Assistant to
him, and to act as his Lieutenant if we landed a party
anywhere under his Command during the Voyage ;
George Underhill and John Parker, two young Lawyers,
design'd to act as Midshipmen ; John Vigor, a Refor-
mado to act as Captain Dover's Ensign when ashore ;
Benj. Parsons and Howel Knethel, Midshipmen ;
Richard Edwards, Coxswain of the Pinnace, to receive
Midshipmen's Pay ; James Wasse, Surgeon ; Charles
May, his mate ; John Lancy, Assistant ; Henry
Oliphant, Gunner, with eight Men called the Gunners'
crew ; Nath. Scorch, Carpenter ; John Jones, his Mate,
with three Assistants ; Giles Cash, Boatswain ; and
John Pillar, his Mate ; John Shepard, Cooper, with
two Assistants ; John Johnson, Thomas Young, Charles
Clovet and John Bowden, all four Quarter-Masters ;
John Finch, late wholesale oileman of London, now
Steward ; Henry Newkirk, Sailmaker ; Peter Vanden-
heude, Smith and Armourer ; William Hopkins, Ship's
Corporal, Capt. Dover's Sergeant, and Cook to the
Officers ; Barth. Burnes, Ship's Cook."

The two young lawyers who were " design'd to act as
Midshipmen," the " Reformado," who would be either
a volunteer or some officer who had been deprived of
his command, but retained his rank, and the " wholesale oileman of London " who—stirred by some prick-
ings of romance, no doubt—had turned ship's steward,

are unusual features of the list. As for Babet, the
Deputy-Surgeon, it is interesting to note that Dampier,
in his recently published *Vindication*, had asserted that
only one of all his officers of the " St. George " had
stood by him when Funnell and the rest deserted with
the barque, and that one was the " doctor "—no doubt
John Babet. It is pleasant to think that Dampier was
able to help him to further employment.

As for the men, one-third of them were foreigners
and the rest, in Woodes Rogers's words, " tailors,
tinkers, peddlars, fiddlers and haymakers "—anything,
in fact, but seamen. Yet they seem to have taken very
kindly to the sailor's way of life, for when the " Duke "
and " Duchess " put into Cork, their first port of call,
Woodes Rogers found his crew " continually marrying "
the girls on shore. He particularly mentions a Dane,
who was " coupled by a Romish priest to an Irish
Woman, without understanding a word of each other's
language, so that they were forced to use an interpreter."
What struck Woodes Rogers as curious was that, when
they left Cork, " this pair seemed more afflicted at the
separation than any of the rest." " The fellow continued
melancholy for several days " ; whereas the others would
" drink their cans of flip " (a sort of hot punch made of
beer and spirits) to the last moment, and then " part
unconcerned."

They had sailed from Bristol on August 2nd, 1708,
Woodes Rogers himself being on the " Duke," a ship
of 320 tons, carrying 30 guns and 117 men ; and
Captain Stephen Courtney commanding the " Duchess,"
which was of 260 tons, 26 guns and 108 men. But on
neither of these crowded ships, says Woodes Rogers,
were there more than twenty real sailors. However he
was nothing if not an optimist, and he looked to get some
useful hands in Cork. On the way there he gave a
taste of his quality by administering a sound thrashing

to an incompetent local pilot, who had sought to lead them into the wrong bay. At Cork there seems to have been something like a rush to join the ships, for Captain Cooke in his book gives their numbers upon leaving that port as 170 men on the " Duke," and 151 on the " Duchess." Indeed Woodes Rogers says that they were " pestered " with applications. It may be noted here that genuine privateering (as distinguished from piracy) was now a more paying proposition than it had been when Dampier sailed in the " St. George," for an Act of Parliament had been passed abolishing the Government's share of one-fifth of the prize money, and transferring whole interest to the owners and crew.

On the morning of September 1st, they sailed from Cork in company with H.M.S. " Hastings " and a convoy of about twenty merchantmen. At first there was considerable confusion on board, " as is usual in privateers at setting out," but Woodes Rogers quickly restored things to order. On the 5th he and Courtney assembled their crews, and for the first time disclosed to them the ambitious design of the voyage, from which they could hardly expect to return in less than three years. It must have been a shock to some of them, but Woodes Rogers had a great " way with him." On board the " Duke " there was no protest of any kind, " except from one fellow who expected to have been tything-man that year in his parish, and said his wife would be obliged to pay forty shillings in his absence : but seeing all the rest willing he was easily quieted, and all hands drank to a good voyage."

So far, so good, but Woodes Rogers now found himself in a difficult position. He knew he must encounter cold weather in rounding Cape Horn ; but as none of his men had been aware of his true destination, they were " but meanly clad " for such a voyage. There are two methods of keeping sailormen warm off the Horn : by

o

giving them warm clothes or by strong liquor ; and as Woodes Rogers shrewdly remarks, " Good liquor to sailors is preferable to clothing." But in this case the stock of liquor also was running low. It was a question, therefore, whether it would not be advisable to put in to Madeira—a name of high standing in this connection —before proceeding any farther, and there procure such a supply of the generous wines of that country as would ensure that the shivering crews would at any rate feel warm inside when they reached the colder latitudes.

Woodes Rogers therefore called a committee meeting of officers on board the " Duke " ; and as this is the first of those discussions, of which we shall hear so much before we have done with this voyage, it is necessary to say a word about the somewhat unusual " constitution " which had been drawn up, with the owners' approval, before the vessels sailed. In that document it was laid down that all " attempts, attacks and designs upon the enemy " should first be discussed in committee of the officers, and the same applied to all " discontents, differences or misbehaviour." Woodes Rogers, though a notably masterful man who cannot have enjoyed being contradicted, carried the principle even further than this. On all important occasions he would call a committee meeting ; and even when nothing particular was happening he would sometimes assemble his officers and get them to sign a kind of general testimonial, stating that they agreed with everything that had been done up to date. He declares that without this rather tedious method of procedure " we could never have performed the voyage," and, remembering the intractability of most crews at that time, we can well believe it.

Dampier's signature appears under the minutes of practically every meeting, and it is clear that his great experience made him one of the most valuable members of the committee. He may sometimes have reflected upon the contrast between Woodes Rogers's breezy tact and his own methods on such occasions—which, according to Welbe of the " St. George," had consisted of setting forth his own opinion at the outset, and losing his temper when anyone disagreed with it. One happy result of these everlasting meetings on the " Duke " was that they effectually precluded the appearance of such books as Funnell's and Welbe's, for the commander was armed with the written approval of the officers for almost everything he had done. As for the discussion about the Madeira wines, it is perhaps hardly necessary to say that the decision was made in their favour ; but I give the minutes of the committee meeting here in full, as a typical example of how this most democratic voyage was conducted :

" At a Committee held on Board the ' Duke ' Frigate, resolv'd by the General Consent of the following Persons :

That both the Ships ' Duke ' and ' Duchess ' do touch at Madera to make a larger Provision of Liquors, the better to carry on our long Undertaking, being but meanly stor'd for so large a Number of Men as are in both Ships ; and in case of separation between this Place and Madera, then to meet at the island St. Vincent, one of the Cape de Verd Islands, to wood and water our Ships. But if we miss of one another at that Island, or that the first Ship finds it inconvenient for stopping, then to proceed to Praia on St. Jago, another of the same Islands ; to wait at both these islands fourteen days ; And then, if the missing Ship does not appear, the other to proceed to the Isle of Grande in Latitude 23 deg. 30 m. S. on the Coast of Brazil, there to wait three Weeks ; and then if we don't meet, let the Single Ship proceed on the Voyage, according to the Orders

*given from our Owners : This is our Opinion this 9th day
of September,* 1708.

THOS. DOVER, *President*   CHARLES POPE
STEPHEN COURTNEY   CARLETON VANBRUGH
WOODES ROGERS   THO. GLENDALL
EDWARD COOKE   JOHN BRIDGES
WILLIAM DAMPIER   JOHN BABET."
ROBERT FRYE

So they steered for Madeira, and on the way overtook a
Swedish ship, which they strictly examined for contra-
band. Some of the crew, who were deplorably drunk,
told the Englishmen that there was gunpowder on
board ; but no one could find it, so they let the Swede
go ; and her master gave Woodes Rogers two hams and
some " rufft dry'd Beef," and " I gave him a dozen
Bottles of Red-Streak Cyder."

While this pleasant exchange was being made, the
first mutiny broke out on board the " Duke." We, who
have had to listen to so much criticism of Dampier,
should note that Woodes Rogers was then only eleven
days out from Cork ! He had taken his crew into his
confidence, and they had heartily approved the design
of his voyage ; he was about to put into Madeira for the
express purpose of getting on board a stock of the
liquor which they loved ; all the omens were propitious ;
and they chose this moment to mutiny—apparently
because they wanted him to make a prize of this neutral
Swedish ship. One sailor was whipped, ten put in irons,
" some begged my pardon, and others I was forced to
wink at," says Woodes Rogers. Woodes Rogers
assembled the rest of the men, and " laboured to con-
vince them " that it would have been a mistake to behave
like pirates at the very outset of their voyage. The
boatswain, Giles Cash, who had been the leader of the

mutineers, was degraded ; and when a deputation of
seamen came to the Captain to plead for him, Woodes
Rogers's reply was to send him on board another
English ship, the " Crown " galley, which had been
accompanying them, for removal to England.

The wind being contrary, they passed Madeira, and
cruised among the Canary Islands. Here they took a
Spanish prize, and extorted ransom from the town of
Oratava, in the form of brandy and wine. Vanbrugh,
the agent, here began to show himself as the nuisance
that he was. He insisted upon going ashore, against
his Captain's orders, and was of course arrested, and had
to be exchanged against the prisoners from the Spanish
prize. Sailing away for South America, much encouraged by their new stock of liquor, they crossed the Line
on September 25th. Here the greenhorns were ducked
from the yard-arm in the customary ceremonial manner,
and Woodes Rogers remarks that it " approved of great
use to our fresh water sailors, to recover the colour of
their skins, which were grown very black and nasty."
Calling at the Cape Verde Islands, Courtney and Woodes
Rogers were annoyed to find the men selling their
clothes (the few that they had) to the negroes for mere
" trifles." The practice was immediately prohibited.

On October 8th, while still at anchor among the
islands, Woodes Rogers held an important committee
meeting on board the " Duchess," at which the delicate
question of " plunder " was considered. The privateers-
man's code distinguished between captured property,
which clearly belonged to the owners, and loot or
" plunder " of a more personal and accidental character,
which was commonly divided among the men on the
spot. There had been so much grumbling and squabbling about the Spanish prize already taken that Woodes
Rogers now found it necessary to modify his " constitution " with the owners, so as to give the men's predatory

instincts more scope. He drew up a scale of shares, from himself down to the humblest sailor, which effectually restored the temper of his crews, though the owners lost something by it. He also offered a reward of twenty pieces of eight to the first man who should sight a valuable prize. And, having done this, he set sail once more across the ocean for Trinidad.

On the way there was another mutiny, this time on the " Duchess." The leader was a truculent individual named William Page, one of the mates. Courtney came on board the " Duke " to see Woodes Rogers about it, and it was decided to remove Page from the " Duchess," in exchange for Babet, Dampier's old friend. But when these orders were conveyed to Page, he refused to budge, whereupon the dignified Captain Cooke, second-in-command, lost his temper and went for him, and " several blows passed." [1] Eventually the man, after jumping overboard and otherwise behaving like a lunatic, was lashed to the main jears on the " Duke," and heartily " drubbed." After which they put him in irons and left him.

Finding themselves unable to fetch Trinidad, they bore away for the island of Grande in Brazil. When the land came in sight, they sent Dampier off in the pinnace to find the entrance to the bay, and he returned presently and piloted them in. He also brought a large turtle—an unfamiliar delicacy to most of those on board. England and Portugal being at this time friends, and the French and Spaniards the enemies of both, it was decided to remain for some time at this Brazilian island, in order to repair their ships, especially the " Duchess," which was in a bad way and needed to be " heeled both sides." They had been in the Bay only a few hours,

[1] Cooke, in his solemn, conscientious account of the voyage, says not a word of this incident, of which he was probably ashamed. But, indeed, his is a dull book—though useful occasionally for matters of fact.

when Courtney had to put eight of his men in irons for refusing to obey orders ; and a night or two later two of his men ran away, but, wandering about the woods in the darkness, " were so frightened with Tygers, as they thought, but really by Monkeys and Baboons, that they ran into the Water hollowing to the Ship, till they were fetched aboard again." Undeterred by this, two Irish " landmen " ran away from the " Duke " on the following day, but were found by the " Duchess's " boats, which had gone ashore for water, and brought back under guard. Woodes Rogers had them " severely whipped and put in irons." After that discipline really did seem to improve.

The ships were now ready to leave their hospitable Portuguese island ; but before doing so, Woodes Rogers went with all his officers to the little town of Angre de Reys to pay a formal visit to the Governor, Señor Raphael de Silva Lagos, who received them " very handsomely." It happened to be a saint's day, and the occasion of a great religious procession through the town ; and the Governor at once asked his English guests if they would like to be present at the ceremonies. " We told him," says Woodes Rogers, " our religion differed very much from his " ; but he waived all their objections aside, and insisted upon their joining in the church service and the subsequent procession. Nothing loath, the English officers, who had just had an excellent dinner, rose from their chairs and sallied out. In the street they collected their ship's band, which they had fortunately brought ashore with them from the " Duke," and it was immediately proposed that the English band should perform a few musical interludes during the service, and should head the great procession to the church. The scene that followed is one of the most remarkable in all the picturesque annals of the privateers. It also illustrates two of Woodes Rogers's special gifts—

his popularity with all sorts and conditions of men, and his gift of vivid narrative. He writes :

" Our Musick play'd, *Hey Boys up go we !* and all manner of noisy paltry Tunes ; and after Service our Musicians, who were by that time more than half drunk, march'd at the head of the Company, next to them an old Father and two Fryars carrying Lamps of Incense with the Host, next came the Virgin Mary on a Bier carry'd on four Men's shoulders and dress'd with Flowers and Wax Candles etc. After her came the Padre Guardian of the Convent, and then about forty Priests, Fryars etc. Next was the Governor of the Town, myself and Capt. Courtney with each of us a long Wax Candle lighted : Next followed the rest of our Officers, the chief Inhabitants and junior Priests, with everyone a lighted Wax Candle. The Ceremony held about two hours, after which we were splendidly entertained by the Fathers of the Convent."

What a scene under the palm trees and the tropical sky ! They stayed the night in Angre de Reys, and next day returned to their ships, taking with them the Governor and " Gentlemen of the town " (there can't have been many, for there were only sixty houses in all). The Canary wine was brought out, and the greatest cordiality prevailed. The guests " were very merry, and in their cups proposed the Pope's health to us ; but we were quits with 'em by toasting that of the Archbishop of Canterbury ; to keep up the Humour, we also proposed William Penn's to them : and they liked the liquor so well that they refused neither."

On the 3rd December, in the afternoon, the two privateers weighed anchor, and set sail from the pleasant island of Grande on their long voyage round the Horn to Juan Fernandez. Before starting they held a committee meeting and removed Vanbrugh from the position of owners' agent on the " Duke." He had been up to his tricks again. Without the slightest provocation, he had ordered the men to fire at an Indian canoe, whereby one of the unfortunate natives was killed, and this was the kind of offence that Woodes Rogers never forgave. They had a terrible passage round the Horn, and the " Duchess " was at one time in considerable danger. When the weather had somewhat abated, Woodes Rogers took Dampier with him in a boat and went aboard his consort to see how she fared. She had shipped a great deal of water, and her men were soaked to the skin ; and since it was now so cold that they expected at any moment to encounter icebergs, their sufferings must have been terrible. But Captain Courtney already had their clothes out drying on the rigging, and by getting some of his guns down into the hold he had succeeded in making his ship more " lively," so that she did better after this. But everyone was glad when Juan Fernandez came in sight on January 31st.

Here occurred one of the most memorable incidents of the voyage—the rescue of Alexander Selkirk. Cooke's account is here a useful supplement to his commander's livelier narrative. The afternoon was already well advanced when they sent in a boat to look for a suitable anchorage. The men were pulling in towards the land in the failing light, the island looming up dim and mountainous before them, when those in the ship perceived a fire among the trees ; and Woodes Rogers, not unnaturally jumping to the conclusion that there must be Spaniards about (with their ships perhaps out of sight behind some headland), recalled his boat by signal. We can guess what must have been the feelings of the unhappy Selkirk, who had, of course, lit this fire as a signal to the English ship—the first he had seen for four and a half years !

Next morning, however, they stood in closer and sent in another boat, which discovered no enemies, but a solitary person running wildly about the beach, " with a white ensign " which he waved to attract their attention. " He was clothed," says Cooke, " in a goatskin jacket, breeches and cap, sewed together with thongs of the same." They called to him to show them a good place for anchorage, and he gave them directions in a strange, stumbling voice, " and then ran along the shore in sight of the boat, so swiftly that the native goats could not have outstripped him." When they had seen the place, they invited him into the boat, that he might return to the ship with them, but " he first enquired whether a certain officer that he knew was aboard ; and hearing that he was would rather have chosen to remain in his solitude than come away with him, till informed that he was not in command." Cooke is too tactful to give this officer's name. It may have been Dampier (I do not know whether he was in the boat at the time), and certainly, if Selkirk was referring only to the officers of the " St. George " and the " Cinque Ports," there was no other who would be likely to be " in command " on this occasion—though there were others, such as John Babet, who had sailed in the earlier voyage. On the other hand, Dampier appeared now as Selkirk's friend, praising him highly to Woodes Rogers and describing him as the best man on Stradling's ship, so that, as we shall see, the castaway was presently promoted to be second mate of the " Duke." There is other evidence, too, that Selkirk was on friendly terms with Dampier. In fact, we are left guessing.

Lieutenant Fry, who was in the boat, stepped ashore, and at Selkirk's invitation, followed him along a circuitous and " uncouth " path over the rocks, until they " came at last into a pleasant spot of ground, full of grass and furnished with trees, where he saw two small huts,

A View of the COMMODORE'S TENT at the Island of JUAN FERNANDES.

THE ISLAND OF JUAN FERNANDEZ

(Showing the tents used by Anson when he visited the island, during his voyage round the world)

indifferently built, the one being the lodging room and the other the kitchen." This is from Cooke. Woodes Rogers says : " In the lesser hut, at some distance from the other, he dressed his victuals, and in the larger he slept and employed himself in reading, singing Psalms and praying, so that he said he was a better Christian while in this Solitude than ever he was before, or than, he was afraid, he should ever be again."

Selkirk told Fry that at first he had been able to eat nothing, owing to the absence of salt, but afterwards subsisted on seals and " other fish," until he had become so hard and nimble that he could run barefoot over the rocky ground at a speed which enabled him to catch the wild goats for his dinner. Not wishing to deplete the stock, he had kept a record of his kills, which showed that he had eaten five hundred goats altogether in the four and a half years of his stay. The goats, of course, were a legacy from some previous visit by a European ship ; so were the innumerable rats which kept him awake at night, " gnawing at his feet " ; and the cats which he fed and encouraged so that they might rid him of the rats ; also the turnips and parsnips, some of which had originally been sown there by Dampier's men. They got him back to the boat and off to the ship, where he was received by the Commander.

Woodes Rogers was keenly interested. At first, he says, " we could scarce understand him, for he seemed to speak his words by halves." What astonished the privateers even more, he refused " a dram " when it was offered to him, " having drank nothing but water since his being there." There was much eager conversation on the quarter-deck, as their uncouth guest stood before them ; and " Captain Dampier tells of a Mosquito Indian that lived here three years alone and shifted much in the same manner as Mr. Selkirk did, till Captain Dampier came hither in 1684 and carried

him off." [1]   I think Woodes Rogers and Dampier must
have gone ashore with Selkirk the next day, for the
former gives us many details of " Robinson Crusoe's "
life on the island—how when the Spaniards came to the
place, he hid in the trees and waited till they had gone
(there was no " Man Friday ") ; how he had " tamed
some kids, and to divert himself would now and then
sing and dance with them and his cats " ; and of how
they tested his fleetness of foot by bringing ashore the
ship's bulldog and setting it to race against him, when
Selkirk always " tired " the dog. The whole incident
of Selkirk's rescue is one which would have been memorable in any case. It is doubly interesting to-day as
showing us so plainly the principal source of Defoe's
immortal story.

The " Governor " of Juan Fernandez, as Rogers nick-
named Selkirk, was now set to catch a plentiful supply
of goats ; and with this diet of fresh meat, with turnips
and parsnips, the men soon began to recover from the
effects of their long journey round the Horn. The
ships, too, were repaired, and on the 12th February,
the little squadron set sail northward for the coasts of
Chile and Peru, Selkirk having been installed as mate
on the " Duke." Their main objective now was the
Manila ship, and Woodes Rogers took the opportunity
of a sudden calm to call his officers on board the " Duke "
for another committee meeting on the subject of plunder.
He had conceived the idea of appointing a representative
of the men on each ship, to share with an officer the
duty of distribution ; and this was accordingly done.

They cruised along the coast till the 12th April,
taking several prizes. One of these was unlucky, for
there exists among the State Papers a petition addressed
to Queen Anne in 1710 or 1711 by the merchant
owners of Bristol, appealing for efforts to be made to

[1] See pages 102-3.

secure the exchange or release of Simon Hatley, mate of
the " Duchess," and other members of a prize crew,
who, going on shore for provisions, had been caught
by the Spaniards and thrown into Lima prison, " where
they now are, together with several others of your
Majesty's subjects formerly belonging to ships under
Captain Dampiere's command." Hatley had succeeded
in smuggling a letter out of prison to his owners. This
letter, which is dated November 6, 1709, concludes as
follows : " Some of our countrymen that were here
before we came, they have made turn their religion.
We live a sorrowful life among them, and always plagued
by the Fathers, putting us in irons and in the dungeon
to make us turn, but we are resolved to dye first.   I and
one more they have had to the gallows, hanged until we
were almost strangled before they cutt us down, this is
what offers from, Gentlemen, your most humble Servant,
Simon Hatley."

Woodes Rogers now decided that, while waiting for
the sailing of the Manila galleon, they could not occupy
their time better than by an attack on the important
town of Guayaquil, which seems to have been a favourite
objective with the English privateers. Anchoring among
the palm-clad islands at the mouth of the river, as
Dampier had done so many years before, they held a
meeting, and, according to their own peculiar custom,
drew up an elaborate set of regulations for the attack on
shore.   Cooke says that " a dispute arising who should
command in chief ashore, at length it was agreed that
Captain Rogers and Captain Courtney should each of
them command a company of seamen, and Captain
Dover a company of the land-men ; that Captain Dover
should give the word the first night, and the other two
captains in their turns." This clumsy arrangement seems
to have worked fairly well.   It was carefully explained
to the men, who by now were spoiling for a fight.

On the 15th they intercepted a French-built ship from Lima, which was re-christened the " Marquis," and placed under the command of Cooke. On board of her they found 500 bales of Papal Bulls, 16 reams in a bale, and a quantity of bones in small boxes, " ticketed with the names of Romish saints, some of which had been dead 7 or 800 years." This was disappointing plunder for a Protestant privateer, and Rogers threw most of it overboard, " to make room for better goods." In the meantime they " rowed and towed " up the river for Guayaquil, and, landing at a village on the way, found there letters to the local governor in which he was warned that an English ship was at sea under the redoubtable " Captain Dampier." As it happened, Dampier had captured this very village on the occasion of his last visit to Guayaquil.

Rogers immediately took measures to spread among the local Indians an exaggerated version of the story of a " squadron " under Dampier. He also saw that there was no time to be lost. But when they arrived outside Guayaquil, they found, as so many English invaders had before them, that the alarm was already given. Beacons were blazing on the hills, the bells of the town were ringing, and volleys of musketry, fired blindly into the night, conveyed a message of defiance from the inhabit-ants. It was a question what to do next, and Dampier was consulted. He said that the buccaneers " never attacked any large place after it was alarmed "—he must surely have meant that they never did so without regretting it !—and Captain Dover agreeing with him, it was decided to remain in their boats in the river, and send a messenger to the town demanding ransom.

It is hard to believe that Dampier can have favoured this latter course, which he had so strongly opposed on former occasions. In the present instance, the usual result followed : the Spaniards prevaricated while they strengthened their defences.   But Woodes Rogers was not to be trifled with.   At the appointed hour he suddenly broke off negotiations, and with seventy men landed and attacked the town.   The Spanish gunners, with more resolution than they usually displayed, stuck to their pieces till the English were " within pistol shot." One of them, an Irishman, continued firing even then, till he fell covered with wounds ; but their shooting must have been extraordinarily erratic, for only two were killed on the English side.   Dampier was now put in charge of the guns, and he quickly turned them on the streets of the town, which were soon emptied of all but the English.

It was, in fact, a handsome victory.   And the best of it was that the Spaniards presently changed their minds about the ransom, and, rather than see their city ruined, sent Rogers a lump sum of thirty thousand pieces of eight.   With which he and his merry men marched down to their boats again, with colours flying and trumpets sounding cheerfully.   On their way down the river, they looted several houses on the banks, and it was at one of these that " Mr. Sellkirk, the late Governor of Juan Fernandez," distinguished himself by his exceptionally " civil behaviour."   For being sent, with a Mr. Connely, to search some charming young ladies who were suspected of having hidden jewellery under their clothes, he performed the task with such modesty as to occasion the fair captives " no uneasiness nor surprise." As Selkirk and Connely were both " young men," Woodes Rogers expresses the hope that " the Fair Sex will make 'em a grateful return when we arrive in Great Britain."

As all the " houses up the river were full of women," and " every pair of legs was spiralled with necklaces and gold chains," the privateers added considerably to their wealth before they got out to sea.   Snuff-boxes, jewelled sword-hilts, plate, silks and laces must have made a gay display in the cabin, when the appointed representatives of the officers and of the seamen assembled there to value the spoil. Already Dampier must have felt that this was a more promising voyage than any with which he had recently been associated.[1] There was only one fly in the ointment : the fatal miasma from the river marshes had proved more dangerous than the Spanish guns, and some kind of malignant fever was knocking the English sailors down like ninepins ; so that it was decided to make for the island of Gorgona (off the coast of Colombia) and try a change of diet and of air, before cruising for the Manila ship. Courtney was taken ill, and Dover " went on board the ' Duchess ' to prescribe for him."

The next excitement was a rumour that the Spanish prisoners and the negroes on board were plotting to " murder the English and run away with the ship in the night." Woodes Rogers examined the Spaniards, who strenuously denied it. Some of the negroes owned to a vague knowledge of a plot, but not till they had been threatened with torture to make them speak. On June 13th, 1709, they anchored off Gorgona, and settled down for a longish stay while they recovered their healths, and refitted their prize, the " Marquis." Woodes Rogers remarks that " Captain Dampier has been here several times, but never rode where we did, which is the best and only good road in the island." Dampier, at this time, appears to have been on board the " Duchess." " My pilot Dampier forsook me," says Woodes Rogers, though for what reason is not clear. Among their prisoners " was a gentlewoman and her family," including an eldest daughter, " a pretty young woman of about

---

[1] When they reached the island of Gorgona, Cooke " reckoned the value we had then aboard for the owners in gold, plate and jewels amounted to about £20,000 and in goods £60,000."

eighteen," who was newly married, and had with her her husband, who " showed evident marks of jealousy, the Spaniard's epidemic disease."   So Woodes Rogers, with a touch of humour, put them in charge of his third lieutenant, Glendall, " for being above fifty years of age, he appeared to be the most secure guardian to females."

On the 7th August, they sailed from the island in search of the Manila ship.   They set their Spanish prisoners ashore on the mainland ; but Woodes Rogers assembled the negroes, and, after offering them their freedom if they would agree to fight for him, " 32 of them immediately promised to stand to it as long as the best Englishmen, and desired they might be improved in the use of arms."   After which they drank the inevitable " dram " all round.   A few days later, a sham fight was staged between the " Duke " and the " Duchess," the latter flying Spanish colours for the occasion.   And everyone, from the captains down to the humblest fore-mast hand, " acted the same part he ought to have done in earnest, firing with ball excepted."   Even the surgeons had " patients " in the hold, splashed with red lead and water to simulate blood.   The negroes must have been vastly edified by this " agreeable diversion," as Woodes Rogers calls it.

As things turned out, they had plenty of time for martial exercises, for the Manila ship persistently failed to come in sight.[1]   More agreements about " plunder " were drawn up, and a painful example was made of " one of the ' Duchess's ' black nymphs," who had proved to be a lady of easy virtue.   " This I mention," says Woodes Rogers, " to satisfy the censorious that we don't countenance lewdness, and that we took those women aboard only because they spoke English and

[1] The great treasure galleon had not been captured by an Englishman since Thomas Cavendish took it in the year 1587. The next success after Woodes Rogers's was to be that of Anson in 1743.

begged to be admitted for laundresses, cooks and seam-stresses." This particular negress was whipped at the capstan. In the course of their wanderings, they sailed over the very spot where Dampier had unsuccessfully engaged the Manila ship in the " St. George," and our hero was in frequent consultation with the other captains. Once or twice we find him at fault as to their exact whereabouts, but Woodes Rogers adds that he could always be relied upon to recognize a place when he got ashore. His transfer to the "Duchess" seems to have caused no ill-feeling. On one of the islands of the Marias group Dampier found a human skull, which he told Woodes Rogers must belong to an unfortunate Indian, who, with one companion, was left there by Swan in 1685 ; " for victuals being scarce with these buccaneers, they would not carry the poor Indians any farther, but after they had served their turns left them to make a miserable end on a desolate island." The long wait began to affect the men's behaviour, and regula-tions were passed which " prohibited all playing at cards or dice " aboard the ships.

On the 20th December, they were cruising off Cape St. Lucas, the southernmost point of California. Every-one was feeling " melancholy and dispirited " ; for all hope of intercepting the treasure ship had been for the moment abandoned, and the committee had already passed a resolution to steer for the island of Guacu and replenish their stock of food, which was running low. The " Marquis " had put into an adjacent harbour to refit for the voyage. This was the position, when, at about 9 o'clock in the morning, " to our great and joyful surprise . . . the man at the masthead cried out he saw a sail, bearing west half south of us, distant about 7 leagues." The " Duke " immediately hoisted her ensign, and bore away in pursuit, the " Duchess " fol-lowing. For a long time they were in doubt as to whether this was indeed their prey, for the wind dropped, and there was a dead calm all the rest of that day. However, Woodes Rogers sent off an armed pinnace, which approached near to the chase, and returned to him in the evening with the news that this was no other than the Manila ship—though, as it turned out afterwards, not the " admiral," but his consort, of slightly smaller size.

Two pinnaces were sent to " tend her all night, and keep showing false fires so that we might know whereabouts they and the chase was." And at daybreak, the " Duke " being now close up, Woodes Rogers " ordered a large Kettle of Chocolate to be made for our ship's company (having no spirituous liquor to give them) ; then we went to Prayers, and before we had concluded were disturbed by the Enemy's firing at us." After all, it was a short and sharp engagement. The " Duchess " was to leeward, and having little wind, could not come up, but the " Duke " poured in broadside after broadside, with volleys from the small arms, to which the Spaniards replied, " but did not ply their great guns half so fast as we." Finally, just as the " Duchess " was coming into action, the " Duke " got across the enemy's bows, and began to rake her, whereupon she hauled down her flag.

It was a great prize, the richest captured by any English ship for many a long year. She was named the " Nuestra Señora de la Encarnación Desengaño," mounting twenty guns and twenty swivels, and carrying 193 men. She had about twenty casualties, and the " Duke " only two ; but of these one was Woodes Rogers himself, who was shot through the left cheek, the bullet carrying away part of his upper jaw, so that his teeth fell out upon the deck. He continued to direct the action, though he was unable to speak, and had to give his orders in writing. That night he swallowed something which he believed to be part of his jaw-bone, and there-after began to mend slowly, though he was in great pain, and could take only liquid food and that with difficulty. Yet the indomitable man continued to attend committee meetings as though nothing had happened.

Of these there were more than usual, for there was a certain amount of jealousy among the officers of the " Duchess " and the " Marquis " as a result of the " Duke's " single-handed victory over the Manila ship. Now that it was clear that there were really two of these treasure galleons (a thing they had not expected), the " Duchess " and the " Marquis " demanded the right to go out alone in search of the other one. And this they carried by resolution, in spite of the protests of Woodes Rogers, who could only set his arguments down in writing. Dampier, as an officer of the " Duchess," voted with the rest. The condition of Woodes Rogers's health may have been a leading consideration with those who voted against him ; but it is clear that he took the adverse decision very much to heart.

So the " Duke," with her wounded commander, remained in harbour, while the " Duchess " and the " Marquis " put out to sea again to find the Manila " admiral." Their luck held. On Christmas Day, very early in the morning, when only a few hours out, they sighted a big Spanish galleon, and crowded on sail to overtake her. It was about 2 a.m. and still dark. The " Marquis " was a " cranky " sailer, and the " Duchess " was the first to come up with the chase. Cooke, from his position in the " Marquis," gives an admirable account of what he could see of the fight. Staring out through the darkness, he could observe the flash of the guns and hear their roar, but could not determine what was happening. Towards dawn the noise of battle subsided, but an occasional shot indicated that the Spaniard had not yet surrendered. As a matter of fact, Courtney, in the " Duchess," had been compelled to draw off to repair his damaged masts and rigging.

In the grey morning light they saw the Spaniard's yellow flag, and recognized her for the " admiral " of the Manila fleet, and a hoarse cheer burst from their throats as they strained every nerve to draw nearer to the scene of action. At the same time, the " Duke," with every sail set, was seen moving out from behind the headland, coming to their assistance. Woodes Rogers also had heard their guns and seen lights out at sea ; and though he was still unable to speak, and his officers had urged him to stay behind, he was now coming out to take his share in the fight.

There was a small breeze from the E.S.E. and the " Marquis " and " Duchess " crept slowly up to the gigantic Spaniard, and began again to batter her sides. " Our ships," says Cooke, " looked like small barks to the enemy." They sailed round and round her, pouring in volleys. The " Marquis " was the first to arrive, and her men gave three lusty cheers before firing the first broadside of the fight. The Spaniard's decks were now seen to be crowded with men, and she answered them defiantly, so that the English began to suffer severely in their masts and rigging. The Spanish gunnery, as in the previous fight, was slow but accurate : they had a ship of above nine hundred tons, equipped with " false decks " to resist the round shot, and forty guns of a heavier calibre than those of the privateers. The " Marquis," indeed, had only eighteen guns, so that, as Cooke remarks, " if the enemy had fired at the hull as he did at the mast and rigging, he must have shattered us almost to pieces." The " Marquis " and the " Duchess " engaged her one after another all that day, firing so many shots into her towering sides that towards evening the " Marquis " began to run short of ammunition, and fell astern with the " Duchess " in order to borrow a fresh supply. Cooke went on board his consort, and found her "much disabled in her masts and rigging and seven men killed." He and Courtney agreed "to yard-arm and yard-arm with the enemy in the morning," and further to fire guns at intervals all night "to annoy the enemy and to give the 'Duke' notice where we were, keeping out lights."

While the two officers sat in conference in the cabin, a boat arrived from the "Duke" asking for news. Woodes Rogers was now close up with them, and he hints pretty plainly in his book that, if he had been allowed to accompany them in the beginning, the three ships must have carried the Spaniard at the first attack, before she had recovered from her surprise. With daylight the desperate fight was renewed. Cooke says : "Captain Courtney in the 'Dutchess' stood close up, gave his broadsides and volleys, and then ran ahead. The 'Marquis' coming up under her quarter did the like, and the 'Duke' next performed the same along her lee side. We kept raking of her, fore and aft, and then wared to get out of the way of the 'Duke's' shot, still firing, as did the other ships."

The "Duke" was unlucky—or else too impetuous—for she got so close that the Spaniards were able to throw their stinkpots on board—evil-smelling contrivances made of saltpetre, sulphur, assafoetida, arsenic, sublimate of mercury, and Goodness knows what else. One of them exploded some gunpowder on the quarter-deck, causing great havoc, and forcing the "Duke" to withdraw temporarily from the fight. The "Duchess" also had to lay by "to stop her leaks and secure her foremast, being much disabled," with twenty-five casualties on board. The "Marquis" carried on alone, and received some stinkpots in her turn, which set part of the ship afire ("but we soon put it out") and got onto Cooke's fine clothes, so that "I stank several days intolerably."

It must have been upsetting to that dignity of his !
When darkness fell, the three captains met on board the
" Duke " in anxious consultation.   Woodes Rogers had
been wounded again, " so that I could not stand, but
lay on my back in a great deal of misery, part of my
heel being struck out, and all under my ankle cut above
half through."

Finally they called the inevitable committee meeting,
which decided that there was " no probability " of taking
this powerful ship, and that it was better to leave her and
" secure the prize we have already took."   So ended a
memorable sea-fight.   Cooke says that on the " Marquis "
alone " we fired above 300 great shot, about 50 cross-
bars and 2 great chests of steel bars, beside abundance of
partridge small shot and above 9 barrels of powder."
He has the grace to add that " to give the enemy their
due they defended themselves very well, but we migh
as well have fought a castle of fifty guns " as this " prodigious strong " ship.   It transpired afterwards that
there was a special crew of 600 men on board the
Spaniard, hurriedly recruited for the occasion, when it
was learned that the terrible Dampier was again in
those seas.

But the privateers were already rich, and under a less
energetic commander than Woodes Rogers (who made
a characteristically rapid recovery from his injuries) they
might well have felt that there was nothing more for
them to do.   Even Woodes Rogers and Dampier clearly
regarded the circumnavigation of the globe, which they
were now about to complete (Dampier for the third
time) merely as the most convenient way of getting back
to England.   Woodes Rogers frankly apologizes for
including in his book a brief description of " this long
and tedious passage."   Dampier could have kept our
interest alive in his old effortless way ; but unfortunately
he had long ceased to make entries in his journal, and

even he, if we may judge from his occasional appear-
ances in Woodes Rogers's record, was as nearly bored
by the latter end of this voyage as by any he ever took
part in.

They sailed first to the island of Guam, in the Ladrones,
and there Woodes Rogers displayed his accustomed tact
in getting upon almost as friendly terms with the local
Spaniards as he had with the Portuguese at Grande.
He entertained the Governor and leading residents on
the " Duke " with " musick and our sailors dancing."
But though they might dance on occasions, the men
were, in fact, " fed up," and their commander found
them more difficult to deal with than any Spaniards.   In
a valiant attempt to cheer them up, he had ceremoniously
observed St. Valentine's Day, drawing up " a list of the
fair ladies in Bristol that were in any ways related to or
concerned in the ships," and sending for the officers to
his cabin, where everyone drew a name " and drank the
lady's health in a cup of punch and to a happy sight of
'em all."

But nothing could make up for the reduction in the
daily rations, which now became necessary, and we get
the impression that they sighted Guam only just in time.
From Guam they sailed to Batavia, stopping at several
islands and suppressing several mutinies among themselves on the way.   At intervals the ship's doctor would
perform operations on Woodes Rogers's throat, removing pieces of broken jaw-bone and " musket-shots."
Also " I had several pieces of my foot and heel bone
taken out."   After refreshing themselves at Batavia,
they made sail across the Indian Ocean for the Cape of
Good Hope.   They had sold the leaky " Marquis " to
an Englishman at Batavia, and were now only three
ships in company, the " Duke " and " Duchess " and
the captured Spanish galleon, which they had renamed
the " Batchelor."   At the Cape, they waited from

December 29th, 1710, to April 5th, 1711, and then sailed with the regular Dutch convoy for Holland and England. It was a wise move, considering the wealth they had on board, and Rogers and Courtney must have felt relieved when, having rounded the Shetlands, they anchored safely in the Texel on the 23rd July. From thence, after some delay, English men-of-war convoyed them to the Downs, where they arrived on October 14th after a voyage of more than three years.

CHAPTER XII

AND SLIPS HIS CABLE

THE cruise of the "Duke" and "Duchess" was one of the most successful ever undertaken by English privateers. We can only hope that the citizens of Bristol, who stood to profit handsomely by it, gave Woodes Rogers and his men a fitting reception on their return. In money and goods, the total value of the booty available for distribution is stated to have reached the impressive figure of £170,000. Of this, the Bristol merchants, who had financed the voyage, took half, and there was a substantial allotment (probably £14,000) to Woodes Rogers himself, who now became a comparatively wealthy man. He formed friendships with Sir Hans Sloane, Sir Robert Southwell (to whom Dampier no doubt introduced him), and other men of distinction, and in 1717 he was in a position to acquire by lease the quit-rents and royalties of the Bahama Islands, of which he was made Governor in the same year. His story of his voyage round the world was published in 1712, and achieved a success only second to that of Dampier's books. Woodes Rogers well deserved these rewards. His voyage, as has been recently pointed out,[1] was in many respects more note-

[1] By Mr. G. E. Manwaring in his introduction to a new edition of Woodes Rogers's *Cruising Voyage Round the World* (Cassell: 1928). He adds that two large silver candlesticks taken on this voyage are now in Bristol Cathedral.

CAPTAIN WOODES ROGERS, WITH HIS SON AND DAUGHTER, 1729
From the engraving by W. Skelton after the painting by Hogarth.

worthy even than Anson's thirty years later ; for whereas Anson was in command of six ships of the Royal Navy and two victualling ships, all fitted out for him by the Admiralty, and lost every one of them on the way, except his flagship, Woodes Rogers brought both his little privateers safely into their home port. We part regretfully with this debonair commander. He was to have many more adventures, and perform many dashing exploits before his death in the Bahamas in 1732 ; but none so completely successful and so deservedly famous as this voyage in which Dampier piloted him round the world. The two men, in fact, so different in gifts and in character, made a remarkably fine combination.

But when all these prior claims had been satisfied, there was still a large amount of prize-money left over for distribution among the officers and men of the " Duke " and " Duchess." Dampier's share, we may be quite certain, was more than sufficient to have enabled him to spend the few remaining years of his life in comfort. Unfortunately, he did not live to receive it. Before the distribution was made, he had gone on the last of all his voyages. Perhaps we may be allowed to express the hope that this time it was not a " warm " one !

Until three years ago, the state of Dampier's finances after his retirement from the sea was a subject of controversy. Many of his early biographers, who ought to have known better, had hurriedly scratched in the familiar pathetic picture of a grey-haired genius left to die in a garret by his ungrateful country ; while others, more conscientious, had replied by pointing out that even if Dampier never actually handled his share of the prize-money, he could surely, on so good a security, have borrowed enough to keep him in reasonable comfort for the remaining three and a half years of his life. All this, however, was conjecture. But in 1925, Dr. B. H. M. Rogers, to whose researches I have already referred,[1] sent a second communication to the *Mariner's Mirror* (volume 11), in which he described a further MS. document lent to him by Mr. Goldney, of Corsham, which, when compared with certain papers in the Library of Congress, Washington, provides a full and apparently exhaustive statement of Dampier's financial position at this time. What is even more important, it gives us a glimpse of his life, and indicates why he now had to reside permanently in town.

The Goldney MS. consists of the report, dated May 9, 1719 (four years after Dampier's death), of the Master in Chancery who had been appointed to inquire into the accounts of the voyage of the " Duke " and " Duchess," and endeavour to arrive at an equitable, if somewhat belated, settlement. These accounts had been the subject of several law-suits by members of the crew and others, and it is clear that the lawyers had been getting their share, whoever else went begging. What Dampier demanded was " eleven shares equal in value with those due to the ship's company," and a further " 1/16th part of the nett profits." He also claimed interest on this sixteenth part of the profits, to date from the day when the owners had divided their portion among themselves without including him. We do not know what the eleven shares would be worth ; but we do know that one-sixteenth of the net profits of this wonderful voyage would be well over £2000, without including interest. So that Dampier was asking for a substantial sum.

He did not get it. Nor did poor Grace Mercer, his executrix and residuary legatee. Indeed the whole purport of the report of the Master in Chancery is that he has disallowed the executrix's claims. He abruptly dismisses all suggestions of interest ; and he fails to find " any such agreement " as is alleged by Dampier's representative in regard to the one-sixteenth part. He adds :

[1] Page 201.

" The owners also offered before me to pay him (Dampier) £500 more than he recd. [So he had received something !] but said Dampier refused such offer unless they paid him down £1000." We begin to perceive in what manner Dampier spent the remaining years of his life. It was a great age for litigation. The " before me " indicates that both he and the owners' solicitors had been privately interviewed by the Master, with a view to some composition, but that Dampier's obstinacy had made it impossible to settle out of Court. Like many unbusinesslike people, who are careless about money (though they may, on occasions, enjoy their " golden dreams "), he could be stubborn enough when he thought he was being cheated. We can see him confronting the lawyers, his untidy hair about his eyes, his head thrown back, his underlip more prominent than ever. A thousand pounds or nothing ! Nothing it was.

But we are not to suppose that Dampier never made anything by the Woodes Rogers voyage. On the contrary, we find among these papers a schedule setting forth the various payments made on account to Dampier in the course of the voyage ; and the still larger sums which he had received since the return to England. This schedule is as follows :

CAPTN. WM. DAMPIER Dr.

To		£	s.	d.
Cash recd. of Captn. Rogers	. .	45	0	0
do. of Ald. Bachelor comm.	. .	11	0	0
Cloathes at Cork	. .	8	17	11
Cash etc. of Capt. Courtney	. .	53	4	10
200 dolls at Batavia @ 5/-	. .	50	0	0
200 more at do @ 4/	. .	40	0	0
Cash in Holland of Courtney	. .		8	4
6th part of (undecipherable)	. .		19	3
Cash of Mr. Corsley	. .	611	10	0
Carry forward	.	£821	0	4

				£		
Brought forward	.	.	.	£821	0	4
Cash of Master	.	.	.	500	0	0
pd. Executrix of do.	.	.	.	20	0	0
plunder money	.	.	.	6	5	6
Agency money	.	.	.	4	0	0
Totle Mo. recd. per Damp.		.	.	£1351	14	0 [1]

That is to say, something over a hundred pounds in the early part of the voyage, ninety at Batavia, and eleven hundred odd since the return to England—all this, of course, to be set off against his claims.

At first sight it looks as though Dampier had been having a gay time at Batavia—deliberately cutting a dash, perhaps, in a part of the world where he had previously been known as a needy adventurer. But we find in Woodes Rogers's narrative that there was a general share-out of " plunder " at this port (Dampier was one of the judges appointed to decide which part of the cargo was " plunder " and which was the owners' property), and also that an allotment of money was there made to the officers, to enable them to equip themselves for the homeward voyage, Courtney acting as treasurer. Dampier's share was two hundred pieces of eight.

What is quite clear is that he cannot, on this occasion, have landed in England penniless, according to his former habit ; and, further, that he drew about £1200 from the owners (the Mr. Corsley, mentioned in the schedule, was the owners' solicitor) after his return. It is, therefore, certain that he must, at any rate, have lived like a gentleman during the remaining years of his life.

It is true, also, that, like most gentlemen of his period, he died in debt. Another schedule attached to the Master's report gives details of his debts amounting to

---

[1] I am aware that this does not add up quite correctly. The arithmetic is that of the Master in Chancery.

£677 17s. 1d., most of it money borrowed on his "expectations" from his friend, Edward Southwell, a certain Capt. Humphreys, and others.[1] But there is nothing unusual in that, though it may have been a disappointing legacy for Grace Mercer. Dampier had good reason to suppose that he would presently be able to pay these debts in full. Unfortunately, we have no evidence to show that his executrix ever got another penny, beyond the £20 mentioned in the schedule as having been paid over to her.

He was not without other resources. The "little estate" in the West Country which he had purchased while in Jamaica, had probably been sold before the voyage of the "St. George." Dampier was induced to make a considerable personal contribution towards the cost of that voyage, and in order to do so he had been compelled to revoke certain financial arrangements which he had made through his friend, Southwell, for the support of his wife Judith ; so that Judith was left with only his pay from the Customs while he was away. It seems unlikely that he can then have possessed the estate. On the other hand, there is no reason to suppose that his salary from the Customs, which was in the nature of a pension and had been paid uncomplainingly by the Government during his two long absences, should not have continued down to the day of his death. Judith, his wife, was now dead, for by his last will he revoked a previous bequest to her made at some date before 1703. His expenses as a widower would not be great, since he apparently had no children.

Finally, there were his books, which were still selling well. A second edition of the *Voyage to New Holland* had appeared while he was away with Woodes Rogers,

[1] Dr. Rogers is quite wrong in supposing these people to be professional money-lenders. But one creditor, Capt. Richard Newton, held some of Dampier's furniture at the time of his death.

while the *New Voyage* had reached its fifth edition in 1703, and was to go into a sixth two years after he died. Whatever arrangements he had made with Knapton, his publisher, there must surely have been another source of revenue here.

In September, 1714, three years after his return from his last voyage, Dampier celebrated his sixty-third birthday. He was not an old man as we reckon nowadays, but his health had already broken down. Forty-two years of seafaring in those hard times was about as much as any man's constitution could stand. He was living in the parish of St. Stephen's, Coleman Street, near Old Jewry, and was apparently being looked after by his cousin, Grace Mercer, to whom he left the greater part of his property. It is typical of the difficulties confronting the biographer of a man like Dampier that he has told us nothing whatever about this cousin—the one woman, besides his wife, who ever had anything to do with his affairs. We may guess that she was the most important female influence in his life—but we are only guessing. That she had been with him for some time is clearly stated in his will; but whether that merely means that his illness had been a long one we cannot tell.

The old sailor's health grew steadily worse, and on November 29th he decided to make his last will and testament, which may now be seen in Somerset House. It begins thus :

" I, Capt. William Dampier, of London, Mariner, being diseased and weak in body, but of sound and perfect mind and memory (praised be God therefore) considering the frailty and uncertainty of this transitory life, and that as nothing is more certain than Death, so nothing is more uncertain than the time of Man's dissolution, do therefore make and ordain this my last will and testa-

ment in manner following, viz : first and principally I
recommend my soul into the hands of Almighty God,
my Creator, hoping by and through the merits, death
and passion of my ever blessed Redeemer to enjoy
eternall life ; and my body I commit to the earth to be
decently buried at the discretion of my executrix, herein-
after named ; and as touching that worldly estate wherewith it has pleased God to bless me . . ."

And he then proceeds to will that his estate be divided
into ten equal parts, nine of which are to go to his
cousin, " Grace Mercer, of London, spinster," and one
part to his " loving brother, George Dampier, of Porton,
near Breadport, Dorset." All his " goods and household stuff," whether in the hands of Captain Newton,
" of Eagle Court, in the Strand," or of Thomas Jones,
or elsewhere, went to Grace Mercer.

You cannot sentimentalize over Dampier—not even
if you have grown to like and admire him as much as I
have in the past few months. He himself would have
resented it as an intrusion. He had a sort of natural
delicacy of mind, an " exquisite refinement," as Coleridge
says ; so that I can imagine nothing more distasteful
to him than the kind of pen-picture one is tempted to
draw—the mighty voyager, the greatest sailor of his age
brought to a stand at last, the grizzled head that has
felt the suns of every continent in the world, from the
West Indies to Cochin China, bowed feebly over the
parchment, while his shaking fingers, probably guided
by a woman's hand, seek to add his signature to the last
words he will ever write. But he does not want us
there ; and we, who owe so much to him, and the
generations yet unborn who will read his incomparable
Voyages with delight, can at least respect his feelings.
Let us softly close the door ! There is no more to say
about the life of William Dampier, except that he died

Q

early in March,[1] 1715, and was buried no one knows where.

But of Dampier, the writer, there are still a few words to say. There never was a more difficult writer to edit, and it is quite impossible that in the few passages which I have been able to quote from his works—though carefully chosen, and all of them highly characteristic—any really adequate idea of his extraordinarily high quality can have been conveyed to the reader. Harris, one of his early editors, made the absurd mistake of regarding Dampier as " prolix " and even " obscure," simply because he was long (Harris prefers Funnell, who is " better digested " and " may be read with more satisfaction " !). He accordingly gets to work on Dampier with the pruning-knife, with the result that all the charming, convincing detail, which is the very secret of his genius, disappears, leaving a bare skeleton of narrative. That is a difficulty (though Harris never saw it) which must confront everyone who attempts to write a biography of Dampier. It has been my object to tell the story of his life, not to summarize his writings ; and I have accordingly endeavoured to keep that story in its proper proportions, not allowing undue space to any one episode merely because he himself has described it at length.

To appreciate him as a writer, therefore, it is necessary to turn to his books, for they cannot be cut or skipped or edited without losing their flavour. In a sense they are the most revealing part of him. When we think that the best thing he ever wrote was produced in the intervals of a buccaneering expedition ; when we picture him studying a flower or a bird, or taking his observations which were presently to recast the map of the Pacific, while serving as a foremast hand among a crowd of drunken, brawling sailors, we appreciate for the first

[1] His will was proved on the 23rd.

time what he might have done for literature and science if Fate had cast him for an easier part in early life.   He lived at the very moment when his special talents were most in demand.   It was during his early manhood that Charles II sent Greenville Collins on a seven years' tour in a yacht, in order that the first decent chart might be made of the British Isles !   James II was equally interested in navigation.   Yet Dampier, at the very time when he might have been enjoying this high patronage, was proving himself the best hydrographer of his age in circumstances which could hardly have been more discouraging.   His appeal is not so obvious as that of Woodes Rogers, for instance ; he has not the professional sparkle of Defoe ; he is emphatically a writer who must be read—*lived with* for a while.   And this applies particularly to his notes on animal and plant life, which are quite delightful to read, but disconcertingly difficult to quote with effect.   I cannot improve on Mr. Masefield's language.   " Dampier's work," he says, " has this supreme merit, that it surveys the lesser kingdoms with a calm, equable, untroubled and delighted vision."

It has been said, on the one hand, that Dampier got his better-educated friends to write—or at least edit— his books for him, and then took the credit ; and, on the other, that Defoe took his ideas, and even his style, from Dampier, and rewarded him with sneers instead of thanks.   Neither charge bears much examination.   I have already touched upon the first.   Dampier may have taken advice.   He had not the slightest idea that he could " write."   He never dreamed that his books would rank as literature.   But no one can now read a page of his writings without feeling that the style—no less than the facts—is his own.

As for Defoe, it is impossible—or I, at any rate, have found it impossible—to discover any passage in his voluminous works which can fairly be said to have been " cribbed " from Dampier. It is, indeed, an impertinence to suggest that he would need to " crib " in this literal sense. But he did go to Dampier—and to Woodes Rogers and to all the buccaneer chroniclers—for his " plots." That was inevitable, and perfectly justifiable. The one passage in Dampier's writings which seems to have made a profound impression upon him was that in which our hero, expecting every moment to be drowned during his perilous canoe voyage to Sumatra, reflects dismally upon his wild and wandering life and the dissolute companionship which is all that he had known since he left the parental roof in Somersetshire.[1] Defoe seizes upon that note, and makes it a kind of *leit-motif*, running all the way through his greatest work, *Robinson Crusoe*, and reappearing occasionally in *Captain Singleton*. He is greatly indebted to Dampier for that idea ; and of course he was indebted not only to Dampier, but to a hundred other adventurers for his facts and his local colour. Yet he could write :

" It has for some ages been thought so wonderful a thing to sail the tour or circle of the globe, that when a man has done this mighty feat he presently thinks it deserves to be recorded, like Sir Francis Drake's. So as soon as men have acted the sailor, they come ashore and write books of their voyage, not only to make a great noise of what they have done themselves, but, pretending to show the way to others to come after them, they set up for teachers and chart-makers to posterity. Though most of them have had this misfortune, that whatever success they have had in the voyage they have had very little in the relation, except it be to tell us that a seaman, when he comes to the press, is pretty much

---

[1] See above, page 134.

out of his element, and that a very good sailor may make but a very indifferent author." [1]

Whether or not that was aimed at Dampier personally— and it rather looks like it—it was, in the circumstances, a shabby, ungentlemanly sneer. But whatever else may be said about this great and original genius, no one ever accused him of being a gentleman ! The fact that he had " lifted " one or two ideas from Dampier certainly would not predispose him to gratitude.

I am hardly competent to discuss the scientific value of Dampier's books. Admiral Burney, writing more than a century ago,[2] observed : " It is not easy to name another voyager or traveller who has given more useful information to the world ; to whom the merchant and mariner are so much indebted, or who has communicated his information in a more unembarrassed and intelligible manner. And this he has done in a style perfectly unassuming, equally free from affectation and from the most distant appearance of invention." So every sailor has thought of him during two centuries. Cook and Philip Carteret, Howe and Nelson have agreed in praising his *Discourse on Winds*, and other notes on hydrography, and in recommending them to the attention of young officers. Like his natural history notes, they are full and informative, without ever being dull. And I cannot resist the temptation to give just one more quotation from Dampier's writings, which affords an excellent example of his manner, when seeking to illustrate a point of seamanship :

" If after the Mizan is hall'd up and furled, if then the ship will not wear, we must do it with some Head-

[1] Defoe's *New Voyage Round the World.*
[2] *A Chronological History of the Discoveries in the South Sea or Pacific Ocean.* By Admiral James Burney. London : 1803-7.

sail, which yet sometimes puts us to our shifts. As I was once in a very violent storm, sailing from Virginia, mentioned in my *Voyage Round the World*, we scudded before the Wind and Sea some time, with only our bare Poles ; and the ship, by the mistake of him that con'd, broached to, and lay in the Trough of the Sea ; which then went so high that every Wave threatened to overwhelm us. And indeed if any of them had broke in on our Deck, it might have foundered us. The master, whose fault this was, raved liked a Madman, and called for an Axe to cut the Mizan Shrouds, and turn the Mizan mast overboard : which indeed might have been an expedient thing to bring her to her course ; the Captain was also of his Mind. Now our Mainyard and Foreyard were lowered upon a Port-last, as we call it, that is down pretty nigh the Deck, and the Wind blew so fierce that we did not dare to shew any Head sail, for they must have blown away if we had, neither could all the men in the ship have furled them again ; therefore we had no hope of doing it that way. I was at this time on the Deck with some others of our Men ; and among the rest one Mr. John Smallbone, who was the main instrument at that time of saving us. Come, said he to me, let us go a little way up the Fore Shrouds, it may be that that may make the Ship wear ; for I have been doing it before now. He never tarried for an Answer, but run forward presently, and I followed him. We went up the Shrouds Half-mast up, and there we spread abroad the Flaps of our Coats, and presently the ship wore. I think we did not stay there above 3 Minutes before we gain'd our point and came down again ; but in this time the Wind was got into our Mainsail, and had blown it loose ; and tho' the Mainyard was down a Port-last and our Men were got on Deck as many as could lye one by another, besides the deck full of men, and all striving to furl that Sail, yet we could not do it, but were forced to cut it all along by the Head rope and so let it fall down on the Deck."

Reference has already been made in Chapter IX to Dampier's keen interest in the problem of the variations of the compass, and to the importance of his observations on this point. While on the "Roebuck," it will be remembered, he compiled an elaborate table of variations, with dates ; but, while offering a few comments of his own, he declined, with his usual modesty, to lay down any cut-and-dried theory, preferring to leave the decision to the scientists, for whom he always shows so much respect. Admiral Smyth, a recognized authority, makes the comment that, "though the local magnetic attraction in ships had fallen under the notice of seamen, he [Dampier] was among the first to lead the way to its investigation, since the facts that ' stumbled ' him at the Cape of Good Hope, respecting the variations of the compass, excited the mind of Flinders, his ardent admirer, to study the anomaly." Speaking generally of Dampier's writings, Smyth adds that " his sterling sense enabled him to give the character without the strict forms of science to his faithful delineations and physical suggestions ; and inductive inquirers have rarely been so much indebted to any adventurer whose pursuits were so entirely remote from the subjects of their inquiry."

About fifty years after Dampier's death, a critic [1] of Boswell's *Tour to Corsica* remarked unkindly (and very foolishly) that the book was a good example of how " any fool may write a most valuable book by chance, if he will only tell us what he heard and saw with veracity." No doubt much the same kind of thing was said about Dampier in some of the coffee-houses. But we, who are confronted with more new books of travel every month than the eighteenth century was accustomed

[1] Gray.

to see in five years, know that the truth is far otherwise.
We know that the travelled fool never manages to see
and hear those things that we wish to be told about ;
or, if he does, he tells of them without a trace of that
inspired veracity which is so different from mere
accuracy, and consequently leaves us cold.   We know
that it is not so easy as it sounds to take your readers
with you in spirit to a country they have never seen,
and keep them as pleased and excited as though they
were seeing it all for themselves.   And if you continually interrupt your narrative in order to discuss
technical points of navigation, we know that you will
require literary gifts of a very high order, if you are
going to score a popular success with your book—as
Dampier did.   In the long list of English travel-writers,
from the best of Hakluyt, Coryat and the eighteenth
century to the more studied manner of the Victorians
and the brilliant impressionism of to-day, a man must
be of exceptional genius to take a high place.   Dampier
is probably in the first half-dozen.   As a travel-writer
alone, his name deserves to be known wherever our
language is spoken.

But I close as I began.   If his voyages of discovery
had been less decisive than they were, if his notions of
hydrography had been all mistaken, if his prose had
lacked the natural elegance and virility which so dis-
tinguishes it and had approximated more to the style of
plain narrative—even then his story would have been
tremendously worth telling.   He crowded enough incident for a dozen adventure books into almost any month
of his life, and gave it the keen tang of truth which most
adventure books so deplorably lack.   Indeed he *lived*
adventure books, and every modern boy between the ages
of sixteen and sixty ought to know of him, and read
him, and be thankful.   Simply to follow the story of
his career is to get an almost personal contact with those

stirring times, of the wild life of the buccaneers in the
west, and the romantic beauty of the Spice Islands in
the east.   No one who has not done it can understand.
It was because Dampier's career was so typical of this
adventurous phase in human life, now lost for ever—
because it was so *typical*, not because it or he was exceptional, though in many ways they were—that I have
found his story so fascinating.   If there are any dull
pages in this book, it is my fault, not Dampier's.

AUTHORITIES

ANON. The Voyages and Adventures of Capt. Bartholomew Sharp. London, 1684.

BOWEN, FRANK C. The Sea : Its History and Romance. London, 1924.

BURNEY, ADMIRAL JAMES. A chronological history of the discoveries in the South Sea or Pacific Ocean. London, 1803-7.

Calendar of State Papers, Colonial Series : " unbound papers."

CLARK RUSSELL, W. William Dampier. London : Macmillan (English Men of Action), 1889.

COOKE, EDWARD. A Voyage to the South Seas. London, 1712.

CORBETT, SIR JULIAN. Editorial notes on the Dartmouth Maps of the Battle of the Texel.

Courts-Martial. Official Minutes. Public Record Office.

COWLEY, C. Manuscript journal. Sloane Collection, No. 54.

COX, J. Manuscript journal. Sloane Collection, No. 49.

DAMPIER, WM. :[1]

> A New Voyage. London : Knapton, 1697.
> Voyages and Discoveries. London : Knapton, 1699.
> A Voyage to New Holland, Part I. London : Knapton, 1703.
> A Voyage to New Holland, Part II. London : Knapton, 1709.
> A Vindication. London, 1707.

DEFOE, DANIEL. Robinson Crusoe, Captain Singleton, etc.

DE LUSSAN. Journal of Le Sieur Ravenau de Lussan. Paris, 1689. English translation, London, 1699.

ESQUEMELING, J. The Buccaneers of America. English translation, 1684-5.

EVELYN, JOHN. Diary. See also his Numismata, London, 1699.

FUNNELL, W. A Voyage Round the World. London : Knapton, 1707.

---

[1] All Dampier's travel writings mentioned in the text, including *A Discourse on Winds*, *A Voyage to Tonquin*, etc., are contained in one or other of these volumes.

Gosse, Philip. The Pirates' Who's Who. London: Dulau, 1924. My Pirate Library. London, 1926.

Gray, Sir Albert. Dampier's "New Voyage Round the World." With an Introduction by Sir Albert Gray, K.C.B., K.G., Pres. of the Hakluyt Society. London: The Argonaut Press, 1927.

Hacke, William. A Collection of Original Voyages. London, 1699.

Harris, John, D.D. (and Campbell). Navigantium atque Itinerantium. London, 1744.

Kerr, Robert. A General History and Collection of Voyages. London, 1811-24.

Lang, Andrew. Essays in Little. London: Longmans, Green & Co.

Mahan, Admiral. The Influence of Sea Power upon History.

Major, R. H. Early Voyages to Terra Australis. London, 1859.

Manwaring, G. E. Article in "The Mariner's Mirror," 1924: The Dress of British Seamen.

Masefield, John. Editorial notes to "Dampier's Voyages." London: Grant Richards, 1906.

Pepys, Samuel. Diary and Correspondence.

Ringrose, B. The Buccaneers of America, vol. 2. From the original journal written by Mr. Basil Ringrose, gent. London, 1684. The original MS. is in the Sloane Collection, No. 3820.

Rogers, Dr. B. M. H. Articles in "The Mariner's Mirror" (Journal of the Society for Nautical Research). Vols. 10 and 11.

Sharp, Bartholomew. Manuscript journal. Sloane Collection, No. 46a.

Shelvocke, Capt. George. A Voyage Round the World. London, 1726.

Smyth, Rear-Admiral. Articles in the "United Service Journal and Magazine," Parts iii and iv, 1837.

Wafer, Lionel. A New Voyage and Description, etc. London: Knapton, 1699.

Welbe, John. Answer to the Vindication. London, 1707.

Woodes Rogers. A Cruising Voyage Round the World. London, 1712.

INDEX

R